THE ILLUSION OF INCLUSION
WOMEN IN POST-SECONDARY EDUCATION

EDITED BY JACQUELINE STALKER AND SUSAN PRENTICE

FERNWOOD PUBLISHING • HALIFAX

Editing: Donna Davis
Cover design: Andrea Dubois
Design and production: Beverley Rach
Printed and bound in Canada by: Hignell Printing Limited

A publication of:
Fernwood Publishing
Box 9409, Station A
Halifax, Nova Scotia
B3K 5S3

Fernwood Publishing Company Limited gratefully acknowledges the financial support of the Ministry of Canadian Heritage and the Nova Scotia Department of Education and Culture.

Royalties will be donated to organizations working to improve the status of women in post-secondary education.

Canadian Cataloguing in Publication Data

Main entry under title:

Illusion of Inclusion

    Includes bibliographical references.
    ISBN 1-895686-17-2

1. Women college students -- Canada.   2. Women college teachers -- Canada.   3. Women -- Education (Higher) -- Canada.   I. Stalker, Jacqueline, 1933-   II. Prentice, Susan, 1961-   III. Title.

LC1567.I54 1998   378'0082'0971   C98-950000-4

Contents

Foreword

This book is intended for readers who are interested in and want to know more about what is happening in post-secondary education. They may be curious about educational issues and what tax dollars are funding, or they may want to learn about the college and university environment for themselves, their children or their grandchildren.

Business, industry, governments and organizations might like to find out why post-secondary graduates may or may not be meeting their needs. They need to know how to collaborate with or influence institutions to ensure that Canada's post-secondary system achieves excellence in all programs and for all students.

Educators also may appreciate learning about the legitimate concerns of the majority of their student population and the minority of their academic staff. Many of the current policies and practices that affect more than half of the population are described, although all post-secondary issues could not be addressed in a volume of this size. Those policies and practices that have a positive effect on women students or all students merit consideration and possibly emulation by other institutions. Those that have a harmful and lingering effect should be changed, and contributors to this anthology offer suggestions for improvement.

Many individuals are astounded when they realize that women, as students and staff, do not have post-secondary treatment and opportunities equal to those provided for men. Women students do not receive equal instruction, consideration, resources, support or learning opportunities in their college and university studies. Similarly, women staff receive differential treatment; even when they are better qualified than their male colleagues, they tend to be paid less and be expected to do more, but they usually are granted a lower non-tenure status. The consequences of these practices are evident throughout Canadian society. University and college graduates eventually become society's leaders and they practise what they have been taught and have seen.

The severity of this situation and the myopia of many of our leaders are confirmed annually when the United Nations (UN) releases its Human Development Index of approximately 170 countries. Canadians are proud of being ranked at or near the top of the list because we have among the highest life expectancy, literacy levels and standard of living. What the media do not report as sensationally is that the UN ranks our country much lower when assessing the quality of life for women. When the Women in Post-Secondary Education (WIPSE) project was initiated in Canada in 1992, the UN's quality of life rating for Canadian men remained high whereas the quality of life rating for Canadian women fell from eighth to eleventh place. Inequities for women were increasing faster than they were being addressed.

The WIPSE project arose from these concerns. This book was originally conceived by Jackie Stalker, a professor of higher education, who recognized the need for essays on educational policies and practices and their effects on women in our universities and colleges. She received support for her proposal from the Manitoba Coalition for the Education and Training of Women, an alliance of women's and educational organizations. The proposal was submitted to the Secretary of State of Canada and seed funding for the project was granted the following year.

WIPSE was launched in the summer of 1992 with the collaboration, cooperation and participation of many women and men across the country, the support of various organizations, and modest funding. Notices printed in university and college newspapers and circulated by organizations across Canada invited individuals to submit articles on federal, provincial or systemic educational practices or policies and their impact on women.

The response was phenomenal, five times greater than anticipated, which indicated people's keen interest in post-secondary education and the effects of its policies and practices on women. Proposals were received from every province and territory as well as from Canadians temporarily residing in the United States, the United Kingdom and Australia. In the spring and summer of 1993, submissions were sent to a national editorial board for a rigorous peer review process. This anthology includes some of the articles that were positively evaluated.

A major objective of WIPSE is to raise national awareness of policies and practices that have an adverse or beneficial impact on women. The WIPSE goal is to promote the equal participation of women in all aspects of post-secondary education and all kinds of formal post-secondary educational institutions.

This book is important because it provides information by Canadian women about their experiences in post-secondary education. Students, faculty, administrators and a national organization each offer their own perspectives on a range of themes. We regret the small number of articles addressing the community college sector. In no way does this indicate a high degree of satisfaction with or a lack of interest in our colleges. Many college staff and students contacted the WIPSE office to express their support and their fears. They wanted to voice their concerns, but feared that the publication of their names might endanger their jobs if they were on staff or impede their progress if they were students. Academic freedom in most of the community college sector is apparently non-existent because of unreasonable restrictions imposed by some institutions or provincial governments.

We can all help to reverse policies and practices that are not in the public interest. Women now constitute the majority of students in Canadian higher education. To be served fairly and well, they must be represented in every aspect of institutional life. The deception, or the illusion of inclusion, concerning women in our community colleges, universities and other post-secondary institutions must be exposed. By learning more about what actually is occurring, readers can use this information to demand change. In doing so, they will help us to achieve WIPSE's two final goals: uniting communities of scholars, practitioners and participants in effecting positive change in higher education, and enabling informed advocacy to improve the situation for women and men in post-secondary education in Canada.

Acknowledgements

Many individuals participated in the various stages of the Women in Post-Secondary Education (WIPSE) project. Their contributions are sincerely appreciated, for without their help this book would not have been published.

Helen Breslauer, senior researcher at the Ontario Council of University Faculty Associations, responded to faxes and phone calls in her usual supportive manner and met with me in Toronto on a busy and rainy Saturday afternoon to formulate the WIPSE concept and call for papers. Marion Vaisey-Genser, former vice-president (research) and executive director of the Women's Secretariat, University of Manitoba, and Carol Fournier Dicks, editor of *The Bulletin*, University of Manitoba, became members of a WIPSE advisory board. Their valuable advice was welcomed; their task was to ensure that no detail was overlooked and that the goals were achieved. From the Coalition for Education and Training, Linda Taylor, Marylea MacDonald, and Mary Scott were there when needed and never lost interest. Successive program officers at the Manitoba Region, Secretary of State, Jackie Friesen, Chris Dobbs, and Pierrette Hébert were always available and supportive. Romulo Magsino of the Faculty of Education at The University of Manitoba provided space for, and faith in, the project.

When the WIPSE project was launched, John Crossley, coordinator of the Learned Societies Conference held at the University of Prince Edward Island in Charlottetown, volunteered his staff's support on short notice and printed the call for papers in the conference newspaper, which was distributed to approximately 12,000 participants. Similar cooperation was shown at the annual Association of Canadian Community Colleges Conference, held jointly with the Association Québécoise de Pédagogie Collégiale in Montréal, where college staff stood at the top of the escalators in the Convention Centre and personally handed out the call for papers to approximately 2,000 delegates. Christine Tausig Ford, editor of *University Affairs*, and many media relations personnel and editors of campus newspapers publicized the project. The phenomenal response and number of proposals received clearly indicated that WIPSE was striking a chord across the country. It also assumed proportions and generated a volume of mail that required the attention of a staff person and more than one editor.

9

An impressive national editorial board was assembled in 1993. Jane Gordon, Mount Saint Vincent University, was deeply involved in the early stages of the project. Other members of the editorial board were Mariette Blanchette, Canadian Association of University Teachers; Sheila A. Brown, Mount Saint Vincent University; Rebecca Coulter, University of Western Ontario; Anne Innis Dagg, University of Waterloo; Beth Westfall Davies, Keewatin Community College; Jane Gaskell, University of British Columbia; Margaret Gillett, McGill University; Susan Jackel, University of Alberta; Sandra Kirby, University of Winnipeg; Ann Manicom, Dalhousie University; Carol McKeen, Queen's University; Ruth Rees, Queen's University; Lois Reimer, University of Toronto; Cannie Stark-Adamec, University of Regina; Christine Storm, Mount Allison University; Peta Tancred, McGill University; Peggy Tripp-Knowles, Lakehead University; and Marion Vaisey-Genser, University of Manitoba.

The editorial board undertook a painstaking review of approximately 150 submissions. Each article was reviewed by three separate peer reviewers. Contributors were subsequently provided with the anonymous evaluations and also an opportunity to revise and resubmit their articles. At the end of this process, a short list was finalized and each article in that list underwent a second review process. The final result is that every article in this anthology has been reviewed by six or more knowledgeable and independent reviewers.

Susan Prentice, Margaret Laurence Chair in Women's Studies, Prairie Region, joined the project as co-editor in the summer of 1995. Her secretary, Helen Osman, provided superb assistance during the later stages of the book whereas Audrey Carroll, secretary for *The Canadian Journal of Higher Education*, worked on both the first and last stages of the project, organizing and maintaining our files, budget and records throughout the prolonged double blind peer review stage. Talented young graphic designer Andrea Dubois creatively translated our abstract idea into a beautiful cover.

Fernwood Publishing provided guidance through copy editing by Donna Davis, production by Beverley Rach and, particularly, support and valuable assistance at every stage from Errol Sharpe and Wayne Antony. Working with this group of people in a supportive, cooperative and independent Canadian publishing house has been a pleasure.

Of course, without the enthusiastic response and patience of the authors and their sharing of expertise and experience, the WIPSE objective of publishing papers on policies and practices in post-secondary education that have either an adverse or a beneficial impact on women would not have been achieved. We are grateful to all those who submitted papers and sincerely wish that we could have accepted and published more of them.

All of the participants and contributors who volunteered their time and services in various ways believe that women's lives are as important as men's lives. They have seen that women comprise the majority of students but only a small minority of faculty and administrators. They know that women's access to universities and colleges does not ensure an education for them. They also know that excellence will be achieved only when the talents and skills of all people are used.

Jackie Stalker

Introduction

Although women purportedly have been admitted to higher education in Canada for over a century, their participation has never been equal to that of men. Numerous studies have shown that women lag behind men on all measures of formal status.[1] Whether as students or as faculty members, women are underrepresented and marginalized on campuses of higher learning. Research into variables as diverse as wage levels and classroom climate, and ranging from sexual harassment to retention rates, demonstrates that women's experiences are different from and markedly inferior to men's experiences in post-secondary education. In 1977, a landmark Canadian study concluded definitively that, for women in higher education, "discrimination is not limited to local areas, nor does it happen occasionally. Rather it is practised daily and on a nation-wide scale."[2]

This collection of essays demonstrates that exclusionary practices are still flourishing, despite formal claims to the contrary. In articles ranging from first-person narratives to research reports, authors document the myriad ways that women—white women, aboriginal women, older women, fat women, working-class women, mothers, returning students, learners, teachers and administrators—continue to be excluded from full participation in higher education. Post-secondary education should be, but is not, a level playing field. Women may appear to be included on campuses across the country, but closer examination reveals a systemic and enduring pattern of exclusion. Like other institutions, universities and colleges purport to provide equality while falling fall short of it in reality.

Discrimination, however, is only one part of the experience of women in post-secondary education. In comparison to most Canadian women, female students and faculty members are decidedly well-off. Women academics are part of a "privileged elite" whose professional careers provide many more rewards than do most women's jobs.[3] Similarly, female graduates of colleges and universities generally go on to workforce participation that is demonstrably better than that of women without higher education credentials. Since universities and colleges also discriminate against immigrants, minorities, First Nations, peoples with disabilities and others, does a focus on women's experiences imply a lack of concern for these other axes of exclusion? Is it elitist to concentrate on the discriminations women face when post-secondary institutions are equally or more unwelcoming to people of diverse racial and ethnic backgrounds?[4]

We believe that a focus on women is appropriate for several reasons. Women comprise more than half of our population and are represented in each of the racial, ethnic and other categories. Additionally, as reasoned almost twenty years ago by Jill Vickers and June Adam:

> A society in which women take their place in the professions must surely result in fewer laws which discriminate against women, in fairer judicial treatment of female offenders and in the more humane treatment of women by doctors, lawyers and other professionals.[5]

Believing that the simple presence of women in formerly male-dominated institutions could bring about fundamental change was overly optimistic. What is incontrovertible, however, is that all belief in a bias-free campus is thoroughly discredited when discrimination against any group is proven. Authentic fairness does not and cannot exist for anyone associated with higher education because the full participation of many individuals is denied on the basis of their supposed "group" characteristics. Thus, ending discrimination is essential for the common good.[6]

The articles collected in this anthology document the costs of this exclusion for the women who live with it: how it affects their career prospects as well as their self-esteem, confidence, productivity and sense of self. Beyond simply describing exclusion, the authors also analyze the chasm between the appearance of inclusion and the reality of exclusion. Contributors weave a complex analysis of historical, organizational and interpersonal factors to show how discrimination against women operates despite formal institutional commitments to equality. In their probing analyses of power, the authors critically examine the prized academic conceptions of formal equality, merit and individualism that are used to justify the substantively inequitable treatment of women and other marginalized people.

In theorizing exclusion, the authors pay considerably more attention to outcomes than to intent, showing that individualistic or personalizing explanations for discrimination against women are inadequate. Policies and procedures that seem most neutral and apolitical hold the key to understanding women's exclusion and marginalization. In this sense, contributors to this collection show how discrimination against women is systemic and institutional. Their critical scholarship demonstrates that the academy is a deeply stratified and inequitable institution, far removed from the idealized image of a placid ivory tower of disinterested scholarship and contemplation.

Despite such evidence, most Canadians cling to the comforting myth that, in academia, individuals rise or fall based solely on their intellectual performance. The evidence proves the opposite. Many people find it disturbing to scrutinize the academy for the same biases that characterize other Canadian institutions. Some academics and their allies so vigorously defend their perception of the university as a democratic and egalitarian institution that they deny all evidence and arguments to the contrary.

One of the most effective tools for resisting women's critique is the damning charge of "political correctness." Under this rubric, women's activism for equality is accused of undermining the academy. This belief enjoys astonishingly wide currency. *The Globe and Mail* expounds that "academic freedom is being sacrificed on the altar of political correctness" and *Maclean's*, the national news magazine, reports that "a new wave of repression is sweeping through Canada's universities."[7] One bemused observer comments that defenders of the status quo have generated a "veritable mass-production industry of hypothesis and speculation," which they ascribe to a "lunatic fringe of politically correct totalitarian thought police."[8] In both Canada and the United States, some proponents of this view argue their case in high-profile, albeit flawed, books.[9] In 1997, several years after a nationally publicized controversy in its political science department, the University of British Columbia hosted the first-ever national conference "Academic Freedom and the Inclusive University." At the conference, some prominent panelists repeated the view that "political correctors" seek to control the university merely to advance their narrow self-interest.

To the contrary, the purpose of equity initiatives is nothing more (or less) than an attempt to ensure that individuals are judged on their own merits.[10] Ironically, defenders of the status quo claim that affirmative action and like measures represent "reverse discrimination" or sexism, even though the goal of employment equity is precisely the opposite. Women who work for equity are demanding that considerations based solely on alleged group attributes like sex or race be set aside. Today, as in the past one hundred years, equity seekers are struggling to break down discriminatory structures and practices precisely so that individuals can finally be seen as unique and valued citizens, unencumbered by stereotypes, myths and prejudice.

The struggle for women's equality has been, and continues to be, painfully slow. Few academic administrators and decision-makers have accepted that post-secondary education is riddled with discrimination. Under the guise of protecting academic freedom and respecting academic independence, change is occurring—but with the speed of a charging glacier. Policy-makers permit higher education institutions to maintain the status quo; inaction is always the easiest route. Thus, aside from relatively minor external legislative and policy directives, Canada's universities and colleges enjoy considerable independence. External factors, including the crucially important issue of funding, play an important role in shaping post-secondary education but institutional autonomy remains the norm.

On the major issues of what gets taught, who gets taught and who teaches, universities and colleges exercise unique control. They determine which women and men are admitted, at what point students have achieved the standards required to earn degrees and credentials, and which academics will be hired, promoted and published. One law professor ridiculed a hackneyed institutional justification for exclusionary practices by quipping, "The university crying that it can't find minority candidates is like General Motors claiming that it can't find Cadillacs: we produce the product that we claim is in short supply."[11] Authors in this anthology demonstrate how women's exclusion has been an outcome of such institutional autonomy. They reveal some of the ways in which our public, and publicly funded, post-secondary institutions treat the majority of the population.

THE MARGINAL MAJORITY

What would it take to transform the exclusive academy into an inclusive one in which all participants are judged and treated by the same criteria? A post-secondary institution is inclusive when its faculty, staff and students reflect the diversity of communities of which they are a part and which they serve. Inclusivity also requires that everyday practices of teaching, learning, research and administration reflect tangible respect and fair treatment of all members. Inclusivity is achieved when "differences are accepted and welcomed, not just tolerated; and where academic freedom is recognized as a foundation of intellectual inquiry that applies across all levels of the academy."[12] Under these conditions, all participants would be judged on their skills, abilities and contributions, and no ascribed characteristics, such as gender, race or age, would delimit or proscribe participation.

Today, Canadian colleges and universities are far from inclusive. Instead, they are characterized by patterns of exclusion ranging from the most overt and institutional to the most subtle and interpersonal. Women and minorities have sometimes named this the "ton of feathers" syndrome.[13] Taken individually, particular practices, procedures or policies may be almost negligible in their effects, but their collective impact is enormous. Without an appreciation of the cumulative effect of institutional practices, all one sees are "feathers." In this sense, women and other equity seekers have been insistent that the object of their critique be the whole "ton."

Equity-seeking women have identified many barriers to women's full participation in higher education. One major discriminatory barrier is the enduring and literal exclusion of women and minorities from the teaching staff of universities. Contrary to the myth of steady but slow "progress," the historical reality is that women's participation rate as faculty members has barely improved across the twentieth century. In 1921, women comprised just 15 percent of the full-time teaching staff in Canadian universities, and this figure has improved only marginally in the intervening years.[14] By 1990, for example, women's representation had increased to only 18 percent of the full-time staff at Canadian universities.[15] In the United States, although women hold 25 percent of faculty positions, their representation has decreased from 36 percent over a century ago.[16] In both countries, exclusion appears to be a standard academic practice.[17]

This underrepresentation of female faculty is frequently attributed to limits in the available pool of women with doctorates or equivalent degrees. That argument might have been valid at one time, but it is inadequate for explaining women's contemporary position. Between 1955 and 1970, women earned approximately 20 percent of master's degrees and 8 percent of doctoral degrees, but these numbers have soared in recent years.[18] The number of doctoral degrees earned by women has increased fourfold since 1971 and, in 1992, women earned nearly one-third of the doctorates awarded.[19] The American story is not much different: women earned approximately 11 percent of doctorates awarded in 1965 and 35.4 percent of those earned in 1986.[20] In both countries, the distribution of women across disciplines is decidedly skewed; women are overrepresented in the humanities and other traditionally "feminine" disciplines, yet have only a minuscule presence in the natural and physical sciences. For example, in Canada in 1991, women represented 33 percent of the education faculty but only 3 percent of the engineering faculty.[21]

These figures are especially puzzling when contrasted with women's steadily increasing rates of undergraduate participation. In 1921, women made up 16.3 percent of all undergraduate enrolments. By 1967–68, women constituted over one-third of post-secondary enrolment, and they reached nearly 50 percent by 1987–88.[22] Today, the majority (56.1 percent) of undergraduate students are women.[23] Within individual fields, women tend to have higher grade point averages (GPA) than men and tend to score as well or higher than men on general aptitude and intelligence tests.[24] Despite their high representation as undergraduates and their demonstrated academic ability, fewer women than men proceed to graduate school. One study showed that 70 percent of male students with A to A+ averages, but only 47 percent of women with similar grades, entered graduate or professional school. Close to half of the male students with a B average began graduate school, compared to less than a quarter of female students with the same grade.[25] The inescapable conclusion is that excellent female students participate in graduate school at much lower rates than less-exceptional men. In her presidential lecture to the American Association for the Advancement of Science, Sheila Widnall summarized the problem with the succinct statement that "the more advanced the degree, the smaller the proportion of female recipients."[26]

In large part, women's ongoing absence from higher education is attributable to objective external factors, such as their family and domestic responsibilities and their lesser expectations of (and diminished sense of entitlement to) a professional career. Women's decisions not to pursue graduate studies, however, are not wholly voluntary. The National Research Council concludes that "objective factors alone cannot account adequately for the career differentials which exist between male and female PhDs."[27] Many women who excelled as undergraduates remember overtly discouraging advice from their supervisors and professors.[28] Other evidence of gender discrimination abounds. Graduate education itself also winnows women out, thus creating problems in the "pipeline" from undergraduate student to doctoral degree holder. In fact, Thelma Lussier demonstrates that women experience almost every aspect of the doctoral program differently than men do.[29] Canadian researchers Thomas Symons and James Page note that:

> One can only conclude that there is a large pool of well-qualified and highly trained talent in Canada that is not being effectively utilized by the universities. One must also conclude that, even though women have become a significant proportion of the university student population, a much lower proportion of women graduates is being encouraged to enter, or being allowed to participate, in university teaching and research.[30]

The inescapable hypothesis derived from these data is that women have been, and continue to be, discouraged from higher education.

One consequence of women's underrepresentation in doctoral programs is that relatively few women prepare for academic careers. Not surprisingly, given women's minority status within Canadian colleges and universities, female faculty also experience very different career paths from those of their male colleagues. More than ten years ago, Symons and Page concluded that gender inequity characterized rates of advancement, distribution across faculty ranks and compensation.[31] More recently, Alison Wylie claimed that matters remained largely unchanged, concluding that:

> women were still more likely than men to be unemployed, underemployed or in part-time or non-tenure track positions; they were concentrated in less-prestigious institutions; they showed substantially higher rates of attrition; they advanced through the ranks more slowly, and at the same rank they were paid less than their male counterparts.[32]

As in the general Canadian economy, the salaries of academic women still lag behind those of their male counterparts. In 1991, Statistics Canada bluntly claimed that "within every rank, the median salary for women was lower than for men, with the largest differential occurring at the full professor level."[33]

Inequality persists. It is demonstrated in universities and colleges by the distribution of women and men by rank. Women faculty hold the majority of junior appointments; men hold the majority of senior academic and administrative positions. Nationally, less than 8 percent of full professors are female, even though women constitute more than 33 percent of the entry-level rank of assistant professors and hold over 45 percent of lecturer, sessional and temporary appointments.[34] According to Sandra Acker, "no other profession has such highly qualified people in such lowly positions."[35] Even more alarming for women aspiring to academic careers is the knowledge that job prospects for part-timers are dim and growing dimmer due to public underfunding of post-secondary education.

Many commentators have reported on the revolving door syndrome, pointing out that female faculty are promoted more slowly than men and voluntarily withdraw from academia at significantly higher rates than men. One study showed that 9 percent of the women but only 2.5 percent of the men resigned voluntarily before their first academic reappointment, and twice as many women as men resigned voluntarily after at least one reappointment.[36] Personal factors contributing to women's "choice" to leave academia include an unmanageable workload, extreme stress, lack of positive feedback, few role models and family demands as well as outright harassment and discrimination.[37] A major institutional factor, in addition to systemic discrimination, is academe's assimilationist viewpoint. Universities "let" women in; they may even recruit them as students, faculty and staff. As no other changes are made to the traditionally male environment, however, women feel alienated, become discouraged and depart.[38]

The campus experience is markedly and demonstrably different for women and men. The chasm that separates their perceptions of the campus experience has been documented and can be quantified. In one study comparing men's and women's experiences and perceptions of discrimination, the results were startlingly different. Nearly one-third of academic women reported adverse experience with promotions compared to 7.6 percent of men; 24 percent of women declared negative experience in hiring practice versus only 7 percent of men; and, although only 0.8 percent of men reported discrimination in processes around nominations, appointments and elected office, 11.4 percent of women did.[39] Researchers also have quantified a chasm in the value and importance ascribed to women's and men's achievements. Studies demonstrate that women have to be more than twice as productive as men in order to be accorded an equivalent peer review rating.[40]

These data provide *prima facie* proof of discrimination. Differential salaries, rank, degrees awarded, promotion and tenure rates conclusively demonstrate systemic institutional discrimination. This differential treatment, however, often arises from practices alleged to be gender-neutral. For example, the "publish or perish" imperative fails to accommodate the life-cycle needs of academics with young children, and thus has the unintended effect of discriminating against women. Other post-secondary education policies and practices are less benign; indeed, many are overtly hostile to women. More and more, these formerly covert practices are being exposed.

THE CHILLY CLIMATE

Stung by the contradiction between formal claims of universal access and their personal experiences, women are becoming increasingly vocal about their treatment by post-secondary institutions. In historical and autobiographical accounts with telling titles such as *We Walked Very Warily: A History of Women at McGill*, female students and faculty marshal countless examples of discrimination against women.[41] Cataloguing a complete list of misogynous practices in academe would be a Sisyphean task, but even a cursory examination makes the point. For example, until 1966 women faculty at the University of Western Ontario were forced to retire at age 60 even though men could work until age 65. That same university also had an informal departmental rule that women should hold fewer than one in five faculty positions and many department heads were outspoken about their preferences for all-male units.[42] Alumnae of Québec's Bishop's University report that their principal prohibited women from using the front door of the faculty common room and barred female students from being on campus after mid-afternoon. They also recall professors unabashedly arguing that higher education for women ought to be restricted to preparing women to teach high school.[43] More than half a century later, similar attitudes persist. At the University of Saskatchewan, a female graduate student reported that her supervisor warned her that "women had to choose" between an academic career or having children.[44] Contributors to *The Illusion of Inclusion* recount similar instances in poignant detail, showing how women's seemingly personal troubles with the academy have roots in the public problem of discrimination.[45]

The enduring marginalization of women in higher education reflects both overt discrimination and more covert patterns of exclusion and devaluation. While proof of discrimination against female students and faculty is a relatively straightforward matter of empirical fact, documentation of the subtle forms of exclusion that shape the everyday experiences of female teachers and learners is less readily available.[46] Subtle harms require a qualitative form of analysis since they are experienced subjectively. Documenting the interpersonal ways in which women are devalued within higher education institutions requires that we actively acknowledge and respect women's experiences. The personal stories in this anthology do just that. The authors explore what might be considered standing conditions of the chilly climate rather than explicit policies of exclusion.

The phrase "chilly climate," coined in 1982 by Bernice Sandler and Roberta Hall, captures the subtle standing conditions that marginalize women. They defined "climate" as the combined effect of a number of practices, each of which is relatively inconsequential or even trivial when taken alone, but which cumulatively communicate lack of confidence, lack of recognition and devaluation. Overall, a chilly climate means that "the campus is a different and far less supportive environment for women than for their male colleagues and peers."[47] Hall and Sandler explain that these micro-inequities are part and parcel of the usual way men and women relate to each other; they are so "normal" as to go unremarked.[48] Often these behaviours are not seen as discrimination even though they frequently make women feel uncomfortable and put them at a disadvantage. According to Hall and Sandler:

> Micro-inequities often create a work and learning environment that wastes women's resources, for it takes time and energy to deal with or ignore these behaviours. The chilly climate undermines self-esteem and damages professional morale. It may leave women professionally and socially isolated, restrict their opportunities to make professional contributions and dampen their participation in collegial and academic activities.[49]

Micro-inequities are "fiendishly efficient" in perpetuating unequal opportunity, in large part because they are beyond the reach of most equity legislation.[50] Mary Rowe explains that micro-inequities cause damage because they are a kind of "punishment" that cannot be predicted in any kind of functional sense. She further points out that, although subtle discrimination occurs in the context of productive work, the punishment is without relevance to performance.[51] The studies in this anthology support a compelling argument that systemic discrimination persists on campuses across Canada.

The punishing effect of chilly campus climates for women and other minorities includes a variety of micro-inequities:

- **Denying the status and authority of women and minorities.** For example, women's authority is denied if male professors are regularly addressed as "Doctor" or "Professor" but female professors are addressed by their first names. Women's status also is minimized when listeners respond to male and female speakers with differential body language, such as nodding affirmatively and smiling at male speakers but not at female speakers.
- **Devaluing women through sexist comments, anecdotes and "jokes."** Frequently when women and minorities object to sexist or racist jokes, they are told they have misinterpreted a harmless comment and are taking offense where none was intended.
- **Excluding or impairing access to information,** such as when important faculty issues are discussed at social events rather than at formal committee meetings.[52]
- **Signalling women's lesser importance** through words, behaviours, posture, tone and gestures that indicate women are not as powerful, intelligent or competent as men and therefore do not need to be taken seriously.
- **Evaluating male and female behaviour and experience differentially.**

For example, a man's non-academic experience is described as "enriching" whereas similar experience in a woman reveals a "lack of focus." Similarly, when comparing two colleagues with identical experience, the male is described as "serving on two departmental committees and even one institutional committee" whereas the female is described as "serving on two departmental committees but only one institutional committee."

- **Undervaluing women's achievements.** Research has demonstrated that women's achievements are systematically undervalued by their peers. As mentioned earlier, one study discovered that women have to be 2.5 times more productive in order to get the same peer ratings as their male colleagues. This discrepancy exists even when objective measures of quality, such as publication impact, are identical.[53]

- **Using gender-biased language** with sex-specific terms (e.g., "Man the Hunter," the generic "he," etc.) when it is inappropriate; alternately, using gender-blind language for sex-specific situations (e.g., "spouse abuse").

- **Administrative pimping.** According to Pamela Milne, this occurs when "the institution receives the benefit of having the administrative work done, and of appearing to promote women to positions of authority, while the woman who actually does the work and makes the institution appear progressive is not rewarded for her efforts." She adds that administrative pimping is the institutional exploitation of women through greater workloads, lower salaries and/or a different quality of education, and it serves as the "very infrastructure of institutional survival" in times of financial crisis in post-secondary education.[54]

- **"Cocooning" women's contributions.** This common phenomenon involves ignoring the comments, ideas and work of women and later giving the credit for them to men (or taking the credit oneself, if male).

Contributors to this anthology explore these issues, showing how chilly campus climates revolve around classrooms, teacher–student interactions, curriculum and even the very definition of scholarly knowledge.

The chilly climate is especially pronounced in classrooms. Poet and essayist Adrienne Rich writes that "the content of education itself validates men even as it invalidates women. Its very message is that men have been the shapers and thinkers of the world, and that this is only natural."[55] Women regularly find themselves and their stories absent from the canon of their disciplines, unrepresented and without role models among the faculty and silenced by pedagogic practices that reward masculinity. Confronted with unwelcoming classrooms, women often experience themselves as "outsiders in the sacred grove."[56]

Male students, on the other hand, receive preferential treatment in most classrooms, and this subtly interferes with the development of women's self-confidence, academic participation and career goals. One depressingly widespread phenomenon in classrooms is the overt devaluation of women. Professors—women and men alike—tend to call on male students more often than female students, tend to make more eye contact with men than with women in the classroom, and give men a greater share of classroom attention.[57] Women students commonly report that professors' lectures are replete with sexist humour and references, that male peers dominate classroom discussions and that professors attend to the comments of male students over female students.[58] In recent years, women have begun to speak and write about this formerly private shame.[59] In one public exposé of sexist classroom behaviour, Deborah Skilliter recounted a humiliating series of student- and professor-induced sexist insults she endured as an undergraduate geology student.[60] Skilliter tells that she learned to wear jeans after her fellow students pulled up her skirt during a laboratory experiment. Along with other female students, she squirmed as a male professor sexualized a reluctant female "volunteer" in a putative demonstration of the reflectivity of light: "Light reflects off her eyes, and my, what beautiful eyes she has! Light reflects off her seductive lips, and light reflects off her A-HEMS, to the accompaniment of loud, mock throat clearing." Such classroom bias may explain why so few female students go on to graduate school. Confronted by unwelcoming classrooms, women may "voluntarily" withdraw their time and interest and elect not to complete first degrees or pursue graduate studies.

Whether in universities or colleges, the traditional curriculum regularly ignores women in course content and omits relevant scholarship by women and minority researchers. The paradigmatic subject of higher learning is still a white, able-bodied, heterosexual male despite the challenges raised by women's studies and inclusive curriculum initiatives. Conventional beliefs in the neutrality of the canon protect the traditional "male-stream" curriculum and pedagogy. Canadian historian Joy Parr claims that male sociability shapes most aspects of interaction within higher education. She points out that "teaching styles are patterned on patriarchal distance [and] . . . research priorities are framed by male concerns, so that findings about women seem specialised and findings about men seem general in interest and applicability."[61] Efforts by equity seekers to ensure a more inclusive curriculum are often dismissed by defenders of the status quo as nothing more than "political correctness" run amuck. Opposition to inclusive teaching and learning practices is sometimes justified as a defense against "politicizing" the classroom—a remarkable reminder that the currently exclusive classroom is perceived as "neutral." Few defenders of the status quo are persuaded of the enormous benefits generated by curricular inclusivity. Roxana Ng makes the compelling claim that anti-sexist and anti-racist initiatives "bring to light the biases with which so-called objective knowledge is constructed."[62] Notwithstanding many institutions' stated commitment to academic merit and excellence, protection of the status quo seems to be more highly prized by our post-secondary institutions than are critical thinking skills.

Even the very definition of scholarly knowledge is shaped by patriarchy. Due to the historical legacy of male domination, masculine concerns construct

22

what is considered "normal." Taking men's experiences as the norm has the corollary of making women appear "different," defined as lesser and inferior. In exploring this issue, Rosabeth Moss Kanter demonstrates that the "majority mentality" generally assumes superiority in knowledge, and "majority" experiences and values thereby become defined as the norm.[63] Dorothy Smith names this the "circle effect," which she explains as the long tradition of men attending to, and treating as significant, only what men say:

> What men were doing was relevant to men, was written by men about men for men. Men listened and listen to what one another said. A tradition is formed in this discourse of the past within the present. The themes, problematics, assumptions, metaphors, images—are formed as the circle of those present draws upon the work of the past.[64]

Women, she points out, can only share in this circle by receiving its terms and relevances, which are the terms and relevances of a discourse among men.

The phenomenon of making male experience central, majoritarian and normal is similar to the processes that marginalize people of colour in the academy. Such practices exclude racialized minorities without ever resorting to overt or personalized racism. Haideh Moghissi explains that, unlike the "man on the street" who practises an easily recognizable racism, most academics:

> disguise their racist attitudes and practices, and hide and suppress challenges to such beliefs more effectively, by resorting to more benign notions and seemingly neutral criteria, such as academic freedom and academic excellence. . . . Underlying the notion of "excellence" in such cases is the belief that being qualified and being coloured and/or female are mutually exclusive. . . .[65]

She attributes systemic racism and sexism to the liberal belief in equality of opportunity and the corresponding conviction that merit alone determines academic success. The proud academic tradition of objectivity, or what has been called the "view from nowhere," draws upon and tends to reproduce the privilege of the majority.[66]

While institutional "neutrality," objectivity and liberal organizational practices explain the lion's share of discrimination, the marginalization of women is not always so benign or directionless. Two decades of feminist scholarship and activism have forcefully drawn our attention to the multiple ways in which campuses are dangerous places for women. Sexual harassment is an unavoidable reality on Canadian campuses, as it is in the nation's homes, workplaces and streets.[67] Study after study in both Canada and the U.S. documents the magnitude of the problem. A Harvard survey, conducted in 1983, found that 32 percent of tenured women faculty, 49 percent of females without tenure, 41 percent of women graduate students and 34 percent of women undergraduates reported at least one experience of harassment by a person of authority while at that university. Disturbingly, 15 percent of these graduate students and 12 percent of the undergraduates consequently changed their academic plans because of the harassment.[68] A 1984 national study showed that one in four female students experienced some form of sexual harassment, which often resulted in severe psychological and/or educational impact.[69] Hall and Sandler (1986) also reported that between 20 percent to 30 percent of female undergraduates experienced some form of sexual harassment, ranging from leers and sexual innuendo to unwanted touching, bribes and threats.[70] Sexual harassment is an issue of discrimination that schools striving for excellence cannot ignore.[71]

Despite nearly two decades of efforts to transform institutions and "warm up" chilly climates, women and minorities have made only the smallest progress. Because of feminist and anti-racist campaigns, we are now more aware of the open prejudice and discrimination that continue to operate against women and other marginalized groups. Most campuses have formal commitments to gender equality and human rights which explicitly prohibit discrimination. Nevertheless, both the evidence and the case studies in this anthology show that nothing has really changed. Authors cover a range of issues, demonstrating that commitments have not been translated into action. Women and minorities are still excluded in academe.

The persuasive evidence has failed to galvanize institutional action, and progress towards equity proceeds at its glacial pace. Everyday practices continue to reinforce the current hierarchy of power. As a part of the regular business of higher education, these practices of exclusion are produced and reproduced. Because the discrimination is simply "normal," those with equity agendas become framed—consciously and unconsciously—as abnormal, unreasonable, rude and irrational. Quite rightly, equity campaigns are seen as serious threats to the main business of the university and to how things have always been done.[72]

TARRED AND FEATHERED: DISCREDITING EQUITY

Women's efforts to address and redress their lesser condition in Canadian post-secondary institutions are met more often with institutional apathy than with sympathy. Administrators and policy-makers may acknowledge the mountain of empirical evidence that proves systemic discrimination, yet they are rarely moved to act decisively to equalize treatment of the sexes. Moreover, as noted earlier, outright hostility frequently erupts in reaction to equity campaigns. According to traditionalists, political correctness is purportedly ruining all that is finest about the academy and women's activism for equality is undermining the very mission of colleges and universities.

A striking feature of contemporary discourse about post-secondary education is the vilification of equity campaigns. Popular, media and learned discussions about higher education in Canada are rife with accusations that affirmative action, employment equity and inclusivity will distort or destroy universities and colleges. In the face of campaigns for fairness, a vigorous defense of academic traditions is being reasserted.[73]

"Tarring" emerges repeatedly as a metaphor, one that is historically linked to racism. Men commonly claim that they are tarred by climate studies and that systemic discrimination implicates them personally. Since most men do not consciously (or do not acknowledge that they consciously) act in discriminatory ways, they frequently assume that claims of differential treatment or chilly climate must be false; hence, in their view, the women and minorities who disclose experiences of oppression must be lying. As liars, such women do not enjoy rights of academic freedom or expression, because the violated academic freedom is that of the aggrieved man who believes his reputation has been diminished. The media find such male claims of injustice particularly compelling. In June 1994 during the Learned Societies Conference, an annual national academic conference, one Calgary newspaper ran the sensational headline "Gender Wars Claim Another Victim," but the report was simply about a white male philosophy professor who was moving to the United States because he was unable to find a tenure track job in a Canadian university and was blaming his situation on political correctness.[74] Traditionalists make the outrageous claim that men are now the victims of reverse discrimination, and call for a return to discriminatory status quo traditions to protect the academy from the dangerous excesses of political activism.

The defense of the status quo, however, throws certain definitions of academic freedom into question. The three essential components of academic freedom are: freedom to conduct and publish research, freedom to teach and discuss and freedom to speak or write as an independent citizen without speaking on behalf of the institution.[75] Traditionally, academic freedom has been defined as an individual right and rarely has it been expanded to cover collective rights and responsibilities.[76] Academic freedom is double-edged; for example, overt sexism may be officially frowned upon but anti-feminism or homophobia are protected as freedom of expression. In terms of pedagogy, traditionalists argue that the canon of a discipline is fundamentally fine even if they must grudgingly admit that the contributions of some "others" need to be "added on." Add-ons, however, are permitted only so long as they do not disrupt the main business of teaching or learning. Sometimes defenders of the status quo continue to use teaching materials and practices that exclude minorities because they say they are protecting the canon and are resistant to "bringing politics into the classroom." This position reflects the naive belief that current practices of the academy are neutral and apolitical.

The widespread assumption that higher education is a meritocracy implies that ascribed characteristics are, officially, not supposed to make a difference to an individual's education or career. If women or racial minorities try to explain their subordination in structural terms, they are perceived as being antagonistic to the whole academic enterprise; since the system is purportedly neutral, the complaints of equity seekers must stem from their desire to demolish post-secondary educational institutions. The insistence by equity seekers that they are campaigning for inclusion in a *reconstructed* academy is lost amid howls of outrage that the treasured academy is under attack. Traditionalists are content with practices of exclusion, and they value their "right to not know."

The "right to not know" undergirds many traditional academic practices of exclusion.[77] Evidence shows that male faculty and administrators ignore the adverse impact of institutional and interpersonal practices on female students and colleagues. If they were to acknowledge the discriminatory effects of apparently neutral practices, then basic assumptions that men as a group take for granted would be challenged and the privileges that also accrue to men as a group would be undermined. When "harm doers" recognize that they have participated in inequitable relations, they tend to one of two reactions: to make restitution or to rationalize their harm through derogation of the victim, denial of responsibility and minimization of harm.[78] Given the evidence to date, rationalization of the harm is the standard reaction on Canadian campuses.

Disinterest and downright hostility to equity initiatives are popularly called a "backlash." This is an inappropriate metaphor since backlash implies the Newtonian inevitability that "For every action there is an an equal and opposite reaction."[79] Although equity campaigns have been met with fierce resistance, defenders of the status quo remain secure in the knowledge that male privilege continues to characterize the academy, as it has for centuries.

As equity seekers turn up the heat on Canadian campuses and produce proof that dispels the illusion of equity and inclusiveness, they also must respond to attempts to discredit their findings. Studies demonstrate how equity campaigns across the country are dismissed, marginalized and vilified[80] by way of a fairly predictable set of processes.

The most common way in which equity reports are vilified is through critiques of their research basis. Overwhelmingly, chilly climate and equity reports are dismissed by virtue of methodological failing or flaws. The commonly accepted scholarly practices of respecting anonymity and protecting the confidentiality of sources are most often singled out as the reason why a climate or equity report must be rejected. The fear is that women and minorities might say anything (or everything) behind the veil of anonymity. A corollary technique of vilification is a critique of the sampling method, which charges that researchers only spoke to the malcontents and thus failed to represent the views of the happy majority. Critiques of sources and sampling are often paired with a concern that men were not surveyed, and confidence is expressed that, had men been consulted, they would have been exonerated. The net effect of methodological questioning is to deny that any problem exists. An associated and perhaps not unintended effect is to discredit the producers of the equity reports. Another way in which the findings of equity reports are rejected centres on men, in general, disliking and refusing to be held accountable for the way their behaviour is perceived. Strong objections are raised to the evaluative criteria that equity seekers apply as proof of discrimination, especially the human rights assumption that discrimination can exist without intent and that differential treatment can occur without conscious design. On this point, Mary Rowe claims that "each person is his or her own expert on what constitutes a micro-inequity in any given instance."[81] Many traditionalists protest that such assumptions license irresponsible and reckless charges. In particular, most men seem largely unable to appreciate the analytic distinction between effect and intent; they respond to critiques of climate and systemic practices as though they were being personally attacked.

To a very large degree, men express their resistance and denial by vigorously attacking equity policies for being *unfair* to them. During the chilly climate upheaval in the political studies department at the University of Victoria, male faculty claimed that they had been harmed by equity policies and began civil proceedings for damages. In other universities, a similar pattern emerges. A 1984 survey of American colleges and universities showed that an "obsession with false complaints" was a "major source of resistance to the implementation of sexual harassment policies."[82] Men's objections centre around the fact that equity policies and human rights legislation make it very clear that individuals in positions of authority will be held accountable for the way their behaviour is perceived. Such accountability is a chilling prospect for those accustomed to viewing professional status as expanding privilege rather than increasing responsibility and obligation.[83]

A third technique for discrediting equity campaigns is the reattribution of responsibility for the harm. Equity seekers tend to be extremely precise in their identification of the causes of chilly climates, and they nearly universally identify institutionalized practices of discrimination and subordination. The overwhelming response is to shift responsibility from the institution to the person or group who named the problem. For example, when a female colleague objects to a sexist comment, she is frequently met with a sharp rebuke that she cannot take a joke and with negative judgments about her lack of collegiality. One woman's reflections on her experiences as a junior faculty member at a well-known Canadian business school supports this point: "responsibility for problems was constantly attributed to me, rather than to the system or my colleagues who perpetuate the negative climate. I have come to believe that such responses . . . constitute the most invidious aspect of the chilly climate."[84]

When the person with power transmogrifies the situation into one of his victimization, the real material and personal harm done to women is denied. The more powerful person in the conflict is usually able to garner greater support and has the weight of tradition and past practice insidiously working to his benefit. This transubstantiation of aggressor into victim is made possible, in part, by the fact that the real victims are generally less important to the institution. Angela Simeone dryly observes that "the fear held by some white males of being penalized by preferential treatment for women and minorities seems to be a groundless one, given the continued domination of white men in virtually every quantifiable measure of success."[85]

After denial, refusal of accountability and reattribution, resistance is often achieved by demonizing women, a phenomenon which sociologists call "moral panics."[86] A slippery slope argument is introduced: traditionalist voices thunder: "'If we let feminists dictate to us what we teach in our own courses, then what will happen to academic freedom? Any woman who is opposed to academic freedom is no colleague of mine!" Professor Sheila McIntyre, whose courageous work has made sexism in law more visible, calls this is the "takeover conspiracy."[87] Men manufacture a conspiracy, characterize the conspiracy as violent, express hostility against the mythical violent conspiracy and thereby legitimize their opposition to equity. With astonishing regularity, equity efforts are described as "anti-male abuse" that "tars all men with the same brush," "punishes young white men" and is practised by the "radical-feminist group think" of "intellectual tyrants."[88] Given the perceived totalitarianism of the equity takeover conspiracy, many men may even convince themselves that their own strong reactions are a reasonable response.

Finally, traditionalist defenses of the status quo are buoyed by appeals to proceduralism. Academic neutrality and carefully worded equity policies frequently have the effect of subverting equity measures. Procedures that are apparently neutral and apolitical are actually extremely effective in maintaining the status quo.[89] For example, until very recently the sexual harassment policy at the University of Toronto used criminal law criteria for ascertaining guilt: findings had to be "beyond a reasonable doubt," as opposed to the human rights test of "balance of probabilities." In a similar vein, the former race relations officer at the University of Western Ontario recounts how the apparently neutral procedure of protecting complainant and respondent confidentiality meant that she was silenced and could not reply to charges that the university was being overrun by "fascists."[90] Much of what makes climates chilly is the often unintended consequence of a collection of practices; thus, procedures that use the test of "intent" prevent action on systemic discrimination, and only permit redress for treatment that is personalized.

Methodological critique, lack of accountability, rejection and reattribution of responsibility, demonization of women and proceduralism combine to discredit equity seekers and their work. Together these techniques comfort those who insist on their "right to not know" about women's second-class status. As business as usual is maintained across Canadian campuses, the illusion and exclusion also are maintained. Women continue to be a tarred and feathered marginal majority.

THE ILLUSION

Belief in something that is neither true nor conforms with facts is an illusion, a false hope. At times illusions, such as a spectacular display of fireworks or a magician's tricks, can be harmless and entertaining. At other times, however, illusions are harmful to and for individuals and society.

One harmful illusion is that women and other marginalized groups are included in post-secondary education. Canada's post-secondary education system is vast and not restricted to ivy-covered campuses and traditional university classrooms; it also includes many other educational settings, such as technical institutes, schools of nursing and community colleges. The latter, established in Canada in the 1960s and 1970s, have become significant contributors to technical and vocational higher education. All of these educational institutions, however, practise "subtle, insidious and damaging forms of sexism;" they marginalize women and contribute to the equity myth.[91]

Although women are a majority in the Canadian population and they comprise the majority of students in post-secondary education, universities and colleges continue discriminatory practices that marginalize them. This illusion of inclusion is vigorously maintained by the institutions and even the public at large, but few actions, policies or practices support the hollow promise of equity.

Another harmful illusion is that the academy is based on merit. As intelligence, skills and abilities are distributed among all people within the population, universities and colleges should represent this diversity. Only systemic discrimination can explain the marginalization of women and other minorities within higher education. Top quality teaching, research and service, for and by both women and men in a climate fostering excellence for all scholars is not only a desirable but an attainable and long overdue goal.[92]

Women's inclusion is real in only one area. As tuition-paying customers seeking education and training, as well as degrees, certificates or diplomas, women are welcomed and their dollars are appreciated. In all other areas, women's inclusion is token, simulated and definitely illusory. If women are included in only one way, as students, but are rarely seen in other positions, as full professors or administrators, the message is strong and clear. If women see other women working only in supportive roles in the academy, how can they be expected to envisage themselves in academic or professional careers? If women are not sharing with men in the development and implementation of curricula, programs and policies, how can institutional practices support the entire student population?

Post-secondary education is irrefutably biased: it teaches and supports a male perspective of the world, operates in a manner amenable to men's priorities, and the status quo continues as masculine privilege is protected and perpetuated. Excuses for the discrimination vary in creativity and credibility, reflecting either intentional illusion or academic delusion. None of the institutional excuses is supported by the evidence, as the articles collected in this anthology conclusively demonstrate.

Just as the attitudes and behaviours of people in an organization make up the culture, so too does an institutional culture determine how well an organization functions. Our predominantly male-run universities and colleges do not function as well as they could or should. In a 1966 watershed report on university governance in Canada, a pithy comment described our university administrators as "men somewhat set in their ways and too busy to have time for forward planning and new ideas."[93] In the same vein but a quarter century later, the 1991 Smith Commission of Inquiry on Canadian University Education stated that "universities are looking rather like places where the women study and the men run the institution."[94] This is the institutional culture that determines how effectively—or ineffectively—our post-secondary organizations function.

The traditional academic culture alienates the majority of the students and restricts women's representation among faculty and administration. Women are being taught, and institutions are being governed and administered, by a predominantly greying and balding white male population. This academic environment has earned the caustic label ascribed to it: "a harem culture."[95] And, despite all the reviews, reports and recommendations on post-secondary governance, universities and colleges continue to protect this institutional culture wherein policies and practices reinforce power imbalances.

The status of academic life in the 1990s was aptly summarized by Sheelagh Conway in the *Globe and Mail*. She dispelled all illusions of merit, inclusion or even vigour in higher education with her statement that "Canada's universities are elite, outdated institutions, sullied by sexism, racism and classism. And they certainly are not healthy."[96] What more can be said? The "old boys" culture determines effectiveness. In turn, effectiveness determines efficiency. Without the former, the latter decreases. Without the latter, personal, financial and all costs increase and political support wanes.

The axiom "What goes around, comes around" may be applicable to this situation. We know that the consequences of the alienating academic culture are being felt by our publicly-funded institutions. When taxpayers are unhappy with some of the products, processes and outcomes they fund, and when the public demands transparency and accountability, legislators act accordingly. Post-secondary funding has been decreasing consistently for more than a decade. As public and fiscal support declines, institutions are neither acknowledging their responsibility nor accepting the equity challenge, even though their very existence may depend upon it.

The consequences of this alienating academic culture are being felt by everyone in society. When the post-secondary status quo continues unchanged, with lip service being paid and exclusion being practised, systemic discrimination is perpetuated. Many graduates go out into the labour force and practise what they have seen and heard. Therefore, for another generation, some personnel practices will continue to be based on preferential treatment, unfair advantages and inequality. The playing field will not be level for yet another generation, because the root causes of discrimination—ignorance, privilege and stereotyping—will marginalize the majority of our human resources.[97] Inclusion, or the merit principle in action, will be the illusion it has always been for more than half the population, the taxpayers, the electorate and the nation.

TOWARDS INCLUSION
With strength and tenacity, women and other equity seekers are working towards the actualization of their dream of an equity culture on campuses, a culture that bases merit on performance rather than on hereditary privilege.[98] Their determination is unshaken by the traditionalists' ever-mounting defense of the status quo. Notwithstanding personal and organizational resistance to equity, women and other minorities continue to strive for equality. They are exposing and confronting the fundamental unfairness of the gap between the illusion of inclusion and the reality of their exclusion.

Articles in the final section of this anthology address the future of women in post-secondary education. Despite the persistent and growing crisis of underfunding and the continental neo-conservative movement to dismantle affirmative action, the authors clearly show that the women's movement and other forces for social justice have made strong inroads into popular consciousness and political discourse. As the presence of female students increases and the number of female faculty grows, the possibility of ignoring us diminishes.

With persistence and humour nurtured by collective action, women are forging strong alliances and garnering public support.[99] Under the rallying cry of fairness and equal treatment, the exclusive academy cannot hold out much longer. In one way or another, the illusion will become a reality; the only questions are when and how. Sooner and voluntarily? Or later and forcibly?

The myth of an inclusive post-secondary Canadian education system has been exposed. We know that universities and colleges are expected and, indeed, ought to lead the way with respect to the status of women in our society. We also know that they do not.[100] We know that the systemic discrimination in post-secondary education causes inequality in society, increases public costs, decreases institutional effectiveness and efficiency and thereby precludes academic excellence.

When the gap between rhetoric and reality is reduced, systemic inequality in academe and its harmful consequences for society will decrease. When merit in higher education is based on performance alone, systemic discrimination can disappear. Finally, when the blustering, prevaricating, tarring, feathering and marginalizing of the majority of the population cease, inclusion will replace illusion.[101]

31

NOTES

1. Simeone 1987: 34.
2. Vickers and Adam 1977: 99.
3. Wylie 1995: 29.
4. Numerous discussions of racism in higher education exist, although fewer analyses of racism than of sexism can be found in the Canadian context. For Canadian reviews, see: MadhavaRau 1995; Carasco 1993a and 1993b; and Monture 1990.
5. Vickers and Adam 1977: 9.
6. Vickers and Adam 1977: 9.
7. *Globe and Mail*, August 10, 1995, and cited in Carasco 1993a and 1993b: 1.
8. Cited in MadhavaRau 1995: 327.
9. For examples of recent books that make a case against current efforts to redress chilly climates, see: Emberley 1996; Fekete 1994; and Marchak 1996.
10. Chamberlain 1988: 183.
11. Cited in Joyce 1991: 30.
12. Daniels 1994: 3.
13. Caplan 1993.
14. Vickers and Adam 1977: 114.
15. Statistics Canada 1993c: Table 1.
16. Simeone, 1987: 29. These figures include faculty at two-year American colleges as well as those in four-year programs, making direct comparisons with Canada somewhat misleading.
17. Women's marginal status as faculty is still better than the low participation rates for faculty of colour and native people. Relatively few Canadian studies document discrimination based on race or ethnicity, although these are crucially important variables. By way of indicating the dimensions of racial exclusion, a 1990 study of the University of Western Ontario showed that people of colour made up 5.3 percent; people with disabilities, 3.4 percent; and aboriginal peoples, less than 0.3 percent of the total teaching faculty (Backhouse 1995: 86).
18. Vickers and Adam 1977: 114; Statistics Canada 1993c: Table 1. "Full-time" is defined as staff at or above the Assistant Professor rank.
19. Statistics Canada 1990; Saunders et al. 1992.
20. Chamberlain 1988: 256.
21. Statistics Canada 1993c: 7.
22. *Report of the Royal Commission on the Status of Women in Canada* 1970; Symons and Page 1984; Saunders et al. 1992.
23. Saunders et al. 1992.
24. Simeone 1987: 9.
25. Simeone 1987: 8.
26. Widnall 1988: 241.
27. Cited in Wylie 1995: 33.
28. See the personal histories collected in Gillet 1981; Parr 1987; and Stewart 1990.
29. Lussier 1995.
30. Symons and Page 1984.
31. Symons and Page 1984.
32. Wylie 1995: 33.
33. Statistics Canada 1993c: 15.
34. Statistics Canada 1993c: 19.

35. Acker 1992: 60.
36. Rothblum 1988: 13. Interestingly, rates of involuntary termination did not prove to be differentiated by sex in this study.
37. Riggs et al. 1993.
38. Tierney and Rhoads 1993.
39. News and Comment 1991.
40. Wenneras and Wold 1997.
41. See, for example, the personal histories collected in Gillet 1981; Parr 1987; and Stewart 1990.
42. Backhouse 1995: 67, 69.
43. Clark-Jones and Coyne1990: 41.
44. Backhouse 1995: 189.
45. For elaboration of this relationship, see Mills 1959.
46. Although learners and teachers make up the focus of this anthology, female and minority academic staff also experience marginalization and confront "chilly climates." Academic staff have rarely been the focus of research; two notable exceptions are Ruchkall 1997 and Looker 1993.
47. Sandler and Hall 1986: 1–2.
48. Sandler and Hall 1986: 2.
49. Sandler and Hall 1986: 3.
50. Rowe 1990: 6.
51. Rowe 1990.
52. Feldthusen 1995: 296.
53. Wenneras and Wold 1997.
54. Milne 1995: 35–36.
55. Rich 1979: 241.
56. Aisenberg and Harrington 1988.
57. Sandler and Hall 1986.
58. Sandler and Hall 1986.
59. York University Women's Supplement 1991.
60. Skilliter 1994.
61. Parr 1989: 2.
62. Ng 1993: 3.
63. Kanter 1979.
64. Smith 1975.
65. Moghissi 1994.
66. Harding 1984.
67. Statistics Canada 1993b.
68. Simeone 1987: 115.
69. Robertson et al. 1988: 811.
70. Sandler and Hall 1986: 10.
71. Robertson et al. 1988: 811.
72. Smith 1989.
73. These movements are actively organized. The most well-known group in the United States is the National Association of Scholars. See Wier and Richler 1994.
74. *Calgary Herald* 1994.
75. Chait and Ford 1982: 55.
76. Drakich et al. 1993.

77. Feldthusen 1995.
78. Chamberlain 1988: 168.
79. Newson 1992 argues that "backlash" is a problematic metaphor.
80. Prentice 1994.
81. Rowe 1990.
82. Robertson et al. 1988: 808.
83. Robertson et al. 1988: 808.
84. Anonymous 1990.
85. Simeone 1987: 44.
86. Hebdige 1979.
87. Cited in Feldthusen 1995.
88. With the support of a University of Manitoba Research Grant, Susan Prentice prepared several documentary histories of the reception of chilly climate reports on Canadian campuses. Quotes cited here are drawn from these documentary histories.
89. Prentice 1994.
90. MadhavaRau 1995.
91. Stalker 1993.
92. Stalker, 1995.
93. Cameron 1991: 306.
94. Smith 1991.
95. Stalker 1995. The concept of the "harem culture" also was discussed at the 1997 University of British Columbia's Academic Freedom and the Inclusive University Conference, in a panel discussion entitled, "Tracing the Discourses on Academic Freedom and Inclusiveness," featuring Jack Granatstein, Fred Shauer and Dorothy Smith.
96. Conway 1991.
97. Stalker and Rubin 1993.
98. Gardner 1961.
99. The PAR-L list, as an example, unites activists, analysts, researchers, academics and others advocating women's equality in discussions of policy, action and research in Canada. The PAR-L site is located at http://www.unb.ca/web/PAR-L.
100. Symons and Page 1984.
101. Illusion has been a recommended political strategy in academe throughout this century. See Cornford 1922, whose advice to young academic men was, "I like you the better for your illusions; but it cannot be denied that they prevent you from being effective." Seventy-five years later, the editors thank Cornford for inspiration regarding the title of this anthology.

Part I
Post-Secondary Education: The Inclusion Myth Then and Now

The Four Phases of Academe: Women in the University*

Margaret Gillett

As we all know, universities are extraordinarily complex institutions. No two are identical. All have different histories, all are the products of their culture and their time, but there are some general things we can say about them. As I have thought about the history of the university as an institution, I have identified four distinct, albeit overlapping, phases as far as women are concerned.

PHASE I
Quite simply, the universities of Phase I were characterized by the exclusion of women. They grew out of the monastic tradition and were essentially elite institutions with male students and teachers, patriarchal values, hierarchical structures and curricula strongly influenced by the writings of the church fathers, Aristotle and, later, neo-Platonism. Phase I was long and slow, dating roughly from the late eleventh century to the early nineteeth century. It spans the time from when informal congregations of students (universitas) clustered around noted scholars became institutionalized as universities, down to the development of separate, secular, post-secondary institutions for women.

The ancient foundations were based on an ideological dichotomy in which male and female were opposites: man was strong, powerful, intelligent; woman was weak, dependent, emotional. From this view, higher learning would fit men into appropriate public or leadership positions but was unnecessary for women. Nature and experience would suffice for them in their supportive domestic and child-bearing roles. These ideas may sound like very familiar clichés, but it is important to realize how they seeped into the very stones of the universities and could not easily or quickly be eradicated.

The general acceptance of male intellectual dominance obscured even the possibility that there could be intelligent women of scholarly bent. Yet intelligent women certainly did exist and some of them could find spiritual satisfaction, refuge from forced marriages as well as access to learning in the nunneries. Throughout the ages there have also been a few exceptional women who attained fame for their intellect, in spite of all the obstacles. One was Trotula, who was said to have held a chair in medicine at Salerno in the eleventh century; another was the redoutable Hildegard of Bingen (1098–1179). In the twelfth century, Hildegard founded a Benedictine abbey, wrote treatises on medicine and theology, composed poetry and music (which we still hear today), and commanded respect from princes and prelates. There have also been intelligent women who protested their exclusion from the world of learning. At the beginning of the fifteenth century, Christine de Pizan (1365–1429) wrote in her remarkable work, *The Treasure of the City of Ladies* (1405):

> If it were the custom to send daughters to schools like sons and to teach them the sciences properly, they would learn as thoroughly and understand the subleties of all the arts and sciences as well as the sons.[1]

But for centuries, it was not the usual custom to send girls to school and women remained locked out of the academy. So Phase I, the purely patriarchal and masculine era of the university, lasted almost 800 years. That was a very long time indeed, a time in which traditions became entrenched and very difficult to change.

PHASE II

The second phase of the life of the university began in the nineteenth century and was the product of fundamental intellectual and social upheavals. The old hierarchies, which had been undermined by the ideas of the Enlightenment and the American and French Revolutions, were further weakened by the forces of science, industrialization and urbanization. The university itself began to change. Largely through American influence, it became more secular, more broadly based with a wider clientele and a more practical curriculum. Through German influence, the academy became more concerned with research and graduate level teaching. Phase II was a period when, in the wider sphere, demands were being made for social reforms such as the abolition of slavery, property rights for married women and the female franchise. In this context, there was at last a chance for the women who had protested their exclusion to be taken more seriously. A nascent belief that women might be entrusted with higher learning was reinforced by the argument that the welfare of future generations depended on educated mothers.

   Of course, there were also countervailing ideas—some of them spread by "scientific experts"—that the education of women would be both individually detrimental and socially harmful. For example, in his book *Sex in Education or A Fair Chance for the Girls* (1873), Dr. Edward Clarke of Harvard drew on an idea from classical physics—that the amount of energy is finite—to argue that because women's delicate bodies have only a fixed amount of energy, rigorous study would divert that energy towards the brain and away from the essential female reproductive organs. Higher education for women would thus result in an excess of brain energy, thereby inducing madness. Conversely, lack of energy in the reproductive organs would produce deformed offspring or, worse yet, a generation of barren women, leading ultimately to the demise of the race.

For men of Dr. Clarke's persuasion, the idea of women in the university was an abomination. Yet the growing clamour for female education was partly satisfied by the appearance of separate colleges for women. Some of these "female academies," seminaries and finishing schools had what were thought to be appropriately "ladylike" curricula, offering literature, music, deportment and the like; others (Vassar, for example) considered themselves "real" colleges with rigorous, intellectual fare that emulated that of the men's colleges. Both kinds of colleges flourished, especially in the United States, and along with normal schools for the training of elementary teachers, they also gave opportunities for the employment of educated women. It might be noted, though, that the presidents of these institutions were quite often men—even if the "lady" principal did all the work.

It was just a matter of time before coeducation in colleges was introduced. It is common to date the trend from about 1837 when women were first admitted to Oberlin, then a small residential college in the U.S. mid-west. However, this development was not quite as enlightened as it might seem. It was not so much an idealistic acknowledgement of women's intellectual worth as unvarnished expediency. The trustees realized that the extra fees women would bring would help defray operating costs, and the women themselves would help with the domestic chores that male students could not be expected to perform.

In the well-established institutions for men, hostility and skepticism still greeted the idea of higher education for women and the "gentler sex" was kept at bay by one excuse or another, right down to the lack of toilet facilities. Among those given in the 1870s by McGill's principal John William Dawson was not that women were not good enough for McGill, but that McGill was not good enough for them![2] Yet those few exceptional women who had appeared throughout the ages still existed and their voices were now being heard. In Montréal, courageous, intelligent and ambitious young women like Grace Ritchie, Rosalie McLea and Nellie Reid, all of whom had won top marks in the matriculation examinations, wanted access to McGill. Their mothers and other women supported them, encouraging them to approach the formidable Principal Dawson. Their cause was also supported by broadminded men in high places—some idealistic, some generous—who used their power to change the rules that excluded women. Lord Strathcona's offer to Principal Dawson of $50,000 for the higher education of women was what made the crucial difference at McGill.[3]

The second phase was one where women were gradually and rather grudgingly allowed to enter the traditional male sanctum. It lasted for about 150 years and has not entirely played itself out. It was notable for its "firsts"—the first women to be admitted to established universities; the first woman to get a bachelor's degree (the first in Canada was Grace Annie Lockhart, BSc Mount Allison, 1875), a master of arts, a doctorate and a medical degree; the first woman professor; the first woman dean; the first woman chancellor.

McGill has the distinction of appointing the first woman full professor in Canada. In 1912, Carrie Derick became Professor of Morphological Botany, but there were certain reservations that take some of the gloss off that story. Her promotion, which involved no salary increase but included the expectation that she should set up her male colleague's demonstrations, was really only a consolation prize and this was made excruciatingly clear to her.[4]

That was typical of Phase II, which was a period of peculiar ambivalence, characterized by "cat and mouse" strategies. For example, after two separate colleges for women were established at Oxford (Lady Margaret Hall in 1878 and Somerville in 1879), women were allowed to attend University lectures but they were "unofficially present" and did not count as students. Chancellor Lord Curzon who headed an inquiry into university reform, admitted in 1905 that "Oxford yielded to the reality while withholding the name."[5] At Oxford, women gradually won the right to take examinations but were not accorded degrees until 1920. At the University of Toronto, the game was even more astounding. In the early 1880s, women were allowed to take exams but were not allowed to attend the lectures. Until 1884 when they were officially admitted, they were forced to eavesdrop on the lectures from the corridors. That year was also the one in which women were admitted to McGill—but only to the Faculty of Arts and on the basis of separate classes, the accompaniment of a chaperone and limited library privileges. Women were "in" but not "of" the university. This had nothing to do with their abilities, for they proved themselves to be very able scholars; it had everything to do with traditional attitudes.

A constant theme found in the writings of the women students of Phase II was loneliness. Pioneer women, for all their boldness, were distressed by innumerable petty humiliations, including booby traps placed in their seats, graffiti scrawled on classroom walls and bawdy stories told by instructors. Elizabeth Smith, one of Canada's first female medical students at Queen's, wrote in 1880:

> No one knows or can know what a furnace we are passing through these days at college. We suffer torment, we shrink inwardly, we are hurt cruelly.... It was so unbearable on one occasion that one of the ladies went to the lecturer afterwards and asked him to desist from that sort of persecution or she would go and tell his wife exactly what he had said.[6]

However, the male medical students had a much stronger counter-threat. They warned that if the women remained in the Queen's Medical School, they would migrate en masse. The administration succumbed to this threat, so women had to go.

If the female students of Phase II were uncomfortable, early women instructors did not have an easy time of it either. They were faced with salary differences, few prospects of advancement, no power but much patronizing, which was especially humiliating when it came from some of the most respected "gentlemen" on campus. Some of the limitations placed on the "ladies" were serious, others laughable. For example, Dr. Alice Hamilton, an acknowledged expert in industrial diseases, became the first woman appointed to the Harvard School of Public Health. So that her appointment would not be considered a precedent, three ridiculous limitations were placed upon it: Dr. Hamilton was not to participate in the academic procession at convocation; she was not eligible for faculty tickets to the football games; and she was not allowed into the faculty club. Initially, women were not eligible for the McGill Faculty Club either. In the history of the club, Frank Scott described "The Great Circle" of discussion around the fire in the lounge as one enjoyed by men exclusively.[7] In 1936 when Dr. Maude Abbott became the first female member she was subject to restrictions, and for many years the Faculty Club Handbook instructed ladies not to loiter in the entrance but to go quickly upstairs. It informed them that they could not ride in the elevator unless accompanied by a [male] member, that they could not enter the main lounge or, except for special circumstances, the main dining room.

Women achieved full membership in the club only after a referendum in 1966. One woman academic who participated in this told me that she voted "no" because she thought "it was nice for the men to have a place for themselves." She represented those Phase II women who humbly felt they were intruders in academia and who still revered male authority, no matter what limitations were placed upon them.

PHASE III

Phase III roughly covers the second half of the twentieth century. (Note that the phases are becoming significantly shorter as change accelerates.) One of the most obvious characteristics of Phase III was the significant increase in the number of female students at universities—the apparent demise of the exceptional few. In the 1970s, women students began to approach half and later more than half of the overall undergraduate population. This was true in North America and many other parts of the world. Currently in Canada, women constitute about 55 percent of the undergraduates. This growth has been sustained and, even though it has been unevenly distributed, women are now studying or teaching in virtually every discipline. The population of female faculty also rose in Phase III, but not in proportion to the students; in Canada it hovered between 15 percent and 20 percent. At present, about 23 percent of the tenured faculty and just under 10 percent of the full professors at McGill are female.[8] This is an improvement over Phase II, but does not really constitute a critical mass—a proportion so significant that it must be taken into consideration when all important decisions are being made and can itself affect the

40

decision-making process.

Another Phase III development was that single-sex colleges began to go "co-ed." In the late 1960s even elite women's colleges, such as the Seven Sisters in the U.S and those at Oxford and Cambridge, began to accept male students. There was also a change in the demographic composition of the female population at most institutions. In Phase II, university women in countries like Canada were usually white and middle-class; now there were gradually increasing numbers of women from other social strata and ethnic backgrounds. These developments obviously reflected changes in the general intellectual, social, economic and political climates of the second half of our century. Movements such as civil rights, the "second wave" of feminism, human rights and multiculturalism have all made a difference in women's aspirations, opportunities, achievements and even the way we dress. I recall a minor incident that is symbolic of the early part of Phase III. One wet Saturday in 1964, a woman faculty member tried to enter the Macdonald College library wearing slacks discreetly covered by her raincoat. Her dress was deemed inappropriate and she was politely asked to leave. Of course, it wasn't the raincoat that was objectionable; it was the pants.

That woman was ahead of her time. From about the mid-sixties on, women not only dared to wear pants on campus and in restaurants and other respectable public places, but they started to speak out. Great numbers of North American women felt liberated from the isolation of suburban domesticity and male dominance by the ideas in Simone de Beauvoir's *La Deuxième Sexe* (1952) and Betty Friedan's *The Feminine Mystique* (1963). In 1967, Laura Sabia, then president of the Canadian Federation of University Women, threatened Prime Minister Lester Pearson that, unless he approved a royal commission on the status of women in Canada, she would march on Ottawa with 2,000 women. She was bluffing, but we got the royal commission. In the 1970s, McGill students brought in radical feminists like Kate Millett to stir things up on campus (Millett gave her view of it in her book called *Flying*, 1974). Later, on a visit to Concordia, Gloria Steinem advocated that women abandon the lady-like demeanour of Phase II in favour of "outrageous acts and every-day rebellions."

Especially in the early days of Phase III, there was much talk of "sisterhood." This was clearly manifest in the flourishing of women's conferences. These meetings had a special aura, one tinged with the glamour of forbidden fruit—women talking to women about things that mattered apart from the personal and the familial. Women academics of the era converted time-worn cliches like: "Behind every successful man there is a woman" to "In front of every successful woman there is a man—in her way" and "Woman's place is in the home" became "Woman's place is in the home and in the House of Commons."

The strength of the movement can be gauged by the fact that 1975 was declared International Women's Year and 1976–85, International Women's

Decade. In 1975 at McGill, we celebrated in several ways including: a special issue of the *McGill Journal of Education*;[9] a campus-wide survey of academic interest in research and teaching on women, which led to the establishment of the Senate Committee on Women and ultimately to the Centre for Research and Teaching on Women; and a very well supported public lecture series. We were honoured that one of our speakers was Madame Therese Casgrain, who had done so much to achieve the vote for the women of Québec in 1940. We celebrated again in 1984 to mark the centenary of women's admission to McGill. One of our forceful speakers that year was Mary Daly, author of *Beyond God the Father: Toward a Philosophy of Women's Liberation* (1973) and other radical books. She shocked many members of her audience when, instead of congratulating us, she chastized the women of McGill for so humbly and gratefully applauding the fact that we were *allowed* in. She thought we should have stormed our way through the barriers and not just waited for men to let us in at their convenience.

Mary Daly was one of the many determined people of Phase III who helped raise women's awareness of their suppressed status and their unrealized potential. As a result of their work, there was a proliferation of conscious-raising or "CR" groups, the development of networks and the articulation of fresh ideas about women's role in academia and their place in the curriculum. Of particular note was the coining of new words such as "sexism" and expressions such as "sexual harassment." Once these phenomena had been named, the Establishment had to acknowledge that they existed and, moreover, that they existed in the gentle groves of academe and not just out in the cruel "real world." Universities then appointed administrative officers or units with particular responsibility for the welfare of women students and members of staff. It is true that official positions such as the deans of women existed in Phase II when the university stood *in loco parentis* for its students, but in Phase III these positions tended to be based more on notions of social justice than on paternalism or protective motherliness.

Phase III was also a period of open demands for things that could only have been whispered in Phase II (and not even thought of in Phase I): affirmative action, salary equity and child care; objections to the Lady Godiva rides at the University of British Columbia and to macho publications like *The Plumbers' Pot* at McGill; maternity leave, paternity leave and job sharing arrangements; the appointment of a few women to senior academic positions (again, those exceptional few); and the publication of a seemingly endless stream of reports, papers and books on women, including a history of women at McGill in 1981. Phase III was infused with action, excitement, change and achievement. It was a good time to be a woman on campus.

However, as positive as all this was, the patriarchal heritage persisted in many forms, including unequal status, power and general attitudes. The voices of some Phase III women still echoed the discomforts of Phase II. In the 1980s one young woman reported, much as Virginia Woolf had in the 1920s, that when she walked into an Oxford library she felt that the knowledge contained there did not and could not belong to her.[10] As for taking a doctorate at that ancient foundation, it was almost a subversive act. In 1989, Mary Catherine Bateson, former dean of faculty at Amherst College, Massachusetts (and daughter of anthropologist Margaret Mead), wrote about the enduring double standard and "the steady drag of disparagement and prejudice pulling [women] toward the acceptance of subordinate roles." She said, "Nowadays, prejudice is relative, not absolute. There is no fixed rule that excludes, just a different probability. . . . . There is always that slight stacking of the deck, the extra stress, the waiting prejudice that amplifies every problem."[11]

Although bias was now more subtle, overt or violent examples of hostility toward women were still evident in occurences of gang rape on campus and exhibitions like the "No Means Yes" banners that boys "just being boys" hung out their dorm windows at Queen's University several years ago. The depths of misogyny were reached in December 1989 when Marc Lepine murdered fourteen students at the Ecole Polytechnique because they were women. Feminists absolutely refuse to believe that the massacre was merely the work of an individual psychopath.

PHASE IV
We are entering Phase IV right now. Just as the other phases have overlapped, so Phase IV is emerging out of Phase III and will probably continue well into the next century. You may wonder what it will be like. Since we have seen a progressive development through Phases II and III, it might be reasonable to suppose that Phase IV might just keep advancing and become a period in which we consolidate our gains. It might be a time when we take gender equity as an uncontroversial given, one that is reflected in all academic policies and practices. Now that enlightened academic leaders are well aware of the harmful and wasteful effects of past prejudices, they might make wholehearted efforts to bring about the just academic society. Recently, the McGill principal actively encouraged women to apply for senior positions at his university, despite the stark budget for 1995–96, the vice-principal (finance) recognized that "provision for pay equity adjustments" is one of the important demands for the future that cannot continue to be neglected.[12] Given these developments it might happen that Phase IV will turn out to be characterized by women's full integration into all aspects of the academic community.

This is something devoutly to be wished, but there are both present and potential problems—"dangers" might be a better word. After all, we live in what seems to be an increasingly violent and constraining world where the media report many discouraging items, such as the elimination of the federal Advisory Council on the Status of Women and the alleged demise of the National Action Committee. Even on International Women's Day 1995, *The Montréal Gazette* quoted a Canadian woman senator as saying women are responsible for the rearing of men who abuse women. Also on that day, the Toronto edition of the *Globe and Mail* headlined, "Women shunted aside in China" and detailed how, at a news conference for the major UN World Conference on Women, eight out of nine people at the head table were men because, organizers said, "We cannot have women organize this work just because they are women!"

These recent examples of regression could be multiplied endlessly, both at home and abroad, giving the impression that our progress in Phase III may have been only a veneer. Paula Caplan's *Lifting a Ton of Feathers* (1993) shows that despite the 110 formal inquiries about the status of women in Canadian universities in the last three decades, patriarchal attitudes are not much changed. The academic context is still infused with a residual belief in male superiority and, even if we achieve what is considered to be a critical mass of women, we have to remember that numbers are not as important as ideology. This is not just a problem for women in universities, as another recent book shows. Sydney Sharpe's *The Gilded Ghetto: Women and Political Power in Canada* (1994) concluded that, despite the record number of 53 women (18 percent) in our present parliament of 295, female politicians still "do not rate." They are still routinely mistaken by attendants for secretaries, wives or visitors, considered fair game for sexist remarks by other MPs, and criticized by the press if they indulge in the rowdy badinage that passes muster for debate among the men. Sharpe's picture shows that we still have a "relentlessly male institution" on the Hill, as does Caplan's for academia. On the other hand, we no longer have the advantage of having a clearly discernible common enemy so we may, paradoxically, become complacent and victims of our own success. While we are very glad to have women's studies classes, which in Phase III were joys to teach, we now find them increasingly difficult and are distressed when some students try, in the name of female solidarity, to impose "guilt trips" on female professors if they give low grades.[13] Phase IV may actually be a more dangerous time for women as we adjust more comfortably to the male norms and the male establishment becomes more accepting of women. Some women now have become "honorary males."

To become an "honorary male" was a response for some newcomers of Phase II and a strategy of others in Phase III, especially those who wanted to be known as scholars and did not want to be categorized as "women" or "women professors." Some of these—perhaps another "exceptional few"—seem to have been immune from any sense of exclusion or loneliness. Whether it is a question of their particular personalities or their good fortune to have had strong mentors and especially sympathetic colleagues, they have been able to ignore what has been identified as "the chilly climate" for women in academe.[14] Some of them contemptuously reject the idea of affirmative action because they see it as both an unnecessary and a demeaning form of special pleading. About two years ago, the McGill Association of University Teachers (MAUT) was considering a moderate resolution to make twenty-five merit-based appointments of women in an attempt to achieve gradually parity of numbers of male and female professors at McGill; two of the most strenuous objectors were women. One was young and in a male-stereotyped discipline, the other was a senior person in a humanities area. The senior woman, who seemed to completely misunderstand the ideal of equity, stridently objected to what she called the "cuntification" of the university. Her extraordinary expression startled everyone; it was difficult to know how much of an impact this had on those present, but the resolution was finally turned down. Parity remains a long way off.

In Phase IV, however, women will have at least two other options besides becoming honorary males. One is, again paradoxically, to acknowledge that women, their opinions and their research interests tend to be marginalized and to accept this marginalization as an inherent part of a valuable but flawed institution. Some women now voluntarily withdraw from the struggle and go about their own scholarly affairs. Dr. Ruth Hubbard, a professor of biology at Harvard, chose this "disidentifying" path. In her book, *The Shape of Red*, she wrote that she actually found strength in the feeling that she was an outsider. Surprisingly, this is an option that Virginia Woolf may have supported. In *Three Guineas* (1938) she said that women must have enough education and power to be able to remain outsiders in order to retain their identities. However, as Ruth Hubbard recognized, this option carries a serious disadvantage. She said, "I have jeopardized my effectiveness in departmental politics and virtually eliminated myself from the decision-making process."[15]

Apart from either becoming "honorary males" or remaining outsiders, there is another choice for women in Phase IV. This third option is to recognize that, over time, we have positively changed the nature of the university and can continue to do so. We have successfully managed to make changes to the curriculum and to get some long-neglected women rewritten into our disciplines; we have challenged the notion that scientific research is necessarily objective, showing that gender bias has lain hidden in the questions asked, the interpretations made and the funds available; we have chipped away at male complacency and shown that we *can* teach, conduct research and contribute to the academic community. Many would agree with the McGill woman who wrote recently: "Women reflect and react differently from men in certain situations—not necessarily more wisely, but differently . . . [and] it makes many of us impatient when men pretend that their way of thinking is inclusive."[16] Women who choose the third option want to retain the difference, want it accepted and respected. They do not want to be made over.

Yet, even if they do not want to become "old boys," they would like the privileges accorded to the members of "the old boys' network." They want to be fully admitted to the scholarly community as a whole and to have this acknowledged; to be given major responsibilities; to have, for example, an all-female PhD committee that is as respected as an all-male one; and to have research on women taken seriously. Still,under the pressures of the new entrepreneurial university with larger classes, fewer professors and less security, some of the very things that women have held most dear will be threatened. These are things that not only permitted the development of individual scholars, but also held the promise of humanizing academia—personal qualities like caring in our dealings with students, qualitative methodologies in the quest for truth, cooperation rather than competition in dealings with colleagues. No one would ever wish to restore the biases and restrictions of Phase II just for the sake of preserving "difference." However, it must be recognized that differences may not only be endangered by overt discrimination, they may be obliterated by three very common contemporary phenomena—stress, fatigue and economic expediency.

In the summer of 1994 (when no one was supposed to be looking), the McGill Pensions Committee reversed a hard-won policy of paying equal pensions to men and women. The three-man committee took up the old, outlawed argument that economic reality and demographics demanded that women should receive lower pensions than men. This incredibly retrogressive step was taken because women as a group live longer than men as a group. No one knows, of course, whether female academics live longer than male academics. Fortunately, the Pensions Committee did not get away with it. The decision was reversed—but only after a great outcry from the McGill community and months of wrangling. Eternal vigilance is still necessary.

As we make our way through the "nasty nineties," the third option for women seems to offer the most. However, women are still vulnerable and we must see to it that institutions do not put their relatively few women on endless, exhausting committees as tokens to "political correctness." At McGill we must be concerned about other women as well as ourselves and inquire into how much a hostile cultural climate contributed to the tragic deaths of Dr. Justine Sergent and her husband, both of whom committed suicide in 1993 in the midst of an intolerably stressful professional controversy at the Montréal Neurological Institute. We must watch closely the effects of "downsizing" on women—for example at McGill, the collapsing of the position of equity officer into the double job of assistant to the principal and equity officer.

Phase IV is not going to be easy. That much is obvious. But it also has marvellous potential, which university women must realize. It will truly be the information age, in which the current conveniences of the internet, CD-ROM and many other advances of science and technology will expand exponentially. Digital concordance will bring scholars of the world much closer together. Women can end their isolation by joining in the work to be done on campus as well as by joining e-mail groups. These range from the new, very general international Women's Policy, Action and Research List, established by the Advisory Council on the Status of Women, to very specialized networks like the Jane Austen E-mail Group, begun by Dr. Jacqueline Reid-Walsh of McGill. It would be a big mistake to think that women will automatically be accorded a fair share of the future. We have to actively stake our claims for it.

While we learn from the past, appreciating the accomplishments of our foremothers and all those who helped us, I hope we will take up the challenge issued to academic women by Caroline Heilbrun when she said:

> I do not believe death should be allowed to find us seated comfortably in our tenured positions. . . . Instead, we should make use of our security, our seniority, to take risks, to make noise, to be courageous, to become unpopular.[17]

We can take pride in the fact that the women of Phase IV include some university and college presidents, some deans, directors, chairpersons and other senior administrators. We must realize that Heilbrun's challenge applies to them as well as to the rest of us. There is no guarantee that they will not be pressured into becoming "adjunct old boys." We need their help and they need ours if we are to make the most of the best chance we have ever had to show that we are truly both scholars and women.

NOTES

* An earlier version of this material was presented as the 1995 Frank Scott Lecture at McGill University and was published in Fontanus (McGill Libraries), VIII, 13–25.
1. de Pizan 1405.
2. Gillett 1981: 33–34.
3. Gillett 1981: 70.
4. Gillett 1990: 74–83.
5. Curzon 1909.
6. Shortt Smith 1916: 1.
7. Miller 1975.
8. Shaughnessy 1994.
9. See the Spring 1975 issue of the *McGill Journal of Education*.
10. Beer 1995.
11. Bateson 1990: 37.
12. *The McGill Reporter* 1995: 10.
13. See for example Pearce 1995.
14. "Chilly climate," a term used earlier in this book, was probably first used by the American Association for University Women to describe unfriendly attitudes and limited opportunities for women on campus. It has been used frequently in Canada. For example, in 1992 a "climate committee" was set up at the University of Victoria "in response to the concerns raised . . . regarding the discouraging and unsupportive environment experienced by graduate and undergraduate women students" in the Department of Political Science (in the University of Victoria, Department of Political Science, Report of the Climate Committee, March 23, 1993: 1); and in June 1993 the Canadian Association for Women's Studies struck a sub-committee to investigate how "chilly climate" reports have been received on campuses across Canada.
15. Hubbard 1989.
16. Williams 1995.
17. Heilbrun 1988: 131.

Strangers in Canadian Classrooms: Native Students and Québec Colleges

Linda Collier

The 1980s saw a remarkable increase in the number of native students attending post-secondary institutions. This trend will likely continue through the 1990s. Those interested in looking at women in post-secondary institutions might well be interested to learn that, according to Statistics Canada, more native women than men attend post-secondary institutions.[1] Consequently, many of the issues arising from native post-secondary education relate specifically to native women. One important issue that emerges is what the overwhelmingly non-native personnel in these post-secondary institutions can do to ensure a fair chance of entry and graduation to this new and growing clientèle.

I teach in the Humanities, Philosophy and Religious Studies Department of John Abbott College in Ste. Anne de Bellevue, Québec. This historic and small village has now become a part of suburban Montréal. For the past seventeen years, I have taught a humanities course called Indian and Inuit Views. Over the years, many of the native students attending the college have taken this course. Since January 1989 the number of aboriginal students at the college has risen dramatically due to the establishment of two special programs for native students. In this college, our experience comes primarily, though not solely, from teaching native women students.

As a non-native, I do not presume to tell native people what they should be doing in the sphere of post-secondary education, nor do I attempt to speak for the students. But I do believe that, as a person who teaches about native people and has been a teacher of native students for the past seventeen years, I am in a position to point to areas where the institutions and teachers can change to make post-secondary education more attractive and "user friendly" to native students.

Before I continue, I must voice a major concern for those of us who talk about "native students." We have to wonder whether such a generalization claims far too much and belittles important cultural and personal dimensions. Clearly, all generalizations should make the wary reader leery. Talk of aboriginal students seems to ignore the vast differences in native cultures. The difference between Haida and Mohawk people surely outweighs that between Canadians and Americans. Indeed, the differences loom larger than those between, for example, the French and Danes. However, without generalizations we cannot think about the world in anything but personal terms. Every time we say "women" we pass over myriad identities and behaviours. In this article, I do not attempt to give solutions for teaching aboriginal students; rather I attempt to bring to the reader some of the reflections I and other educators in three Québec colleges have made about teaching the native students in our institutions.

First, I provide a context for discussing native education. Second, I give a brief overview of relevant events in the Québec college where I teach. And, finally, I draw on my own experience of teaching native students, working with others who work with native students, and researching the topic to point to some avenues for change.

NATIVE EDUCATION: THE HISTORICAL CONTEXT

Perhaps I should begin with a rather obvious comment: before non-natives came into contact with native Americans, the first peoples educated their own children and people. Education existed. Non-natives did not discover it or "give" it to the native Americans. Contrary to popular belief, Mayans used a form of writing[2] and owned many books, almost all of which the Spanish burned. We know, too, that Mayans calculated using a zero, an essential mathematical tool that the Europeans lost in the Dark Ages and later regained from the so-called Moors, or Arabs of Spain. Any visitor to the wondrous, extensive Mayan city of Tikal in Guatemala knows that at least some Mayans had been to a kind of architectural school. The immense pyramids stand as irrefutable witnesses. Similarly, in the immensity of the northern hemisphere, a place that southern Canadians have been educated to think of as "barren," with all its connotations of nothingness, emptiness and hostility, we find that many peoples lived and flourished. They did so because, to an *educated* person, the land was not barren and empty but full of resources. Where the Franklin expedition members perished and died with their ship's chests full of silver and crystal glasses, Inuit used their knowledge and skills (which is what education supposedly gives us) to survive, love, laugh, joke and sing. Those who say aboriginal people were uneducated before the Europeans arrived ignore these basic facts.

The issue of education for native people should be considered differently from the way it is so often portrayed. Since non-natives first involved themselves with the education of native people, they have tended to define the issue as problematic, and native children as difficult to educate. Even today, many articles in academic journals concentrate on the learning difficulties of native children and adults. The problem lies, though, not in the children, but in the refusal of the dominant society to accept the native people as equals. Instead, Canadian policy has decreed that those who did not perish should become like

49

the non-natives. They should assimilate to the Canadian norm. Yet that very norm has excluded, and still does exclude, "the aboriginal" from the definition of "Canadian." The foreign tourist, looking at the windows of souvenir shops in Montréal or Toronto, sees plastic dolls dressed in stereotypical deerskin and feathered headdresses. But when we look for an authentic native presence in government, business, culture or even our consciousness, we draw mostly blanks. Canada grew on the dispossession and exclusion of its first peoples, not on their inclusion.

This exclusionist ideology naturally carries over into the educational system. Education prepares the state's youth to perpetuate the prevailing institutions and ideology, and teachers act, for the most part, as guardians of that ideology. Fortunately, not all students and teachers comply, so we have, for example, women challenging dominant myths and accepted norms. But the vocal and negative reaction to books proposing non-sexist language clearly indicates how long and arduous the struggle for equality will be. The struggle of the aboriginal people will be even longer and more arduous.

Since the arrival of the first missionaries in Canada, non-natives have been working on two fronts concerning education and native people. On the one hand, these first European teachers tried to inculcate into native peoples certain non-native or European–American beliefs, values and ways of doing things. On the other hand, they worked very hard at abolishing, undermining and making illegal the existing aboriginal educational system. Missionaries railed against the influential and respected position of women in various Indian nations, such as the Mohawk and Montagnais, and encouraged men to treat women as inferior beings. The Indian Act made certain Indian ceremonies and customs illegal. Indians were jailed for maintaining their traditions and for educating their children in their ways by taking them to important ceremonies such as the potlatch, which was a time for feasting and giving away goods and an occasion by which many West Coast nations marked important events.

Furthermore, residential schools were aimed primarily at separating children from their parents, grandparents, communities, elders and teachers. Government policies of forcibly taking away children from their homes and laws like the Indian Act stand witness to the conscious effort to halt native education in their language and in their ways of doing, being, feeling and thinking. We know, too, of the many cases of abuse in residential schools and can only guess at the impact that generations of such abuse has had on native people.

One should hardly find it surprising, therefore, that in Canada today we are more likely to meet an adolescent native male in prison than in a post-secondary institution, or that an adolescent native female is more likely to be a mother than to have a high-school leaving diploma. However, since native people have been allowed to take over more and more their own educational systems, some encouraging trends have begun to emerge. To say "allowed" brings home with some force the extent to which native people have been excluded from mainstream society, for the Indian Act decreed that native education would be controlled by non-native bureaucrats. With some notable exceptions, when native control of educational institutions does exist, it stops at the end of high school. Until recently, only a handful of native students attended post-secondary institutions throughout Canada.

THE NEW CLIENTÈLE

The students now in our classes represent a whole new phenomenon and a whole new responsibility. While many argue for the necessity of native-run colleges and post-secondary institutions, few exist and most aboriginal people attend post-secondary institutions run by non-natives. Those of us involved in such institutions must act, in the interim, to try to serve aboriginal people better than educational institutions have done in the past.

Some of the issues most often identified with post-secondary education are as follows: low enrolment; low success rates, i.e., high failure/drop-out rates; unsuitability of programs and course material; pressure to assimilate and consequent student unease with "losing their culture"; and being away from home. The two last points become especially important for students coming from remote areas, such as the Cree and Inuit of northern Québec.

Currently faced with major changes, Québec colleges or CEGEPs (Collèges d'enseignement général et professionnel) have, over the past twenty-five years, performed the task of preparing high school graduates for university while simultaneously providing training in professional programs, such as nursing and aircraft technology.

JOHN ABBOTT COLLEGE: PROGRAMS FOR MOHAWK, CREE AND INUIT

At the far western end of the island of Montréal, John Abbott College, with a student population of about 5,000, stands in beautiful grounds overlooking the St. Lawrence River and facing both the Mohawk reserve of Kahnawake and the infamous Mercier bridge which links the island of Montréal to the South Shore suburb of Chateauguay. Here and in the North Shore suburb of Oka, or Kanehsatake, in the Indian summer of 1990, blockades and bunkers took the place of picnic lunches, and more soldiers drove around in jeeps, armoured personnel carriers and tanks than served in the Canadian forces of the Gulf war.[3] Newspapers blared headlines like "Mohawks on Warpath," calling upon some archetypal Canadian image of savage Mohawks. Many commentators pointed to this confrontation as the beginning of a new era in Canadian politics, and a clear indication of the enormous frustrations of native people at being systematically excluded from society and seeing longstanding grievances remain unaddressed.

Until 1989, John Abbott College offered no special program for native students. While several Mohawk students had passed through since the college's inception, they had been few in number. Then in January 1989, ten Cree women from the James Bay area entered the nursing program, making up one third of the new class. The arrival of these patently "different" students, coming from remote native communities and speaking Cree as a mother tongue, created a great learning opportunity, which some members of the nursing faculty took up with enthusiasm and dedication. From the determined efforts of some of the faculty and the administration, together with some sympathetic government bureaucrats, emerged a program known as the James Bay Nursing Project. This program aims at ensuring the necessary academic support for native students and provides a training program suited to the kind of nursing that they will eventually do in their communities. Two nursing teachers, released from their teaching jobs, act as project coordinator and special counsellor, and maintain close communication with the Cree school board, one of Canada's first native-run school boards, which was established under the James Bay Agreement.

The next year, the Kativik School Board, set up for the Inuit of Québec under the James Bay Agreement, approached John Abbott College to ask for its cooperation with a post-secondary plan they had envisioned. Consequently, in the fall of 1990, Inuit students began attending John Abbott College. This turned out to be an inauspicious start, coinciding as it did with the events at Oka/Kanehsatake and an accompanying outbreak of racist events; as a result most of the Inuit students returned home within the first weeks of the semester. Fortunately, the next semester started on a completely different basis, and Kativik's new program began to look extremely promising. Kativik requires all its college students to live either in a residence or in designated apartments. A special counsellor/teacher works intensively with them especially in their first year, providing extra language instruction and attending some of their classes so as to be able to give them additional help.

January 1993 marked the college's third year of working with the Kativik School Board and its fourth year with the James Bay Nursing Project. Many changes have occurred in the past few years. Although the Kativik program still flourishes at the college, the Cree school board stopped payment for its part of the James Bay Nursing Project in May 1996. As a result, the project stopped and Cree students now benefit from no special support. Meanwhile, two other programs have started up in the Continuing Education Department; one for upgrading nursing assistants to nurses in the Mohawk community of Akwesasne, which straddles New York state, Ontario and Québec; and another for upgrading nursing assistants in the Inuit community of Kuujjuak in Ungava Bay. All but one of the students involved in the nursing programs are women and in 1992–93, of eleven Inuit students who started the year, one young man and five young women registered for the winter semester.

COLLEGES OF SEPT-ILES AND HERITAGE

This pattern does not necessarily repeat itself in other colleges. In the College of Sept-Iles on the north shore of Québec, the Innu or Montagnais, who have

French as their second language, comprise about 10 percent of the student clientèle. According to the Delagrave report published in 1990, Innu men and women attend the college in about equal numbers. The report also notes that Innu women students tend to withdraw from fewer courses and pass more courses than the men.[4] More First Nations women than men attend Heritage College in Hull, a college with a high percentage of aboriginal students. Consequently, women figure pre-eminently in this discussion of native students at post-secondary institutions.

ADDRESSING THE NEEDS OF NATIVE WOMEN STUDENTS
In the fall of 1992, I conducted interviews with teachers in both John Abbott and Heritage Colleges to discover the teachers' perceptions, insights and comments on teaching native students at the college level.

Childcare
Many teachers pointed out that the women have special needs revolving around their role as caregivers and, often, providers for their families. On average, native women give birth at a younger age than do other Canadians and they have more children,[5] so this issue emerges as more important for them than for other non-native women. As several teachers pointed out, if we really want native women to have access to post-secondary education, we must ensure the availability of necessary services like daycare. The Kativik School Board's program demonstrates one effective way of dealing with the issue. First-year students live in a residence but the young women with children are placed together in apartments and baby-sitting is arranged.

Native students have told teachers they did not attend class because of baby-sitting problems or sick children. Moreover, in situations where the teachers themselves would opt to leave a child, for example, with a runny nose and cold at a daycare, native women tend to choose to miss school and stay with the child. Often parents or older children bring up other children, so some of our students not only have children with them, but also may have children back in the community. These kinds of extended families, stretched over distance, place on the native women demands that are often unrecognized in an institution primarily conceived of as providing education to recent school–leavers. Many teachers commented that talking to native women students had really opened their eyes. "I felt like this woman had lived far more experiences than I had, yet I'm more than twice her age" encapsulates the way many of them felt.

Financial, Language and Cultural Problems
Women responsible for children also bear greater financial responsibilities and burdens, and this too has to be addressed if they are to be given access to post-secondary education. The James Bay Agreement of 1975 set up Inuit and Cree school boards that subsidize students attending college in Québec. Many other

native people fall under the Indian Act and the vagaries of federal government funding. The Delagrave report from the College of Sept-Iles noted some of the inherent problems. When Innu students arrive in college, they have to work in a second language and in a cultural system radically different from their own. Very often, they have not completed high school and need to make up certain courses. They simply require more time than other students do. Yet the funding for their college studies, received from the Department of Indian Affairs and Northern Development, does not take this into account. Thus, they risk dropping out simply from lack of funds.

The Cree, Innu and Inuit have to leave their home communities to attend post-secondary institutions. Imagine, if you can, a seventeen-year old girl from a community of 350 inhabitants arriving in a city of two and a half million people. Unless she has already travelled "down south," she has never seen buses before, and does not recognize a bus stop; she has never seen escalators or elevators except in films; the unpaved roads of her community probably have no stop signs, let alone traffic lights. In her community, she knew everyone and was related to many of them. Add to all this the fact that she is living and attending school in a foreign language and culture and you begin to have some idea of the incredible adjustment demanded from these people. All suffer from homesickness, and their close communal ties mean that most feel they must go home for circumstances incomprehensible to the average southerner, as for example, the funeral of a next-door neighbour.[6]

Native students experience many of these same feelings as students coming from remote villages in countries such as Iran or Pakistan. It is the responsibility of educators to accommodate and be sensitive to the concerns of all students, native, non-native and new immigrants. Unlike newer arrivals, though, native people have aboriginal rights and special calls on the state. Thomas Berger puts this issue squarely when he writes: "Native people are not simply a rural proletariat, nor just another ethnic minority."[7] As the original inhabitants of this land they inherit particular rights, and the past years have seen more and more acknowledgment of their special status both by the courts and the government.

The fact that native students survive a semester in college speaks to their tenacity and courage. In my own college's limited experience with native students, some of their names figure on the Honours Lists; when two graduated from nursing in May 1993, they potentially tripled the number of Cree nurses in the province. Though others may never graduate with a diploma, the experience and extra schooling they have acquired through one, two or three semesters singles them out in their communities and provides them with opportunities from which they would otherwise never have benefited. For this reason, we should hesitate to label such "drop-outs" as "failures," which is what we do when we judge success only in our terms.

IMPLICATIONS FOR EDUCATIONAL POLICY AND PRACTICE

Even if we can usefully generalize about aboriginal or native students, that does not mean we can write a native policy or how-to manual for post-secondary institutions. Each of the three colleges mentioned here has a different program for its aboriginal students. In fact, John Abbott has distinct programs for the Cree, Mohawk and Inuit students. People working in all three institutions maintain communication with different native communities and stress the importance of those links. A major policy implication perhaps emerges: each institution must find a close link to the aboriginal community or communities it serves and work with them to establish an appropriate program or policy. As for pedagogical practice, the one thing teachers unanimously agreed upon was the danger of generalizations about these students. Yet certain comments recurred so often that it is worth examining some of them.

Support Programs

The need for a support program for native students emerges from the experience of all three colleges mentioned in this article. The teachers I interviewed both at John Abbott and Heritage Colleges pointed out the necessity for, and importance of, a counsellor for native students. This counsellor acts as broker between students and teachers, helping each to understand the other. Such support programs work best when agreed on by the communities and students involved, and each program may have to be specially tailored. As well, colleges need to show a certain flexibility in their programs. Strict adherence to time limits in which to complete a program discriminates against students with family responsibilities, far-away homes and major cultural adjustments to overcome.

Walking a Fine Line

Teachers of native students have to walk a very fine line. Many teachers worry about forcing the dominant society's values, attitudes, behaviour and ways of being onto their native students. Yet, for those students to succeed in the non-native post-secondary institutions, they have to operate by our norms and be judged by our standards. Examples of this abound in the scholarly literature. As mentioned earlier, many journals contain articles written about the "difficulties" of teaching native students, often relating these difficulties to native learning styles or some other inherently "native" variable. The "difficulties" usually refer to a list of characteristics attributed to native students: an unwillingness to speak up in class, a lack of eye contact, different body language and so on. Discussions of these characteristics are almost always couched in negative terms. When I first read some of these articles, I did not recognize them as describing those classes in which I taught native students. Several factors could account for this difference. Perhaps this is a question of perception. I perceived these studies as having a negative bias, whereas I felt my experience was positive. Furthermore, most of these studies referred to children, whereas I teach adults, from adolescents to forty-year-old women. In addition, most of these studies referred to schools in native communities; I teach students who have come from their communities to study in an urban environment, so my students are very different. Also, I teach a course about native people in Canada. While this does not absolutely guarantee students' interest, it certainly gives me a head start.

This brings me back to the point I made at the beginning of this article about the systematic and systemic exclusion of native people from Canadian consciousness, ideology and institutions. Children still learn in school that Columbus "discovered" the Americas, ignoring the history and reality of native Americans. And those who now teach in schools and post-secondary institutions themselves learned that same history, with its concomitant ignorance of the present aboriginal population. Apart from those of us interested in the subject, most teachers, like most of the Canadian population, would be unable to identify the different places from which come Cree, Inuit, Dené and Innu. I do not blame the teachers, but point to this as indicative of our exclusion of native people. If the educated and the educators of Canadian society do not know about our first peoples, how are we to work towards their *inclusion* in our society, consciousness and institutions? Imagine the young Cree woman studying history or philosophy, for example, and reading in her textbook phrases such as: "We Canadians find the roots of our culture in Socrates and Plato." Imagine the Inuk (Inuit) student coming from one of the most sharing and cooperative societies being told by his teacher that: "Our culture is one based on individualism." Surely they feel as alienated as I do every time I read a phrase like "the average Canadian and *his* work habits." When I read this, I sense it has nothing to do with me, and I switch off. How many native students switch off when faced with such obvious "non-senses" for them?

We must, somehow, work towards including native people in our worldview, our history and our consciousness if we want to provide an environment conducive to their success in post-secondary institutions. At best, most schools' curricula still exclude them, denying their existence, importance and diversity. At worst, they promote and maintain stereotypes of war-like savages. More TV programs like CBC's "North of 60," in which the native police officer is a woman and which shows native people as regular human beings, would go a long way towards helping Canadians to absorb the reality of native people in Canada.

We must also be aware that all native people, and thus our students, live, work and attend school in a society structured by racism and sexism. Sometimes that racism takes the form of mobs burning an effigy of a "Warrior" hung on a streetlight; sometimes it appears as a few metal-studded youths calling out the slogans of White Power fascists. Other times racism appears in more subtle forms. All of us struggle to come to terms with the difference of the Other.

In interviews of teachers of native students, one phrase recurred time and again: "I can't read them." Most of these teachers had many years of experience and were reputed to be excellent and sensitive teachers yet, independent of each other, many echoed that same phrase. They meant that, as teachers, we keep in touch with our students in all kinds of verbal and non-verbal ways. Most students recognize our non-verbal language and return appropriate, or even inappropriate, signs—but they speak a recognizable body language. When they yawn and roll their eyes up, we translate this as boredom, we're not catching their interest. We can recognize and process these signs. But what happens when the One faces the Other? The teachers interviewed could not see the usual non-verbal signs they look for to gauge how well their students are understanding them. Most teachers expect, want and seem to need certain behaviour from their students. Most teachers insist on the importance of punctuality, attending class on time, handing in assignments on time, doing examinations and quizzes on the appointed day on time.[8] As well, teachers like to see bright, eager faces staring back at them and hear immediate responses to their questions; this helps them believe that the students are indeed paying attention. Such expectations and behaviour stem from a particular culture, that of the majority, and in some ways reflect only one part of that majority, mostly the men.

Feminist criticism has helped us to realize how much the classroom environment reproduces the sexism and culturally determined attitudes and behaviour of society. The video "Inequity in the Classroom," produced by Concordia University's Status of Women Office, shows how long-established teaching practices discriminate against women. When teachers ask questions to the class generally, the white males tend to dominate the session. Women students tend to take longer to respond and are less comfortable in settings perceived as competitive. Many native students share these characteristics. As well, many speak only when they believe they have something to say, which may not happen in an entire semester.

Feminist theory and criticism of pedagogy contribute in an essential way to making the teacher and classroom more appropriate for native students (as well as for women and minority students). By breaking down the power structure in the classroom—for example, sitting in a circle, encouraging more group work, avoiding situations where a few dominant students orient the class to their needs and becoming aware of hidden biases—teachers can contribute to a more comfortable learning environment for native students.

While non-natives tend to visualize life as a kind of ladder, native people see it as a circle: the sacred hoop, the sacred circle, the medicine wheel. If we provide some opportunities for them to do so, native people can close this particular circle by educating us, the non-natives. As more native students attend regular post-secondary institutions, experience tells us that several teachers will make the effort to find out more about these new students and so become more aware of the place of natives in Canadian society. More non-native students will also realize that native Canadians have neither completely disappeared nor been completely assimilated. By simply attending our institutions, native students help to heighten the other students' awareness and alter their perceptions of natives in our society. We begin to understand that people have not just one way but many different ways of relating to the world. Eventually, perhaps, the circle will spread more widely, the Canadian consciousness will include native people in more than just folklore and institutions will adjust to serve this reality. We could learn here from the Dené of the North West Territories. First, dream, then it becomes reality.

Twenty years ago, the National Indian Brotherhood put forward many of these same ideas in their publication *Indian Education in Canada*. One phrase was particularly poignant and appropriate, so much so that it provided the title for this paper:

Non-Indians must be ready to recognize the value of another way of life; to learn about Indian history, customs and language; and to modify, if necessary, some of their own ideas and practices. Only then will Indian children no longer 'be strangers in Canadian classrooms.'[10]

Let us hope that we have different concerns twenty years from now.

NOTES
1. Tables in the 1986 Statistics Canada publications illustrate a marked tendency for more female than male native Canadians (Indian, Métis and Inuit) to attend post-secondary institutions. Unfortunately the same statistics are not available from the 1990 census at the time of writing, so the figures are quite outdated. The number of registered Indians enrolled in post-secondary institutions has increased quite dramatically, from 11,170 in 1985–86 to 21,442 in 1991–92. It will be interesting to see what percentage of these students now is female.
2. Schele and Freidel 1990.
3. For an excellent treatment of these events, see York and Pindera 1991.
4. Delagrave 1990.
5. Indian and Inuit communities display quite different age pyramids from that of non-native communities in Canada. In particular, Inuit and registered Indians have a younger population and higher fertility rates than the Canadian norm.
6. Minnie Freeman (1978) gives a good idea of what this all felt like to her and I recommend her book to interested readers.
7. Berger 1991: 24.
8. The non-native understanding of time, as a thing to be managed and manipulated, creates problems for native students, who tend to perceive time in a quite different manner.
9. Ridington 1988, 1990.
10. National Indian Brotherhood, *Indian Control of Indian Education*, cited in Barman et al. 1987: 17.

Part 2
Women as Students: The Marginal Majority

Making the Grade Against the Odds: Women as University Undergraduates

Judith Blackwell

How well are women getting along in university in the late twentieth century? This was the fundamental question that prompted our study of women in post-secondary education.[1] We spent many hours talking to female undergraduates in a mid-sized Ontario university, in hopes that these women would help us to understand the "highs" and the "lows" of their lives in academia. We thought we might also discover how the university could enhance what it was doing right and avoid what it might be doing wrong.

In the past, women have been discouraged from pursuing more than rudimentary education, have been denied access to educational institutions and have encountered numerous barriers to professional and intellectual development. As this century draws to its close, some satisfaction can be obtained from the increasing female enrolment in higher education, from the visibility and number of female faculty in these institutions, and from other encouraging trends indicating vibrant and visible participation of women in post-secondary education. Nevertheless, most university women have no illusions: true gender equity has not been accomplished.

We set out on our task with a sense of optimism. After all, we had already encountered so many intelligent women who were obviously blossoming from their undergraduate experience. In lectures and seminars, they expressed their ideas with confidence, raising lively issues for debate. They were doing well in their studies and their future prospects were so promising.

Furthermore, women are much better off than their sisters of previous generations, those who first broke down the barriers and gained entrance to the "ivory tower." Universities are no longer expected to be male-dominated institutions designed to train the sons of the elite classes to take their places in positions of power in society. In principle, all academically-qualified students are meant to have equal access to university education, regardless of gender, race, religion or socioeconomic status. Certainly, many social conditions conspire to discourage certain people from taking full advantage of educational opportunities. However, more and more students of diverse social backgrounds continue to appear in universities and go on to high profile, successful careers.

We wondered if the women who were obviously benefiting from the system were succeeding because the institution had adapted to accommodate them. On the other hand, they might be particularly skilled at what one observer has called intellectual "cross-dressing,"[2] that is, skillfully clothing themselves in the ideas and modes of expression that are the passport to success in a male-oriented institution. If so, what were the problems of women who might be less adaptable in this way? Are there still aspects of the university experience that discourage women and that decrease their chances of success?

BARRIERS TO UNIVERSITY SUCCESS

Clearly, many life experiences will influence whether or not a woman will even contemplate the option of entering a university degree program. Conversations with "mature" students provide anecdotal information about why they did not go directly to post-secondary education after high school. Some married or became pregnant at a young age, or they were supporting husbands or partners who were preparing for their own careers. Some families are reported to support further education for sons, but not for daughters. Some mature students also ruefully report that their early educational experiences had convinced them that they were intellectually incapable of obtaining a post-secondary degree.

In our study, we encouraged students to describe the perceptions they brought into the university setting, the factors that influenced decisions at crucial times in their educational lives, and the evolution of their thinking about the value of their education. We also were curious about students' sources of encouragement, and whether they had been discouraged from making certain academic decisions. We asked general questions about gender socialization, gender-based ideology and their combined impact on women's educational careers.

Our research focuses on the experiences of women who were fortunate enough not to have run up against barriers to university entrance or who were able to overcome those they encountered. Enrolment in university, however, does not guarantee that the student will graduate. We were interested in the influences that might discourage fulfilment of women's academic potential or encourage them to withdraw from university. Are women gaining the skills they will need in the future, not only knowledge and critical analysis but also intellectual confidence? How do they perceive their academic potential and has the university had a positive impact on their perceptions of their abilities? Is the university environment fully encouraging the education of women?

In addition, we were interested in the impact of the academic experience on the aspirations of students. Three decades before our research began, it was a common idea that a woman went to university to get her "MRS." degree, that is, to acquire a husband who had promise of economic success and societal respectability. To our surprise, this idea was still alive and some students had been subjected to "jokes" of this nature. This suggested that female undergraduates should be given the opportunity to discuss their reasons for seeking a university education and its place in the larger context of their lives.

Women's understanding of the value of an undergraduate degree, and their educational and career aspirations in general, may be influenced by lifelong exposure to attitudes that slot women into particular roles in life. We were familiar with research that suggested that many undergraduate women in both female traditional and non-traditional disciplines value their degrees only as a ticket to a job that will be readily abandoned when the time comes to have children. This is very different from considering a degree to be the first hurdle on the way to a successful and rewarding career. Students undoubtedly bring such ideas into the university setting. If they leave with them unaltered, the university is not doing its job of encouraging students to consider the full range of avenues open to them.

Post-graduate education is becoming increasingly important, and universities should be expected to encourage education at all levels for both women and men. In recent years, over half of bachelor and first professional degrees have been awarded to women. Almost half of master's degrees go to women, but less than one-third of doctoral degrees. Therefore, another area of investigation centred on post-graduate educational opportunities for women, and the factors that may discourage women from taking second or third degrees.

We frequently hear about the "chilly climate" of the university setting. This metaphor identifies behaviours and the use of language, both in the classroom and on the campus in general, that can create detrimental learning environments for female students. Such climates communicate different expectations for women than for men. They can impede personal, academic and professional development by creating an atmosphere in which classroom participation is discouraged. In extreme situations, a woman may feel that her very presence in the course is not of serious concern; she may avoid certain programs, or she may choose not to take courses from individual instructors. The degree of "chill" experienced may also influence decision-making with regard to remaining in university or continuing to the post-graduate level.

Do universities indoctrinate students with male-biased knowledge, as some feminist scholars claim they do? Is the "reality" women are asked to study a reality formulated by and structured for men? Women's studies programs, courses taught from a feminist perspective or focusing on women's issues, as well as tutorials, reading courses and independent research may go some way towards redressing an imbalance. These alternatives, however, are in turn dependent on a critical mass of academics willing to teach these courses and to supervise students in thesis or research work.

This concern underlies arguments for encouraging women to become academics, providing more faculty mentors and female role models for undergraduate women. One of our research questions, therefore, addressed the exposure female undergraduates have to female faculty. Since gender does not necessarily determine sensitivity to women's issues, feminist course content or female-sensitive pedagogical methods, we were also curious about whether students perceive differences between male and female professors or teaching assistants.

When planning this research, recent events in Canadian universities, ranging from offensive demonstrations by male students to the deliberate massacre of female engineering students in Montréal, suggested to us that the "chilly climate" metaphor may have been inadequate to fully encapsulate the psychological impact of female students' encounters with post-secondary education. Nevertheless, we hesitated to include direct questions about sexual harassment or the more blatant expressions of sexism that might still be displayed by faculty or by male students. Rather than "leading" our respondents, we preferred to hear their voices and understand what they perceived to be barriers to their education. As we shall see, the women in our study did not need prompting to report sexism in the classroom and sexual assault on the campus.

Despite the prevailing notion that one's university days are halcyon years, the degree to which this dream can be a reality often depends on time and money. Needless to say, students receiving full financial support need worry only about cyclical academic deadlines and management of the funds available to them. For the remainder, time and money problems can become barriers to education. Such pressures are experienced by both male and female students, but they can be of particular concern for single parents, working students, married students and mature students. These categories overlap, and the extent to which females are overrepresented in any one of them suggested problems to be explored in our research.

As living costs and tuition fees increase, the financial barriers to education are exacerbated. When family support is not available, the student chooses between going into debt and maintaining full-time student status, or working and attending part-time. When debts are incurred, the lower wages of women exact a heavier repayment toll than will be experienced by male graduates with an equal debt load.

Single parenthood is a particular burden. Recent concern has been expressed over the many single mothers on social assistance who graduate from university with large debts accumulated from federal and provincial student loans. The single mother juggles her course load and her family responsibilities. She may decide to take a full course load, supported with meagre student loans that limit her part-time earnings. Alternatively, she can enroll part-time and have the freedom to juggle all three: as much paid work as she can handle, family duties and the demands of her studies. Therefore, we were also interested in discovering whether financial problems or family responsibilities were making the lives of female undergraduates more difficult.

THE LIVES OF FEMALE UNDERGRADUATES

Because we seemed to have more questions than answers, we decided to talk only to a small number of students but to spend a good deal of time with each of them. We had a list of questions and topics to discuss, but we wanted to give our respondents maximum opportunity to tell us, in their own words, about their experiences and their concerns. We opted for open-ended conversations, rather than structured interviews.

Our findings are based on a selection of the issues discussed in interviews with eighteen undergraduates. Eleven of them were in the traditional age range: twenty to twenty-two years old. The remaining seven were aged twenty-five years or older. With regard to their domestic status, eleven were unmarried and living in residence, with their parents or with friends. Five were married or cohabiting (two with children). Two were single mothers. We began interviewing social science majors (thirteen), but the sample grew to include four humanities majors and one science major.

SENSITIVITY TO GENDER INEQUITIES AND FEMINIST ISSUES

When we began to study the transcripts of the first eighteen interviews, we were particularly impressed by the differences between younger and older students. The women aged twenty-five years or older were much more sensitive to gender inequities and feminist issues, and they appeared more appreciative of the value of female academic role models. They also seemed to react more strongly to overt sexism in male faculty and other problems they had encountered.

Only among the younger respondents did we hear, "I really don't think I have been treated differently because I am female." One twenty-year-old, a scholarship student, did allow that her own attitudes were a possible barrier to complete realization of her abilities:

> This is terrible, but when I think of the future, I think that I'll probably get an above-average paying job, not a lot . . . and, I expect to get married and I would expect him to have a half-decent job. And I do assume that he will make more than I would. That's the way I like to think of it, and then I could take time off to have kids.
>
> I've thought about that, interestingly enough . . . that if I were a male I wouldn't have this attitude. I would have to achieve more at university and would definitely be thinking "money" and "career." But because I'm female I don't have to think about it that much. . . . (Respondent 01)

Responses such as this one suggest an emerging awareness of women's issues. By this we mean that the individual notes special concerns for female students relative to their male counterparts, but she does not see that they may have a significant impact. It is simply a matter of personal choice. Here is another example: "Math and science I wouldn't even approach. I think it's that stereotype of 'girls don't do well in math and science' . . ." (Respondent 05). We see in these words clear evidence of a woman's choice of courses and, ultimately, of her career options being limited as a result of gender stereotyping.

Students with only emerging sensitivity to gender issues reported concerns about campus safety, anticipated potential career problems, thought it would be a good idea to have a place for female students to get together or reported sexist remarks made by professors and male students. However, they took pains to distance themselves: "As females, we encounter a lot of sexism in this world, and I feel that if you can't deal with it now, you'll never deal with it" (Respondent 07). This statement reveals a commonly reported tendency to bravely ignore the "inconvenience," rather than to confront the issue of whether it is fair to be exposed to it.

Six of the younger respondents showed emerging sensitivity to gender inequities; in the remaining five, little or no awareness of feminist issues was evident. Indeed, one student expressed open hostility; she described one course, as follows: "God, I couldn't believe how they went on and on about feminist stuff. I can see giving both sides, but I really resent it when they shove it down your throat that way" (Respondent 13).

In contrast to our younger respondents, all of the women aged twenty-five years or over had either emerging sensitivities or a clearly articulated feminist consciousness. Among the older women, even among those who were only beginning to clarify their thinking, we heard genuine expressions of anger, an emotion that was notably absent from the voices of the younger women. For example, a respondent who had been strongly influenced in her thinking by one of her courses said:

> This year was like a crash course on feminism and in many ways I'm very traditional and I resent being pushed into the nineties. Life [now] is so much more complicated because of it. And suddenly I was seeing, and I was very angry a lot of the year, and I still don't know what to do about it. I guess I was aware of feminism before this year, but I didn't call it that. I just called it individual outrage at something.
>
> I'm all of a sudden aware of being a woman now. I almost wish I didn't know anything. (Respondent 17)

Four of the seven more mature students had acquired political consciousness and could articulate their concerns. They argued the need for services for women: better child care, support groups, a women's studies program and a women's centre on campus. They made no excuses for the behaviour of certain male professors. They said that the university needed more female professors and women in the administration of the university.

FEMALE ACADEMIC ROLE MODELS

Although older respondents more frequently expressed appreciation of a supportive female presence among the university faculty, we heard positive comments from younger students too: "I see these women at Brock [university], like the profs, and I think 'Hey, I can do that!' . . . I think I can, anyway" (Respondent 06). Other respondents said: "I've always been encouraged by women in higher positions. Seeing them there, working under them and having their support and encouragement is always so much more valuable than males" (Respondent 17).

> I've seen how far some of the women [faculty] have come. In a man's world, these women are making headway and nobody can take that away. . . . Women need a lot of support and help to get anywhere and to get above the stereotypes and stigma . . . and I'm one who can help. (Respondent 02)

Differences in teaching styles also were observed, not only in female professors, but also among female seminar leaders: "Females can communicate that they know what they're talking about without 'putting on a front'" (Respondent 03); "Males are more task-oriented. The females are more concerned with feelings and take time for students" (Respondent 08). "The male teaching assistants are more like the prof, the sarcastic remarks hidden beneath comments. The females are more open to either sex. The way they teach . . . the females are more sympathetic" (Respondent 07). One respondent told of seeking help with a personal problem from a female teaching assistant and noted that "It was good she was there, because I wouldn't have gone to a man."

The students were certainly not uncritical "fans" of women in academia, and did not hesitate to report, for example, that individual faculty members could be "just as boring" as their male counterparts. Some of these comments communicated a particular disappointment: "I have a prof now . . . , and you would never know she was a woman." We also received reports of female seminar leaders who deviated widely from acceptable standards of behaviour:

> One was on a power trip. She liked to show us how smart she was all the time. It got so bad that almost no one talked [in the seminar] except the two guys. She would always let them make a point, but if . . . [one of the female students] said something, she would cut you off. Even if you were right, she still finished what you were saying. (Respondent 16)

Some of the younger students were notable for not even having "noticed" that they had female professors. They were also more likely to explain any difference in terms of "personality," and to minimize male–female differences in teaching. In line with their less clearly articulated feminist consciousness, they would be more vague about why they liked having a female professor, simply saying, for example: "I feel more comfortable, I guess."

Interestingly, two students much preferred having male teaching assistants:

> Male seminar leaders expect women to not have very much important to say. They don't expect you to contribute anything much . . . like, you're just there. So, if you say something silly or not right, it doesn't do anything to what they think. (Respondent 06)

Female instructors, on the other hand, were perceived to have high expectations of their female students: "with the female leaders, if I say something wrong they might think I was . . . dumb . . . or something. I was just more afraid of looking dumb" (Respondent 06). Another said that females made her feel "like she was being tested, or something."

OVERT SEXISM IN THE CLASSROOM

We began this research with high hopes that the situation of undergraduate women was much improved. At the close of the twentieth century in Canada, universities have policies on sexual harassment and regarding racist or sexist language in education. One assumes that men are keenly aware of, and would be sensitive to, potential gender inequities. We were therefore surprised at how many reports came to us of overt masculine bias and sexist "humour" among male students, seminar leaders and professors.

One student noted how male professors interrupt conversations between women, even when one of the women is also a member of faculty. A male teaching assistant was accused of cutting off the arguments of females in the seminar, and then criticizing them for not contributing more to the discussion. A professor was reported to say unabashedly that he did not want "the women's perspective" discussed in his course. Another was said to "humorously" and deliberately humiliate female (and only female) students in the public forum of the lecture hall. One of our respondents, seeking advice during office hours about what she perceived to be contradictory messages concerning essay topics, was told by her professor: "Now run along, and be a good girl." She noted: "Even my father doesn't call me a 'good girl!' He [the professor] really gets on my nerves, and I have to force myself to go to lectures now."

In both the social sciences and the humanities, we heard of male professors making sexist "jokes" in lectures. Apparently, these professors take special delight in historical accounts of women's subservience in past eras, make "wisecracks" about how women's status has changed, and "humorously" suggest that changes in the direction of equality for women and reproductive choice represent a retrograde move.

I had a couple of men that made remarks about things through the course. . . . They are not immediately sexist, but the academic jibber is there. The female professors never say things like that. . . . I felt like, what is this guy getting at? What is his goal? What does he want us to do? What does he want us to believe? I get a little nervous. (Respondent 08)

Older students are more likely to get "a little angry" than to get "a little nervous," but no student felt it was in her interest to make an official complaint. Indeed, the general tendency is for undergraduates to blame themselves for not responding in an appropriate manner:

Not only was he not a very good lecturer, he would make some very strange remarks. Chauvinistic, racist, some odd things to say. And he thought these comments were very funny. . . . He laughed more than the class did. . . .
Much to my surprise, I started not going to lecture. I skipped one. It was the first time I had ever done that, and I felt guilty. So I went the next time. But after a month I didn't go very often. The next thing I knew, it was time for a term assignment and I wasn't ready. So I withdrew. . . . I could have kept that course, so it was my own fault really. (Respondent 19)

Women are loathe to lodge a complaint about this kind of problem, although they discuss it among themselves and, at times, with their seminar leaders:

[A professor] was really down on females. He used to make jokes about . . . well, sexist jokes. A lot of girls saw it as crass and only showed up for major lectures and the exams because they couldn't deal with the remarks he would make. . . . I wasn't impressed by his comments either. . . . (Respondent 07)

This student, under the guidance of one of the seminar leaders, reinterpreted the professor's behaviour as follows:

His comments were a way of getting females to . . . think about the courses they're taking and what they're doing. . . . [A] lot of the girls in the course had it in mind to be in university to get their "MRS.," so to speak. . . . That's the way it was explained to me by one of the TAs. . . . He said that the sarcastic remarks were just to get the girls thinking.
Now, for me, I just looked at it that way. Some of [the professor's] remarks were fairly hurtful, but I think you have to look over that in order to proceed. (Respondent 07)

At the outset of this study, we hoped that gender-related problems in the curriculum would be confined to exclusive use of male-oriented examples in lectures or neglect to employ gender-neutral language. We did not expect to receive so many reports of women (from ten of eighteen respondents) being asked to silently submit to offensive comments or, through intellectual contortions, to bravely attempt to justify them. We also were not prepared for the problems that students impose on one another.

OPPRESSION FROM FELLOW STUDENTS

One of the problems reported by our respondents was the reverberation of sexism outside the classroom. In its least offensive form, it requires female students to justify to their male peers the discomfort caused by professors' remarks. Thus, we heard reports of being accused of being "pushy" and being asked to defend themselves against the charge of having "no sense of humour." One of our respondents attempted to resolve this problem by concluding that the professor "meant no harm" and that his behaviour was "no worse" than that of those who tell racist or ethnic jokes.

Of far more concern were reports of sexual aggression by male students. Although no member of our sample reported personal problems in this regard, two chose the setting of our research to discuss the concerns they had about unreported sexual assaults on their friends. As one of these stories involved a single perpetrator and the other more than one, we believe them to be separate incidents. Both of the victims lived in a campus residence. By the reports we received, both of these women had been assaulted by "friends" or acquaintances. These are two cases related by two of eighteen women in confidential conversations.

None of our respondents was directly encouraged to discuss sexual harassment or sexual assault. That they brought up the subject reflects a "ripple effect" these events have on other students. These women were upset on behalf of their friends and disturbed about how the male perpetrators had escaped identification and punishment.

> I'm still furious about it. He's still here. She didn't come back this year. I mean, he could do it to someone else.
>
> But, I didn't find out until much later that it wasn't the first time she had been raped. It was some uncle or some relative, when she was younger, and no one believed her. So she figured no one would believe her this time either, and she didn't want to go through it again. Pretty horrible, eh? (Respondent 12)

WOMEN'S EXPERIENCES IN UNIVERSITY

What was the overall impact of the university experience? Many of the respondents were unsure, but others felt that they now saw more educational options ("When I went into university, I didn't know about a Master or a PhD or even Honours. I knew I wanted to go on, but I didn't know how.") or had new career options open up to them. Some women also mentioned their personal growth.

> Being here . . . I've learned and grown quite a bit. . . . I've been self-sufficient as far as I concern myself, and that's helped me to see what lies ahead in the future.
>
> It's opened my mind, I see more than what I came to university seeing. I'm not as narrow-minded as I was when I came through the front door. (Respondent 07)

Another woman put it this way: "[The professors] show both sides of the issue when they present something . . . which is good. If you go out in the workforce with only one side of the story, you become very biased" (Respondent 08).

When it came to considering their futures, there were clear differences between the younger students and their more mature counterparts. Of the women aged twenty-five or older, only one was uncertain about her plans beyond her immediate expectation of spending the summer "keeping busy" with her children. She differed from the other mature students in the study, in that her husband's income meant that "we don't have to worry about money anymore." The other mature students ranged from concern to extreme anxiety over their financial affairs: "It's terrible. I worry about it all the time. I worry about the everyday bills. I've skipped two payments of rent already" (Respondent 02). Nevertheless, all but one hoped to go on to further education after attaining their bachelor's degrees, even though for most of them this would mean amassing a large debt.

Those who came to university directly from high school were much less certain about what their futures might hold. Some were playing with the idea of graduate school or considering different possible careers. None of them expected to owe more than $2,000 upon graduation, and all of them were receiving financial support from their parents. By and large, the students under age twenty-five looked forward to an open-ended future with a range of possibilities available.

Interestingly, only three of the single women interviewed mentioned traditional female aspirations of marriage and motherhood. Of course, the research was oriented toward academic accomplishments and university life, and the respondents were not asked directly about their expectations in this regard: "Yes. I would like to have a family, but I would like to have a career as well. My Mom does it, so I just figured I can do it too" (Respondent 12). Perhaps other students share this woman's optimism that, one way or another, a career and family obligations will be worked out to the satisfaction of everyone.

Our preliminary investigation indicates that women have come a long way in higher education but that their situation is less than ideal. We were very disappointed to discover that professors and male students were making life difficult for female undergraduates. These barriers to education were being bravely overcome by our respondents, but they could not speak to us on behalf of the women who may have dropped out of university because the struggle became too onerous. We were also unable to measure the degree to which the students who took part in the study might have accomplished more, or might have had more far-reaching aspirations, had they obtained their education in an atmosphere free of these barriers.

Universities can respond in a number of ways to special problems of female undergraduates. Personal safety can be increased by constructing a well-lit campus and providing escort services after dark. No university should be without a sexual harassment office. Provision of child care services can decrease the burdens on single mothers. Courses in women's studies provide a forum in which students can situate their gender-related problems in the larger context of feminist theory and research.

Some problems, however, are more difficult to solve. Of utmost importance is the number of students who suffer in silence. Unreported sexual assault or harassment is a profound concern. We also cannot ignore the students who do not report sexism in the classroom or in faculty offices, and whose personal well-being and academic success may be compromised as a result. Our observations suggest that problems go unreported because students fear their grades will be adversely affected if they appear to be "troublemakers" or because they believe that nothing will come of it.

The challenge for universities is to assure students that their problems will be taken seriously, even if these problems are of a sensitive nature and may be difficult to express. Without overly dramatizing the situation, universities must bring gender-related issues to the forefront and communicate the message that policies are in place to deal with them. There is a good deal of consciousness-raising yet to be done, with university faculty and students alike.

NOTES

1. Special thanks to Sandra McIsaac, who assisted in this project from its inception in 1989 through to the transcription of the interviews. Her interviews were conducted with sensitivity and sensibility. Support from the Department of the Secretary of State and consultation with Joan McCurdy-Myers are gratefully acknowledged.
2. See K.L. Fulton 1991. References to the academic literature on women in higher education have been kept to a minimum.

It's Still a Man's World:
Women and Graduate Study

Vande Jane Vezina

In the past twenty years Canadian universities have experienced a substantial increase in the enrolment of women both at the undergraduate and graduate levels. From 1981 to 1994, the number of women enroled on a full-time basis at universities increased by 60 percent.[1] While the increase in the participation rate for women at the undergraduate level appears to indicate that equal representation of both sexes exists in higher education, an examination of enrolment figures at the graduate level reveals that the opposite is true: males and females are not represented equally. Although 54 percent of full-time students enroled at the undergraduate level were women in the 1993–94 academic year, only 41 percent of full-time graduate students were women.[2] Women students are underrepresented in graduate programs.

Some feminist scholars suggest that this inequity can be addressed through an examination of the university.[3] As a social institution, the university promotes the stereotypical roles attributed to men and women within the larger society. The awareness of prescribed sex roles begins in early childhood. It is the socialization experiences of male and female children that serve to reinforce the sex role stereotypes in our society. While the typical male child is taught the skills necessary to prepare him for his role as breadwinner in the family, the typical female child learns the domestic skills necessary to prepare her for her role as wife and mother.

> [These] distinct and unequal roles are sanctioned by long custom and convention which hold that the proper sphere for women is the private and domestic one. The sphere in which women are to make their contribution is, however, not merely separate, but also less powerful than the public world inhabited by men insofar as their private domain affords women no role in the formation of public policy, in the shaping of the institutions that in turn largely shape and govern our culture.[4]

Within this society, men have played a major role in the way social institutions, such as higher education, function. Women, however, have had little, if any, say in how the university has been structured.

As one scholar suggested, despite the growth of higher education in Canada in the last twenty years, the university structure continues to operate "to preserve the place of privilege."[5] Unfortunately, the place of privilege has always been afforded to men, not women, whether in the student body or at higher levels of the administration where procedures governing the university are developed and implemented. The result is a university structured on the basis of men's perceptions and beliefs, where women continue to educate themselves in a cultural, intellectual and social environment from which they have been almost entirely excluded. But, in an era when women are entering higher education in increasingly larger numbers, when the press for equal rights for women is a dominant political issue and when, among institutions of education, the university vehemently declares that equal access is a primary consideration, it is extraordinary to find that women continue to be underrepresented in graduate programs.

The majority of studies on women in university are concerned with explaining the existence of a male bias within the university structure and its effects on women students at all levels.[6] Relatively few studies have examined male bias in graduate programs and its effects on women students and the choices they make within their graduate programs. In an attempt to fill this gap in the literature, a study was undertaken (1) to look at male bias in the structure of the university, and (2) to focus on the perspective of women graduate students.

Twenty women students enroled in various master's programs at a southwestern Ontario university were interviewed about their experiences as graduate students. Specifically, these women were asked to discuss the curriculum and classroom interaction, their mentoring relationships, their exposure to sexual harassment and their future plans. Women students appear to encounter a number of barriers to their success as academics and these barriers are linked to the male biased structure of the university. They are found in both the curriculum, where women scholars' contributions are undervalued and trivialized, and in the negative attitudes that some male faculty and students have towards women. There are also far fewer female than male professors to serve as advisors, role models and/or mentors for women students. In addition, the high rate of sexual harassment against women in universities (more than 20 percent of women in universities across Canada claim to have experienced sexual harassment in one form or another[7]), and the difficulties associated with raising a family while enrolled in graduate school can discourage women from pursuing doctoral work.

CURRICULUM AND CLASSROOM INTERACTION

Many of the women interviewed were aware of a male bias in the curriculum. These students recognized that most of the literature introduced and the issues discussed in the classroom reflected men's ideas and perspectives. The participants believed that women's scholarship has been trivialized or taken less seriously than men's, and their concern with and interest in women's issues has been largely ignored. A sociology student described the nature of the curriculum in her discipline: "In general, I would say . . . most information is written by men about men for men's issues. The course content selection is purely biased towards men" (Interviewee 5). Another student in political science explained that, not only were there no courses on women available within her discipline, but: "There [was] no gender dimension to my courses at all. There [was] no mention of feminist scholarship and there's a lot of good feminist scholarship out there, and not a mention of it at all" (Interviewee 4). A communication studies student identified the method by which one of her professors chose to introduce women's studies in his course: "In another course I did, there was . . . a paper for discussion on . . . Steiner's oppositional decoding as active resistance. And, that was like the token feminist paper for that course" (Interviewee 11).

The use of the term "token" here suggests that, as well as being aware of a male biased curriculum, this student realized that women's contributions were being trivialized and that the study of women in higher education was not considered a legitimate academic activity by this professor. Similarly, a history student at the end of her program commented:

> There's little or no evidence of women . . . in the courses I have taken a lot of the time. They [professors] don't consider women a legitimate category of study. So, they unconsciously ignore it and wipe it off their outlines or syllabus (sic). . . . All the readings, all the lectures are just constructed about issues that pertain to men. (Interviewee 2)

This exclusion has ultimately affected these women's sense of self-worth as students. A philosophy student explained how she and other women in her class were made to feel inferior to male students during most of their classroom interactions:

> Some of the other students in our faculty started to get together . . . and we started talking and we realized that we perceived the form of argumentation that we take differently than the men. And, we thought, ourselves, that it was just us, individually, that we were somehow feeling inferior. . . . Very few women . . . spoke up in class. We felt sort of intimidated. (Interviewee 6)

According to some of the women interviewed, the interaction between women students and male professors in the classroom frequently brought to light the attitudes, values and evaluations some male faculty have of women students. At least two women said that they were not treated the same as male students.

I really don't think he [the professor] treated me seriously when I was talking about how important it is to talk about gender differences and things like that. He really didn't think that it was a big deal. Probably because we are women, we are not taken as seriously or as intelligently as men. (Interviewee 5)

I feel that my comments in a lot of classes have not been treated as seriously as they should have been. (Interviewee 10)

Clearly, many of the participants in this study were forced to deal with the fact that women are not equal members of the academic community. Furthermore, these women realized that the obstacles they face are not only found in the curriculum, where the inclusion of feminist scholarship and discussion of women's concerns could lessen or eliminate barriers, but also in classroom interactions with male students and faculty. The attitudes of these individuals are generally reflected in their behaviour towards women inside, as well as outside, of the classroom. Whether in or out of the classroom, sexism is generally expressed in the form of support for the "traditional" roles associated with men and women in our society and a questioning of women's legitimacy as members of the academic community. This can be especially problematic in smaller and more specialized programs where enrolment levels in graduate courses are lower and women are afforded closer contact with male colleagues and faculty members.

MENTORING EXPERIENCES
The kind of relationships that students, both men and women, have with their professors ultimately affects their academic performance, either positively or negatively. This is especially true in graduate education where students work more closely with faculty, often on a one-to-one basis. Such a close working relationship with professors in graduate school is made possible largely because fewer students are enroled in these programs than in undergraduate ones. For example, in the 1993–94 academic year, 499,549 students were pursuing undergraduate degrees across Canada on a full-time basis, whereas only 74,765 students were enroled in full-time graduate programs.[8]
    One of the many obstacles women graduate students face is the lack of women in faculty positions who serve as role models, advisors and/or mentors. In the ten year span from 1984 to 1994, the proportion of women among full

professors in Canadian universities increased by only 6 percent and these individuals now constitute less than 8 percent of faculty members.[9] In a study at the University of Western Ontario, women graduate students were asked if they felt that a sufficient number of women faculty were available with whom they could identify or from whom they could seek support and advice. Over 35 percent of students said that the underrepresentation of female role models was of considerable concern to them and nearly 33 percent felt that there were not enough women professors available to support and advise them.[10] The very presence of women professors not only serves to legitimize women's place in the university community, but it also serves as an example for women students, verifying that, with hard work and determination, they too can become successful academics. Several of the women interviewed for this study talked about female professors as positive role models. For example, two social science students said of their female professors:

> She really takes what she does seriously. I just see her as a really hard worker. She's committed. She perseveres. . . . I see her as a strong woman. (Interviewee 12)

> Definitely a really good role model for women in general because she is very competent. . . . I admire her and the work that she does. (Interviewee 18)

For these two women, the competency of the female professor in question, combined with her position as a faculty member, were the characteristics used to define her as a good role model. A student in the arts, however, evaluated her woman professor as a positive role model in a different way:

> She knows what she wants. She doesn't let herself be intimidated by anybody. . . . It's just sort of an all around, sort of a confidence about her. . . . She gets involved in all the academic stuff around here and she has a voice, which is very important. (Interviewee 6)

As advisors to students, female professors also play an important role in students' successful completion of graduate degrees. Generally speaking, faculty members who supervise graduate students spend a considerable amount of time reading, critiquing and providing feedback on the research efforts of the students under their supervision. However, the shortage of women faculty members works to limit the choices of those women graduate students wishing to work with a female professor. These students must either ensure that their own interests closely reflect the specialization of available women faculty members, or work with a male faculty member who has similar interests to their own. Yet, research has shown that about 75 percent of students prefer same sex advisors.[11]

One student completing her degree in philosophy noted that: "There is no female faculty member in the area" (Interviewee 6). A political science student mentioned that the sole woman faculty member in her department did not specialize in her area of interest: "She's not an expert on that topic. . . . I wish she was a little bit more in tune with the literature" (Interviewee 4). Yet, this same student chose to work with this woman anyway simply because she was the only female professor available to her. Another student who recently completed her degree in sociology explained why she decided to work with a male faculty member: "I never thought of a woman in this department because, first of all, there are not many of them. And, second of all, there were no women that I thought specialized in [this area]" (Interviewee 12).

Similarly, a psychology student, interested in working with a particular woman faculty member, talked about why she chose a male supervisor instead:

I know I would love to work with Ms. X. That's what I thought when I applied. I thought, gee, I would love to work with her . . . I like the work that she has done . . . but he specializes in the area that I am most interested in . . . (Interviewee 19)

As mentors, faculty members are able to encourage female students to complete their degrees and to support them in their academic choices. Female mentors can relate to the stresses young women face, such as sexual harassment, more easily than males can.[12] A geography student described the nature of her relationship with a part-time woman instructor:

She has actually been a really big help. . . . She's actually partly responsible for me focusing on this—gender neutral studies. . . . She is incredibly supportive, not just academically, but also personally because I had a lot of problems within the department this year. . . . And, it made life a living hell, and I went to her and I talked to her a lot about it. She was incredibly supportive. (Interviewee 7)

The presence of support is a factor in women students' decisions to pursue graduate degrees and in the progression of many women through graduate programs. Indeed, research indicates that women who lack a mentor have a lower self-esteem among the female student population.[13] This also was true of some of the women participating in this study. A mother of two, in the faculty of social science, said that the mentoring relationship she had with a woman professor helped raise her self-confidence and ultimately affected her decision to pursue graduate work.

I never really believed that I could do it [go to graduate school]. I kept feeling like I really don't belong here and, if anybody ever sees through this, they are going to throw me out because I really shouldn't be here. And then, she gave me this confidence to believe that, yeah, I could do this. (Interviewee 16)

Of the few women master's students in this study who did have mentoring relationships with women faculty members, the importance of these interactions did not go unnoticed. Upon reflection of her graduate experience, one student noted:

> I come from a very small town with very traditional attitudes. . . . And, here I am, and she is encouraging me to do a PhD. And, for me, this is just incredible. She makes me realize that I can do it . . . that I can go to that level, you know . . . that I don't have these barriers because I am a woman. (Interviewee 6)

For other students, the relationships they had with women professors also had a significant effect on their decisions to continue in graduate school.

> I never gave any thought to being a graduate student before she started telling me that I was graduate material. In that respect she has really helped me to begin thinking of myself as a professional—not just as a professional student, but as a professional person. (Interviewee 17)

> She's made an inestimable contribution [to my education]. I would not be in graduate studies if it were not for her. I would not have thought that I could have done it. (Interviewee 2)

SEXUAL HARASSMENT ON CAMPUS

Sexual harassment has traditionally been defined in broad terms, ranging from the most severe (outward physical attack) to the least threatening (continual use of words or statements meant to demean women). Most consider the exchange of sexual favours for job promotion or the threat of job loss for refusing to have sex with someone as "classic" examples of sexual harassment. Yet, many women are exposed to sexual harassment in more subtle ways. For example, staring at a woman's breasts while talking to her can make her very uncomfortable and, therefore, could be considered a more subtle form of sexual harassment. While this form of sexual harassment is often taken the least seriously, researchers have found that "subtle and/or inadvertent incidents can sometimes do the most damage because they often occur without the full awareness of the professor or the student."[14]

A study at the University of Western Ontario showed that at least 22 percent of women graduate students on that campus had been sexually harassed.[15] Similar findings were discovered in the present study: 20 percent of women interviewed indicated that they had experienced more subtle forms of sexual harassment either by a male faculty member or student. However, none of these women chose to report the matter to the sexual harassment advisor, to confront the accused or to bring it to the attention of another person in authority. Rather, all of the women chose to ignore these incidents. Their reasons for not reporting the incidents were influenced, at least in part, by the nature of the harassment and whether the encounter involved another student or a faculty member. The women who felt that they had been harassed by their colleagues were not surprised by the way these men treated them and, therefore, decided not to report the harassment:

> Well, I really didn't think it was necessary [to report the incident] because it just happens all the time. I'm not saying it's right. It's not right. I'm not saying I shouldn't go. But, I just felt that it's so common that I just didn't think I needed to. (Interviewee 5)

On the other hand, women who had been harassed by professors were reluctant to report the episode because of the power faculty members have over students. One woman noted:

> When you are a student and there is a professor, you are not in a position to say, "Could you not look at me like that. It makes me uncomfortable." That's outlandish. Maybe that is what I should have done. But there is no way I could do that. (Interviewee 12)

Another student explained why she did not lodge a complaint against a professor who sexually harassed her:

> Well, there's all this talk about women coming forward and reporting it. The reason I didn't do anything about it was because of that fact that I was coming back here the next year . . . and I didn't want to have this black cloud hanging over my head. (Interviewee 17)

This same woman tried to minimize the effects of her experience by saying, "it wasn't like he ever made an attempt to touch a part of my body that I consider private or kiss me or sexually assault me." For these women, as for many individuals, sexual harassment has been defined only in its "classical" form and therefore the experiences they describe do not warrant making a formal complaint. These women also realize that their complaints will not be given serious and legitimate consideration.

Their reluctance is reinforced by a perception that, even when professors are found guilty of harassment, they will not be punished. The atmosphere of collegiality that often exists within the university seems to deter other faculty, or members of the administration, from confronting these individuals in order to make them aware that sexist behaviour will not be tolerated. At least two of the women participating in this study knew of male professors in their departments who did not change their sexist attitudes, despite the recent implementation of a sexual harassment policy on campus. One of these students noted that, while her professor had been brought in front of a disciplinary committee and charged with sexual harassment, he continued to teach and to make statements that made women in his class very uncomfortable.

> Our professor, who is known for being sexist—apparently he has been
> called up against a committee for harassment . . . so, you know, [he
> says] "Feminism is just a bunch of dysfunctional dykes who don't
> know what to do with their lives." (Interviewee 7)

This same student felt that women were basically powerless to deal with harassment in the university:

> The biggest problem is that the majority of professors are older men;
> and they are just bringing women in and making retirement mandatory
> now . . . it takes a lot of time. These guys have a strong foothold. They
> have been here thirty years. You don't tell them what to do. (Inter-
> viewee 7)

Another woman spoke of the attitude that one of her professors maintains towards women students: "He's notorious for sexism, notorious for giving A's to males and A-'s to women; notorious for silencing women in the classroom" (Interviewee 10).

Unfortunately, the fact that these two professors were not formally disciplined for imposing sexist attitudes on their female students indicated to these women that neither other faculty, nor the university as a whole, take such practices seriously. Many women who are sexually harassed choose to minimize the effects of these experiences. Since they know that they will not be supported by either the professoriate or the administration, women often find it easier to cope with harassment by ignoring the behaviour, blaming themselves and/or downplaying its effects.

CHILD CARE

The issue of child care also is a primary consideration for many women who choose to pursue graduate degrees. This is particularly true for female students with small children who are too young to attend school. Research demonstrates that, for many of these women, the decision to continue is largely based on the quality and accessibility of child care services.[16]

At most universities where child care is available, there are extremely long waiting lists. For example, as recently as 1989, one Ontario university had at least 150 names on a waiting list that had only ten spaces available. Pregnant women at this institution were advised to add their names to the list before the birth of their child; and it was suggested that they also leave their names at the preschool centre. For many of these children, a space would not be available until they were too old to attend the infant/toddler centre.[17] Moreover, of those colleges and universities that do provide adequate and affordable daycare, most operate only between the hours of 9 am and 5 pm. This schedule means that those students taking evening classes or doing library research at night do not have access to child care services. Some researchers have suggested that drop-in centres should operate from early morning until late evening so that women students can have adequate access to library materials and other resources.[18] Others suggest that "flexibility in the hours of child care delivery can make the difference between succeeding . . . or failure or withdrawal."[19] Moreover, the costs of child care, given the limited number of subsidies available, are often beyond students' economic means. As one participant in the present study commented:

> My experience has been that it is just too difficult with three small children to juggle between family and academia. The combination of the children and the workload has held me back. When I can find more time, then I will pursue a PhD. (Interviewee 1)

Four of the women who participated in this study were parents at the time of the interviews; however, only two of these students had small children under five years of age. These women recognized that, if it were not for their friends and family who provided free and unlimited child care services, their progress through the master's program would have been slower and more difficult. One mother of two recognized that, although both of her daughters were in school:

> Carrie practically raised her sister. When I first started back at school I was taking two courses. That's four nights a week. Plus I was working shiftwork. So, I was gone a lot. So, my oldest daughter practically raised the little one because I was at school most of the time. . . . To be honest, I don't think it would have been so easy with younger children. That's really hard. . . . I have my family. . . . I have a lot of friends too that I have known for a long time. (Interviewee 16)

The issue of child care is of no less importance to those women who do not have children. In fact, it can be a notable factor in a woman's decision to have a family and/or pursue doctoral work.[20]

FUTURE PLANS
The decision to start a family while enroled in a graduate program can be difficult for both men and women when the demands of higher education are considered. These include long hours spent on homework and research, inadequate financial assistance, time limits on degree completion and the open-ended nature of graduate work. Women, unlike men, face an additional constraint. Deciding to have a family is more difficult for women because it is the women who must take time out from their studies to give birth and women who are responsible for the majority of child care duties. Furthermore, women entering graduate school are usually in their mid to late twenties, fast approaching the end of their optimal childbearing years and, therefore, must choose between starting a family or continuing their education.

Fifteen of the women who participated in this study were between the ages of twenty-three and thirty and did not yet have children. These women were affected by what they saw as the increased demands of graduate work at the PhD level as opposed to the master's. One psychology student expressed concern that the lengthy time it takes to successfully complete a master's degree usually means that a woman has to choose between a family and her education. Upon completion of her degree, if she obtains a faculty appointment in a university, she must then decide between career advancement or spending time with her family. The point to remember is that many women graduate students must choose between career or family. Unlike their male colleagues, they cannot easily have both. This represents a real dilemma for many of these women, as the following student commented:

> I am of the opinion that I want to do my PhD and I want to be a professional . . . and I also want to have a family life. I want to get married and I want to have children. I don't want to sacrifice a career for that. But, I also don't want to sacrifice my family for a career. I want a happy balance. Whether I can achieve that, I don't know. More and more I am questioning whether it is possible because the women I do see with PhD's are working so hard and putting so much time into their careers that their families are suffering and secondary. And I don't want that. (Interviewee 18)

The rigorous time demands of advanced graduate work, which often become more intense in a professorial position, are enough for some women to seriously question such a career path.

> The one thing that I have learned is that they [professors] put too much time in and that they are almost discouraging me to go on because you think, "Oh my God, do I have to work that hard in order to get through?" I am not going to do that in order to go on or be a prof or whatever. If

I can get through without doing that, then I will go on. But, if it's going to take that much of my life, then I am not going to do that. (Interviewee 15)

These comments show the career choices that women must make. The university has placed women in a position whereby they are forced to choose between continuing their education or becoming mothers. Within the university structure, the two become contradictory. One result is that many women choose to delay having children until they are older and more established in their careers. Many women would prefer not to delay having a family, but the demands associated with graduate school leave them with few alternatives.

SUMMARY AND CONCLUSIONS
The stereotypical roles that men and women play in society are clearly reflected in the structure of the university. As a result, barriers have developed, which impede the progress of women students and, in some instances, lead to their failure or withdrawal. Nowhere are the effects of these barriers more pronounced than at the master's and doctoral levels.

Women students face barriers to their success in the curriculum, where their contributions to the literature are relatively ignored or trivialized when discussed, and in the classroom, as reflected in the attitudes some male faculty and students have toward women. The university could take a major step in eliminating male bias by acknowledging that women's studies is a legitimate area of study and by including research written by and about women in the curriculum.

The underrepresentation of women faculty members who serve as advisors, role models and/or mentors for women also acts as a barrier to these students since these individuals provide support and encouragement to women students as they progress, and ensure that the interests of women in general are not ignored. Not only are more women faculty needed to address this imbalance, but women must be promoted to higher ranks of the professoriate and to administrative positions where the development and implementation of university policies are a primary responsibility.

The high incidence of sexual harassment on campus shows that the university as a whole has, up until now, been unable to fully incorporate women students into its environment as equal participants since women continue to be devalued and insulted in this manner. A heightened awareness of sexual harassment alone is not enough to encourage women to lodge formal complaints. Punitive measures must be taken to ensure that women are not treated as second-class citizens.

The problems that many students with children face in their efforts to juggle family responsibilities with the rigorous demands of graduate work can also have an effect on their career choices. And for those students who are not yet parents but are thinking about starting a family, the economic constraints and time demands associated with graduate school force them to make a choice between having children now or finishing their degrees. The difficulties associated with combining graduate studies with a family life could be alleviated by providing flexible, affordable and accessible child care, by making reading courses available to students so as to enhance flexibility in scheduling and by expanding part-time studies at the graduate level to make it more financially feasible for parents to study on a part-time basis.

NOTES
1. Statistics Canada 1992a.
2. Statistics Canada 1992a.
3. Filteau 1989; Aisenberg and Harrington 1988.
4. Aisenberg and Harrington 1988: 3.
5. Guppy 1984.
6. Compare Chamberlain 1991; Gaskell, McLaren and Novogrodsky 1989; Stanworth 1988.
7. Morris 1989.
8. Statistics Canada 1992a.
9. Statistics Canada 1992a.
10. Morris 1989.
11. Gilbert 1985.
12. McKeen and Burke 1989.
13. Gilbert, Gallessich and Evans 1983.
14. Hall and Sandler 1986.
15. Morris 1989.
16. Klodawsky 1989; Dagg and Thompson 1988.
17. Klodawsky 1989.
18. Dagg and Thompson 1988.
19. MacDonald and Morris 1986.
20. Klodawsky 1989.

The Academic Shunning of Fat Old Women

Bobbi Spark

I am a fat, old, silver-haired university student. My story, although full of stressors, is also a story offering comic relief in the form of a vicious humour, which my experience has made me just perverse enough to appreciate. Needless to say, I do not fit the stereotypical image of a student.

Using the library intimidates me because the entrance boasts very small entry and exit turnstiles. When I am in the library, I miss meals rather than embarrass myself entering or leaving more than is absolutely necessary. I survive meal times by sneaking in sandwiches and juice in my backpack, and consuming them furtively or hiding them behind computers and large piles of books. The hateful turnstiles are designed for six-foot, flat-chested, slim-waisted males with 60 percent of their body weight in their upper torso. I, on the other hand, am all of five-foot-five inches, have breasts and am an ample-waisted female with 60 percent of her weight in her lower body. I try to squeeze through the thirty-five-inch library gate featuring rapier-sharp, windmill-like protrusions aimed directly at my pubis. As the turnstile's arm rotates relent-lessly, it imperils my right breast. Wriggling sideways to avoid the impending attack, I thrust myself through the barrier by centrifugal force. I stumble, regaining balance but not dignity. With heavy backpack and arms loaded with text, pre-requisite environmental coffee mug and umbrella, I pause. I consider the devilish device as a young male and slender female slip successively through the turnstile. I approach the obstruction with caution, hoping that I am saunter-ing nonchalantly. I am immediately poked in the stomach by a gate appendage. Undaunted, armload precariously balanced shoulder high, I will myself out the other side. Problematically, my generously proportioned body is abruptly halted by the gate's assault upon my coat pocket. A young man, never imagining someone could not slip effortlessly through the turnstile, fails to negotiate his stop and we collide. The melee characterizes life here for a woman of size. I do not fit university turnstiles.

Nor are gateways my only physical handicap; my backpack is surely made for an alien creature. If the straps are shortened, they bind while the pack is being shrugged onto my wide back. Once in position, the pack rests too high and feels as though a wrong move will flip me flat on my back. All women know this is a dangerous position regardless of one's size. However, when the straps are too long, the heavy backpack rests uncomfortably on the ample curve between my short back and abundant bum. Furthermore, I know that I am cursed, because the few times the straps are adjusted perfectly, they immediately slip their fastenings and the backpack falls off. Straps meant to secure it around my waist do not meet because they are too short. And so continues the endless struggle between myself and the indispensable backpack designed for another species. I do not fit backpacks.

Lecture hall seating with long strips of tables ten inches wide are too narrow for my notes, text and dimpled arms. The cramped chairs or benches are tiny, hard, and often broken. A cracked seat is a nightmare for a person of size, allowing two options; looking silly as you try to replace it, or looking silly as it unceremoniously dumps you on the floor. Another type of seat is the old-fashioned 'grade school' desk that opens on one side and features a postage-stamp writing area. All the seats are much too small for me, an indignity as I contort my shape by sucking in my stomach and holding my breath. I tumble in, then exhale and I hope that the chair neither splits nor explodes. It requires a half twist from the waist to allow writing, hence I take terse notes. I do not fit university seats.

There are more than physical barriers to remind me that I am not welcome in academe. I think that I should be celebrated as a student, but instead I am insulted. By design, convention and practice, the institution neither encourages nor recognizes my skills and experiences. I am alternately marginalized and rejected; my years of work in community animation (itself a topic of academic scrutiny) are not appreciated, my reminiscences neither acknowledged nor given uptake. Professors lecturing on 1960s activism brush me off when I tell them that I helped organize public housing tenants, poverty activists, women's groups and welfare rights movements. They prefer the accounts of academic "experts." Women's studies instructors also are dismissive when I share the excitement of real, lived experiences, such as my arrest for interrupting the House of Commons over the issue of abortion. Experience does not fit academe.

I am deeply bitter about the lack of financial, educational or practical support offered for intelligent mature students with limited educational back-grounds. I recall that I cried for two days because I didn't know how to use the library but was too intimidated to ask for help. My first essay assignment terrified me. First catatonic, then frantic, I scrambled to find out what a bibliography was and, more urgently, how to use spell-check to hide my working class inadequacy. It was agony to examine topics of incest, abuse, reproductive technology and poverty. The anguish of personal experience sprang to my consciousness, closing my throat and inhibiting my keyboard. Academe demands a smothering of life experiences to reach an objectivity that is impossible for me to achieve without lying. This dilemma mirrors the lives of all women, but is especially poignant as a cache of experiences assault the emotional fragility of aging women. Aging women's experience does not fit academe.

No one else on campus looks like me; the few female professors do not share my rounded shape. I look rooted and sturdy, but strong substantial women do not fit university norms. As a matter of fact, nothing here fits or is designed for me. High steps, long walks, snowbanks, steep stairs, breathlessly tiny bathroom stalls, long slow lineups, unsafe stacks in the dreaded library, petite school clothing, contact sports, student dorms, rowdy social events, rock concerts and loud pubs confront me. What the hell am I doing here? University is exclusively a male, white, youth-oriented hegemony. Should I consider a sex-change operation or just cross-dressing? Liposuction and diet milkshakes to congratulate myself on disappearing? Perhaps lucrative and illegal drug sales to guarantee my welcome at rock concerts and campus pubs? A reality check says that still I would not fit academe.

I am deeply insulted by my university. Administration bows to traditional misogyny, men benefit from what I call "the inalienable rights of the cock." Male administrators, staff, professors and students are permitted to practise harassment, discrimination, rape and assault on women without meaningful penalty; one might argue that it is more than tolerated, it is sanctioned. This year, my university refused to fire a professor convicted of sexually assaulting a family member. Other male and female professors, known as pillars of the community, spoke of their concern for their colleague and his civil rights. They offered no similar care for the ravaged child, or for the impact this professor would have on students who were themselves incest or rape survivors. Institutionalized male power is merely tacit permission to practise prejudices and the academic subordination of women. Feminist ideals do not fit university practices.

My campus is poorly lit with lots of shrubbery, dark parking lots and indentations, and an inadequate, insensitive security staff. The university's recent acquisition of a partially unused property adjacent to a newly-relocated bus shelter should have been predicated on their making the property safe. The area was littered with derelict vehicles, and the parking lot was ominously dark and isolated after six in the evening. One year ago on the first night of classes, I was sexually assaulted by three young men at a poorly lit, newly-located bus stop. It ranks as one of the most appalling experiences of my fifty years. When I first saw the men, they made me think of my own high-spirited sons. Then they taunted me with explicit sexual invitations, and informed me of the acts they would force me to do. They tore my clothing, grabbed my breasts, bruised my chest and clutched at my vagina. The arrival of the bus stopped them from raping me. When I could not afford a counsellor, the university administration declined to assist with costs and denied permission for me to search for the attackers in student identification photographs. Let me review this. I look like a mother/

wife, they look like my/your sons. Scary, isn't it? Nothing was done. The area is still improperly lit. Women's safety does not fit institutional priorities.

Many older returning students are working-class people with childhood and work experiences characterized by poverty and hardship. However, many are the most poor upon returning to university. They go hungry, use food banks, get welfare during the summer and have to beg and borrow money, clothes and food. They are often deeply in debt for student loans. While they celebrate an indefatigable feminist spirit, their lives are hard. Poverty does not fit a university designed for elite norms.

Astonishingly, although more than one half of students are women and one-third mature, they cast no reflection in the larger campus tapestry. They arrive or return to post-secondary education for a multitude of reasons, including economic need and family breakdowns coupled with a passionate and sincere desire to learn. They are single parents, career women and older women. They are usually part-time, since few can afford to attend full-time. They are often single parents responsible for primary child care; women do not have wives to provide free child care. Their needs for child care, academic support services, family housing, counselling, and family, professional or social networks are conveniently overlooked. University does not fit mature women with families.

There is no bright line of change in academe; all women find discrimination. Their concerns and issues are trivialized, silenced, denied or ignored. I, as a student, am punished for being female, critical and public; this makes university a painful ordeal. I am mocked, my experiences denied or rewritten by academic theorists. My analyses and methodologies are questioned, and I am told that I have no writing skills. I have been threatened with failure for non-compliance (read defiance). My letters have been sanitized and I have been vilified in campus publications. For example, I was branded as a "straight-privilege-user-breeder" because I was a heterosexual mother married to a white man. I am targeted by professors who alternately attack me for my views or force me to be the unpaid feminist educator and defender of all feminist ideologies. I am silenced by the classism and elitism of feminist and non-feminist, male and female professors. I expect more of feminist professors, and I do complain when I don't get it. I resent any professor's collusion with academic androcentrism as problematic to me. While some feminist professors do strive to be innovative, inclusive and supportive, many use power as do traditional males. The practical result of their complicity is that for twenty-eight years I was a feminist, but my worst marks are in feminist courses. In a genuine learning environment there will be respect for both abstract theory and grounded experience. Unfortunately, I do not fit feminism "à l'académie."

A feminist consciousness is an anguished consciousness, so I use my pain to empower me. Many theorists claim that women are victims with little alternative to their complicitous support of patriarchy. I know the reality is that we always have a capacity to resist domination. I not only resist, I invite others to join me. Resistance does not fit academe.

My introduction to an androcentric academy occurred when the university principal "inadvertently misinformed me" about the process of making feminist backlash a theme at a major international conference. The result was that a timely opportunity to discuss the issue of campus backlash to feminism was lost, as was my naivety. The confirmation of androcentrism was reinforced in my second year. Although my school is rated by *Maclean's* magazine as a "top university," it is nevertheless renown for the trivialization of an anti-rape campaign during which male students hung out banners with sexist slogans such as "no means hit the bitch." Three of those many offenders were convicted, but not until fully three years after the incident and then too late for penalty or denial of graduate status. Also in my second year, a male student was charged with raping three women students on campus. The administration allowed the alleged perpetrator computer access from prison to encourage his studies, and then night-time access to the actual university grounds. Meanwhile, the alleged victims were shunned in class and vilified by male professors. Male rapists fit academe, but victimized women do not.

I have emphasized my majestic image, but I am more than just a woman of size with a wide back and generous breasts. In addition, I am intelligent, street smart, compassionate, funny, generous and loving. I am a good student, a radical feminist, a leader, an organizer and a political confrontationalist. I am also a mother, an aunt, a grandmother, a partner, a friend and a sister. I have been a chef, an animator, a researcher, a business woman and an adjudicator. My life has always been eclectic and multilayered. In academe I am simply an assinine, fat, old woman, but in reality I am a sixties feminist with twenty-five years of community work. I am a woman of distinction who possesses both power and a herstory. I myself accepted the matronly stereotype, until I saw pictures of myself on campus. I beheld a commanding fifty-one-year-old dignified woman with long silver hair, fashionable glasses and chic clothes. I am graceful, well-groomed and attractive, and have a warm and sincere smile. Surprise, I like myself! What a lesson to one who should be wiser at age fifty-one. Wise old women do not fit student stereotypes.

If we mature women students knew our numbers, we would know our potential and our power base. We would know one another and we would share the reasons we are attending university so late in our lives. We would demand change, inclusion and representation. We would insist that information about menopause, child abuse, eating disorders, impotency and wife abuse be available at the student health clinic. We would question the allocation of money for drunken, violent, raping orientation and homecoming brawls. We would establish women's centres as well as high-tech libraries and scientific research laboratories. We would demand comfortable desks for all, and library entrances that admit more than a 145-pound male. We would surely change the face of academe. We need to recognize, however, that we will be even less welcome as the significant feminist threat we pose to traditional academe becomes obvious to male academics and administrators.

At university, impertinence is blasphemous, questions are suspect, and academic versions of inclusiveness actually dismiss many people. My experience of otherness is that of being female, working-class, poor, old, fat and silver-haired at my privileged, white, male, slender-identified, youth-oriented, heterosexual, hegemonic university. At times I despair, thinking that I should just leave university, since I am not a young rugged white male. In academe, difference is a poor fit.

Until we mature women recognize our number, validate our existence and seize power, academe will continue to ignore, exploit and de-value us. To make academe fit feminism, I want to insert my reality and experiences. I want to force recognition of my physical differences and to challenge the assumption that we do not belong. I want to compel recognition of the value of our epistemologies, our ways of knowing and our special skills. I want to demand that administrative and patriarchal types reply to my challenges. I am determined to remain in academe; I will not disappear. I will not speak weakly or be silenced, but I do speak of my bitterness. It is time to recognize that my size, age or class is not the problem. These factors are both challenges and a crystalline clue in the quest for an inclusive solution. I categorically refuse the impossible task of trying to fit an androcentric academe, but I am resolved to make academe fit me. If successful, I will leave it a hell of a lot better place than I found it.

POSTSCRIPT
Several years have passed and I am still old, fat and silver-haired, but I am now a graduate with a master of arts. Some things have changed: my university now has a new, high-tech library with wide doors and ample entrances. The new library doors are impressive—massive, regal and dignified. They also are heavy and difficult to open, especially for physically-challenged students. Additionally, the electronic door mechanisms are often turned off, broken or frozen. The university's new library entrance does not accommodate difference. I am still a poor fit.

I therefore didn't get mad; I got even. I was elected president of a student government and presented alternate ideas and "in-your-face" opinions that officials, boards and committees were compelled to hear. While a few genuinely compassionate administrators "got it," too often the most commonly held opinion or insensitive stereotype prevailed. Despite my attempts, I am unsure that I left the university a hell of a lot better than I found it.

An Education At Last

Gail De Chateauvert

I am an aboriginal woman attending an off-campus extension centre of a major western university. All of the students here are mature students who, because of academic, social or financial need, were not able to go to university earlier in their lives. I am in the third year of a four-year education program and I am presently funded by the university.

I am also a single parent of four children. My eldest son is twenty and the youngest is eleven years old. The Education Centre has been a wonderful learning experience for me, an opportunity I never would have expected, due to the fact that I had only a grade eleven education.

Prior to attending university, I had been employed for nine years by a crown corporation. The last five years were on the midnight shift. I did not have enough seniority for the day shift and the midnight shift allowed me to be at home with my family in the morning and in the evening; however, I often cleaned house, ran errands or kept appointments when I should have been sleeping.

My job entailed working on an automated assembly line and in that kind of work, once you did a particular work order a few times, you could practically do it with your eyes closed. There was also a great deal of hostility between management and regular employees. In that atmosphere I didn't feel proud of my work or get any sense of fulfilment from it. I began to feel like a zombie juggling my family, work and *sleep*. Sometimes I even questioned my own sanity.

I began to realize that, in my job situation, my potential for the future was just frustration. My teenage children had begun to have friends over on school nights and parties when I worked on Friday nights. I could see that their education was beginning to suffer. After a great deal of agonizing over giving up a good pension, I quit my job. I stayed at home on unemployment insurance for one year. During that year I spent a great deal of valuable time with my children. I felt as if I were picking up pieces and I was wide awake and alert for the first time in years. I found that I had time to think about what I was going to do with the rest of my life, and I knew that, at my age and with my past experience, it had to be something that was meaningful. I knew of the Education

Centre because my co-workers and I had often talked about going back to school. I also discussed it with my cousin, who had attended this centre and graduated from university.

In March 1991, I applied to the Bachelor of Education Program. A few weeks later, I received a letter to attend personal interviews and, later, a three-day selection process. I didn't think that I would be accepted for the simple reason that I was a nervous wreck during both the interviews and the selection process. In May 1991, I was accepted into their four-year program. I was ecstatic!

My mother congratulated me, and my kids were happy for me. My one brother still thinks I'm out of my mind for quitting my job and the other one thinks I can pick up and move to Vancouver, where he lives, at a moment's notice. My cousin, Sheila, has given me the most support and I call her at any hour of the day or night. I hope that all my classmates have someone like her.

This program has renewed my self-confidence and opened many doors for me. In the past, when my children began to encounter problems with regard to their schooling, I felt powerless as a single working parent. My two younger children will receive a far different education than the older two did because I know what questions to ask and will insist on being involved in obtaining the best for them. The older boys are gaining a new respect for education because they see me working at it every day. On completion, I will be able to provide a secure future for my family and myself.

As a student at an off-campus centre, I am required to perform like any other student on campus with regard to grades. In fact, we spend more time in practice teaching than do the students on campus. The classrooms, unlike those on campus, are smaller, twenty to thirty people at the most. In this small classroom setting my classmates and I interact on a daily basis and receive the individual attention from our professors that we would never get anywhere else.

The students in this program range widely in age, culture and life experiences. The program has a mandate to provide access to at least 50 percent aboriginal students. Aboriginal women, as well as other women in Canada, who have not had the opportunity to attend university should have access to similar programs. Universities need to continue their support for programs such as this. The ideal would be to have more of these programs. Many people who apply do not get in, simply because there is not enough funding.

Part 3
Women as Faculty: The Marginal Minority

The Changing Space for Women in Academe: The "En-gender-ing" of Knowledge*

Rose Sheinin

I have often been asked what difference it would make if there were women at every level of the university, including its senior academic administration. Would the presence of women in the professoriate, as chairs of departments, as provosts and as presidents, have any impact on the nature and excellence of knowledge being sought, stored, shared and disseminated throughout society? Would women, as role models in these important positions, influence the recruitment and retention of women as undergraduate students and as graduate students? Would they change the gender distribution of the several guilds of scientists, scholars and creative artists, from whom are drawn the members of the professorial guild? And would they, therefore, have an impact on the recruitment and retention of women to the professoriate?

To address these queries, we must ask what is knowledge and does it have a gender? If so, what is the gender and when and how did it become a characteristic of knowledge? In the academy, knowledge can be and is being endowed with gender; it is being "en-gender-ed," particularly by women and feminists who serve as academic administrators.

WHAT IS KNOWLEDGE?
Knowledge is the term applied to a body of information and thought, developed or created by human beings about ourselves and the universe in which we now live or which we have inhabited in the past. As an individual, one intuitively understands that the parameters of such knowledge are defined by and derive from the specificity of micro- and macro-climates of belief, culture, gender, geography, nation, religion, sex, etc.[1] In addition, they are pre-determined by the variety of mechanisms used to collect information.[2] This comprehensive concept of knowledge has not always been honoured within the ivied walls of academe. Rather, there has been overwhelming pressure over many centuries to narrow the definition, the utilization and the sharing of knowledge in a number

of dimensions, only one of which is gender.

Two key factors have impacted significantly on the "en-gender-ing" of knowledge: the concept of "man"[3]; and the so-called "scientific revolution," ushered into Western Europe in the sixteenth and seventeenth centuries.[4] The concept of "man" continues to insist that all knowledge to do with "man" is gender-inclusive, because it is deemed to subsume the female. The scientific revolution introduced the "scientific method" as the only methodology to be applied in the search for knowledge.

These two determinants have, until recently, come to define any and all knowledge included in the canon, or dogma of learning and lore, as accepted by the specified guardians of the human heritage, whether appointed by some authoritative body or self-designated. The dictionary defines canon as "Church decree, a list of Bible books accepted by the Church."[5] Dogma is defined as "Principle, tenet, doctrinal system, especially as laid down by authority of Church; arrogant declaration of opinion; a set of authoritative, *a priori* principles not based on induction." Clearly, the canon and its supporting dogma define the specific body of knowledge deemed appropriate by the authoritative guardian; to be discovered or created, to be cared for in perpetuity and to be propagated and disseminated to society through the ages.

The authorized guardians of societal knowledge have changed over time. The original authoritative guardian was the Church, in its many manifestations. However, for the last 1200 years, the university has been a key member of this particular guild. Initially the body of knowledge to be thought and taught comprised theology, law, the arts and letters, the humanities, the natural sciences and medicine. Since the latter half of the nineteenth century, the functions of scientific research and scholarly enquiry have been deemed crucial functions of the academy.[6] As a result, the university has taken on a dominant and dominating role in the construction, search for, protection and transmission of knowledge to society. For this reason, it is important to understand the concept and gender of the academic canon which has loomed large in the past five years or so, particularly among those who introduced the ideas, language and modern mythology of "political correctness."[7]

THE UNIVERSITY: A GUILD OF SCHOLARS AND PROFESSORS
In order to fully comprehend the concept of "en-gender-ing" of knowledge, it is important to understand that the university is "a corporation or guild of masters and scholars." It is, therefore:

> the whole body of teachers and students pursuing, at a particular place, the higher branches of learning; such persons associated together as a society or corporate body, having the power of conferring degrees and other privileges, and forming an institution for the promotion of education in the higher branches of learning.[8]

And so, at one and the same time, the university is a corporation of the professoriate and its academic leadership, as well as a place in which students receive the professions of this teaching corps. The concept of the university as a guild is an important one for understanding the changing space for women in academe. A guild is a "confraternity or association formed for the mutual aid and protection of its members or for some common purpose," or perhaps both. Universities were given the status of a medieval guild in the sixteenth century in the Bavarian Hanseatic towns, by the Princess Elizabeth of Bavaria, as she sought to bring order and law into the battles between the towns and the gowned men of academe. The medieval guild often became "an incorporated society in a town or city having exclusive rights of trading within the town." Indeed, the guild even became "the governing body of the town."[9]

With a slight change in wording, such that "town" and "city" are replaced by "university" and "college," one begins to understand that the professorial faculty associations of today, like their ancestors of yesterday, should and do have very considerable power in, and responsibility for, their community. The professorial guild, like its forerunners, self-defines and self-selects in all dimensions, including gender. And this is the key to the changing space for women in academe.

EARLY "EN-GENDER-ING" OF KNOWLEDGE
In order to comprehend the "en-gender-ing" of knowledge today, we must understand the male gender dimensions of the academy from its very beginnings in the prehistoric shules, scholas and akademias. It will, perhaps, suffice to begin in the twelfth and thirteenth centuries, during which time there emerged the paradigmatic universities, starting in 1179 with the University of Bologna. Of specific relevance to the North American experience, and especially for the double Franco–British origins of Canada, are the Université de Paris and Oxford University, founded respectively around 1200 and 1215. Both were the creation of the Roman Catholic Bishop of Paris and his Augustinian followers, who served as a nomadic professoriate to the two institutions. Over the next 700 years the structure, function and operation of these universities were replicated in every major nation state and bourgeois city, and then in every country of Europe, Asia, Africa and South and North America, including Canada and the United States.[10]

Of course the primordial university model has had many modifications, dependent on time, place, culture and a variety of political, ethnic and societal exigencies. However, *le plus ça change, le plus que ça reste la même chose* in regard to gender. This undoubtedly reflects two major modifications in the very early development of the university. Both were outcomes of several hundreds of years of struggle within the Roman Church, concerning political philosophy, religious canon and the place of women.

In 1255, the Pope decreed that the university was henceforth to be governed only by the theory and practice of knowledge embodied in the misogynistic natural philosophy of Aristotle. By separate bull, all women were henceforth to be excluded from the university as masters or as students. This, then, was the initial "en-gender-ing" of the university and its custodianship of knowledge; the gender was male.[11]

To the present, the male gender has continued to describe, define and determine all aspects of the life and activity of universities. Even in those institutions and during those periods in which women shared in the academic pursuit of knowledge, the dominant gender remained male.[12] The university, the guardian of authoritative knowledge of the day, was structured on a male, monastic lifestyle and learning regimen. It also was structured on a career development timeframe for male individuals who could single-mindedly devote their lifetime of work to the pursuit, replication and sharing of knowledge, with a support system (often female) to serve all other needs.

Scholarship came to define that enquiry, research and creative activity done by male scholars, and to specifically exclude the activity pursued in "separate spheres" reserved for women.[13] It is, therefore, not surprising that knowledge acquired male parameters of interest, expression and need. The analogous determinants of the female were not, and could not be, accommodated by the original university mould of scholarship and knowledge.

The depth and intensity of the male palette of knowledge was deepened as Europe moved into and through feudalism, the reformations of religious thought and practice, and the bourgeois revolutions in the economic, philosophical and social domains.[14] As already noted, the "scientific revolution" replaced all other generation of authoritative knowledge by the "scientific method." What was deemed rational was to replace what was characterized as emotional. Induction and reduction were to overwhelm intuition, no matter how well-informed it was. Experiment was to displace empiricism and the experiential.[15] Thus, that defined as male was to displace all that was interpreted as female.

At the end of the nineteenth century, the struggle for higher education and professional training for women came from the ranks of those women and men who fought for freedom, justice and equality, for suffrage for women, for their education and for their right to earn their own livelihood in any profession. The call for higher education for women originally went out from Germany, and then swept through Europe to Britain and on to the U.S. In Canada, this struggle was first launched at McGill University, where John Clark Murray began a twelve-year battle with Dr. J.M. Dawson, principal of McGill University, to render the university accessible to women in the same way that it was to men. Dawson was representative of those who served as advocates, if such can be the word of choice, for separate and decidedly unequal higher education for women. Only after Principal Dawson's death did McGill University open its doors to women.[16]

A more significant and productive battle was being pursued at about the same time by women in Ontario. In the 1860s, twelve women knocked on the doors of the University of Toronto, but were rejected. By 1883, one had been graduated from the Victoria College School of Medicine. Others entered science and arts programs in subsequent years. And finally in 1907 with the initial political battle won, the Ontario University Act proclaimed that women would no longer be disadvantaged with respect to higher education in Ontario.[17] This pattern of demanding and gaining access for women to higher education was reproduced elsewhere at the dawn of the twentieth century.[18]

During this early period, the entry of women into the universities occurred in three modes. In the model that least challenged the status quo, women were hired as assistants (or simply given the honour of assisting) and technicians for male professors, collecting data in a variety of emerging and labour-intensive fields including astronomy, botany, zoology, statistics, genetics, psychology and eugenics. As the doors of the universities were forced open to women, a relatively small number became students. In some instances, women entered existing institutions and disciplines, mentored by sympathetic men. Other universities saw fit to create new disciplines of study, deemed suitable or especially adapted to women, e.g., the newly-established departments of household science/economics, schools of nursing and teachers' colleges.[19]

As it became clear that existing universities would not welcome aspiring female students and scholars, visionary women and men built new institutions of higher learning expressly for women. It was here that a majority of the earliest North American female scholars and academics obtained their first, and often only, entry into the academic workplace.[20]

With the pressures of several waves of feminism since the early nineteenth century, the all-male university ultimately had to give way to the integral presence of women as students and as academic scholars. Today, in Canada, women make up well over 52 percent of the undergraduate student body, averaged across all faculties and disciplines.[21] At the graduate level their participation is much lower, especially in PhD programs. The female student body is continuing to insist on changes in academe that recognize women, now and forever, as creators, discoverers and consumers of knowledge, both inside and outside the university.

At its highest levels, the professoriate comprises 18–27 percent women, and this figure is climbing. Notwithstanding, the university community as a whole is faced with a dilemma that continues to haunt it, as it addresses the question of the changing space for women in academe.

WOMEN AS SCHOLARS AND SCIENTISTS: CRITERIA OF EXCELLENCE

As women declared themselves scholars and academics in the latter half of the last century, two parallel streams of scholarship and professoriate evolved. One was in the classical university structure; the other comprised the marginalized or excluded women's departments, faculties, colleges and universities. The separate streams applied the same objective standards of excellence to completely distinct subsets of the guilds of scholars and academics. The subjective criteria were, however, markedly different, the differences being largely determined by imperatives of gender, real or imagined.[22]

Since 1900, women as scholars, scientists and academics have become increasingly aware of a significant problem that confronts them, due to the subjective application of apparently objective criteria in the differential assessment of excellence of women and men by a professoriate that is largely, often exclusively, male. The outcome of such assessment affects not only the individual scholars, but also the definition of what kinds of scholarly and scientific work will be done in the universities and elsewhere in the country. This has resulted in the almost total exclusion of women, women's issues, and scientific problems of immediate or even more theoretical relevance to women, from the body of knowledge which is accumulated and disseminated by the scholarly and scientific professoriate.

One important response to this major problem was the establishment of women's studies programs and feminist research centres, and the insistence that experimental studies of male mice cannot be extrapolated to the female human being. These endeavours, carried out most extensively in the U.S. and Canada from the 1960s to the 1990s, are important milestones in the transformation of knowledge and the methodology for its accumulation, so that these have begun to include a number of dimensions of the female and the feminine.[23]

WOMEN'S COLLEGES

The women's colleges and medical schools provided the first modern university models for the "en-gender-ing" of knowledge. Historical analyses have revealed that a key contribution of these institutions was the generation of novel thrusts of research and pedagogy in well-established disciplines and fields.[24] But, in addition, they engendered entirely new disciplines and fields of study and research, employing the tools and thought of what has come to be known as "maternal feminism." This form of knowledge included areas of interest to the "feminine condition," and therefore was acceptable to the then male guardians of the knowledge of the day. Examples include household science, household economics, nursing and teaching.

Initially these outcomes were the fruits of the labours of the pioneer women academic administrators serving at all levels in the "women's colleges" and medical schools. Their successes provided paradigms and exemplary leverage for similar, often tentative, initiatives in the already long established, all-male universities. Conversion of the latter to co-educational institutions was partly an attempt to capture and control the growing body of female academics and paying students. It was perhaps more significantly the result of the efforts of many men and women who strove for educational equity for women.

Because of the all-pervasive sexism in the academy of the period, women were largely unwelcome anywhere but in the "women's colleges." There, they became members of the professoriate, chairs and heads of academic units and members of the cadre of senior academic administrators, dedicated to the higher education of women and the generation and dissemination of knowledge appropriate to women's needs.

One can readily trace the impact of the initial cohorts of academic women who emerged from these various experiments in the higher education of women. Some began immediately to engender and beget scholarship, knowledge and teaching of, about and for women.[25] The linkage of their feminism in all political domains of their lives, including those of academe and their scholarly and scientific guilds, was tight to the point of almost total identification.[26]

At one end of a spectrum, their feminism could be characterized as minimalist and benign. This approach focussed on barely ruffling the status quo; their goal was simply the integration of women into a knowledge structure determined by men and already approved by the male custodians. At the other end of the spectrum were found the radical feminists, bent on the transformation, whether from within or without the academy, of epistemology, scholarship, research and creative activity, so that it would be fully inclusive of and determined by women as well as by men.

WOMEN'S STUDIES AND STUDIES ON WOMEN

What is often not appreciated or assessed is the linkage between these early steps in the "en-gender-ing" of knowledge and those that have been taken during the 1970s, '80s and '90s. The establishment of women's studies programs, and centres and institutes devoted to the generation, maintenance and dissemination of knowledge of relevance to women was very important.[27] Most recently, we are beginning to see the full integration of studies on, for and by women into the total accepted disciplinary and non-disciplinary body of knowledge. This is the ultimate goal for knowledge. Perhaps two examples will suffice. One is the full "en-gender-ing" of American history through the sustained and determined efforts of feminist scholars of all cultures and ethnicities in the American Historical Association and in history departments across the U.S.[28] A second is the insistence that the clinical and medical sciences must acknowledge and include the sexual differences of men and women as determinants of health and illness.[29]

In large measure, this desired outcome has resulted from a significant increase in the number of feminist scholars and scientists who have been able to insist on gender inclusiveness as an index of the excellence of the field of knowledge and of its guild of scholars. A second kind of outcome has emerged from the growing number of women in administration and management of all institutions in society.[30] This has engendered entirely new fields in the pursuit of knowledge. These include a focus on women in management, administration and leadership in general, as in academe and in the linked guilds and arenas of activity of research, scholarship and creative activity.[31] Such investigations have provided evidence that men and women bring different perspectives, management skills, leadership and visions of success and of shared power for the implementation of the missions of their respective organizations, including those in academe.[32]

ACADEMIC ADMINISTRATORS: WHO AND WHAT ARE THEY?
Academic administrators are those, at any level of university leadership, who accept an administrative role that is outside of the usual tripartite functions of the professoriate, i.e., to teach within the undergraduate and graduate contexts; to do research, scholarship and creative activity; and to contribute to the community both within and outside of the university.[33] Thus the guild of academic administrators could be taken to include undergraduate and graduate co-ordinators or secretaries, chairs or heads of departments (or analogous units), along with assistant or associate chairs or heads, deans and members of decanal teams, rectors, principals, presidents, vice-presidents and provosts and their associates.

Academic administrators serve as representatives and mirrors of universities and colleges. They are recognized by the academic and societal communities to be fonts of knowledge and scholarly leaders in their respective fields and disciplines. They are expected to serve as catalysts in the development of the faculty, staff and students whom they lead. They are mentors in the precious apprentice–mentor relationship, which is the key to the engendering of successive generations of the creative corps of those who seek, generate, care for and disseminate knowledge both inside and outside of the academy. They are expected to have plied their respective academic and administrative trades with integrity and commitment. In short, they are leaders of the academic community and of society. They are representative of the custodians of knowledge for society.

The most influential officers in the university in terms of its academic mission are the president/rector and the vice-president/rector academic. The president or rector, as chief executive officer, provides the supreme model of academic endeavour, academic integrity and expression of the university mission in the pursuit and dissemination of knowledge. This role is supported by the vice-president academic who is the senior academic officer, responsible for continually expanding the academic mission of a university and for ensuring that this is fully implemented in all sectors of the particular academy. Together, they provide the appropriate role models, mentors and prods to the other members of the cadre of academic administrators and to the university at large.[34]

THE HISTORY OF WOMEN IN ACADEMIC ADMINISTRATION
The history of women in academic administration traces back to the Middle Ages and the convents and monasteries devoted to the pursuit and dissemination of knowledge, and headed by women abbots and anchoresses.[35] But most

important for our present are those institutions of higher education and learning for, and of women, established throughout the world in the latter half of the nineteenth century.

The women who provided academic leadership to these universities and colleges were confronted with opportunities and creative tensions, which derived from the first phase of modern feminism.[36] This, in turn, resulted in the mobilization of progressive forces embracing both men and women, who coalesced around the issues of suffrage for women,[37] the economic advancement of women and their entry into the labour force in increasingly large numbers.[38] Above all, their insistence was that women must be able to earn their own living in a world committed to equality, rationality and enlightened thought and practice.

The opportunities for these pioneer female administrators derived from acknowledgement, for the first time, of the need for organized colleges and universities to provide higher education and professional training for women. The creative tensions arose then, as they do today, from the continued restrictions placed by some elements of society on the advancement and the empowerment of women.

Throughout the first half of the twentieth century, small but significant strides forward were made by individual female scholars and groups of scholars in "en-gender-ing" knowledge in the academy and in the relevant guilds of research and scholarship. Nonetheless, the overall gender of these human activities continued to be male until the arrival of the phase of feminism known as the women's liberation movement.

The women's liberation movement grew from a base of liberal individualism focussed on the enshrinement of the rights, freedoms and responsibilities of men and women in theory and practice, which welled up during the Second World War. At the same time, this movement became anti-colonial, anti-imperialist, pro-liberal democracy and irreversibly committed to the rights and freedoms of every single individual.

Crucial to the successful outcome of this emerging radical feminism was the growth in number, scope and impact of women and men who engaged in the several struggles for political and economic equity, particularly in the U.S. and Canada. Their actions were eventually embodied in legislation in the domains of civil liberties, civil rights, educational equity, employment equity and pay equity.[39] In Canada, these are evidenced in the Canadian Charter of Rights and Freedoms,[40] and analogous provincial legislation. These laws, especially when transferred to universities and colleges, provide a necessary bulwark against the backward slippage of the status of women in academe, a process that has occurred so frequently in the past and to which too many are committed in discussions of "political correctness." The enactment and implementation of such university legislation is the key component for "en-gender-ing" knowledge in the present and in the future.

ISSUES FOR ACADEMIC ADMINISTRATORS IN THE "EN-GENDER-ING" OF
KNOWLEDGE IN ACADEME

A number of key issues continue to challenge those who would and should lead
in the "en-gender-ing" of knowledge in academe. Perhaps the major impediment to achieving this goal is the implicit, and sometimes far too explicit,
assumption that the "en-gender-ing" of knowledge and of the academy, to
include the female along with the male, is equivalent to rendering both non-
excellent. Academic leadership must address this matter.

This thorny issue is perhaps best placed in the context of the following
questions:

1. How excellent can a department/faculty/university be if its curriculum
    disseminates to students only a very minuscule, highly-selected, self-
    perpetuating, gender-biased representation of our collective knowledge
    about human beings and the world in which we live?
2. How excellent can a department/faculty/university be if it continues to
    neglect the 52 percent female fraction of the student body?
3. How excellent can a department/faculty/university be if it does not, in its
    faculty, reflect this gender distribution in society?
4. How excellent can a department/faculty/university be if its faculty does not
    provide two crucial elements of excellent education: positive, gender-
    specific role models; and positive, gender-specific mentors?
5. How excellent can a department/faculty/university be if it persists in
    providing only very negative, gender-inappropriate role models and men-
    tors to its students and to society?
6. How excellent can the senior administration of a university be if it allows
    the criteria for entry into the male-dominated, extra-university guilds of the
    humanities, social sciences, physical sciences, life sciences, engineering
    and mathematics to continue to determine the gender-inclusivity of our
    universities?
7. How excellent can the senior academic administration of a university be if
    it continues to accept, as the appropriate paradigm of academe, the monas-
    tic, all-male model created and enshrined in law in 1255 specifically to
    exclude women?
8. And, finally, how excellent can a university and its entire senior academic
    administration be if they do not implement the various laws of the land and
    the Charter of Rights and Freedoms of the land which guarantee that we
    shall:
    *   provide equality of education to all of our young, and even older men
        and women;
    *   provide them equally with economic equality;
    *   provide them with equality of mobility in every workplace, including
        our very own academe.

For purposes of developing strategies and tactics for the implementation of gendered academic excellence, one could apply the following general equation:

Academic excellence is a function of all of humankind.

In the case of the academy, its excellence would be proportional to all of its faculty members, i.e., the sum of its female and male professoriate. Since the available evidence indicates that the intellectual capacities of men and women are comparable, it is clear that academic excellence should be dependent upon the endeavours of a professoriate that is 52 percent female and 48 percent male, since this is the current sex distribution of society. If one considers academic excellence in terms of knowledge, then excellence of knowledge must be equivalent to the total body of knowledge of humankind, the sum of our knowledge of men and women or the total body of knowledge amassed by men and women throughout the world.

A number of mechanisms are at the disposal of academic administrators to ensure implementation of inclusively-gendered academic excellence. They all depend upon the shifting of the equilibrium of the above equations towards the ultimate goal of 100 percent excellence by increasing the variable relevant to the number of female faculty members and their excellent performance. With such understanding, it is both possible and incumbent upon the academic administrator to ensure that all missions, goals, objectives and methodologies for their implementation are gender-inclusive.

The tools available for implementation of such an approach are few, but powerful. Example and moral suasion from all members of the senior academic administration are absolutely mandatory, whether they are men or women. Employment and pay equity legislation, as translated into the university sector, must be scrupulously endorsed and implemented. This is not merely to be in compliance with the laws of the provincial and federal governments. More significant is the necessity to recruit and retain women to faculty positions, particularly those women who are willing to take up the challenge of the "en-gender-ing" of knowledge. It is equally important to ensure that men, already in place or newly hired, be cognizant of and committed to, the linkage between academic excellence, educational equity and the "en-gender-ing" of knowledge.

WHAT CAN AND SHOULD WOMEN IN ACADEMIC ADMINISTRATION DO TO ENGENDER KNOWLEDGE?

What do women bring to the matter of "en-gender-ing" knowledge? First and foremost they bring their understanding and experience of a truth often considered a truism: that younger and older men live the lives of men, whereas younger and older women live the lives of women. This is so even in those overlapping sectors of life experiences which are shared. Because of gendered life experiences, women in academic administration can and must insist that the acquisition and sharing of knowledge reflect this reality.

Women presidents and vice-presidents send the appropriate message to the university and to society. They become part of the image and the authenticity of gendered role models, mentors and representatives of the current authoritative guardians of knowledge. As a group, and individually, they are recognized as experts in the entire array of disciplines and fields of research, scholarship and creative activity. Girls and young women who are still planning their lives and careers see a reflection of themselves in these important activities, previously reserved for men and boys. And boys and young men will learn to adjust their visions to a reality that includes women in all arenas of life, and acknowledges their contribution as generators, teachers and custodians of knowledge for society.

It is gratifying to observe that in 1997, as in 1993, seven (7.7 percent) of the ninety-one presidential chairs of Canadian universities and colleges are filled by women. Those who occupy vice-presidential seats have decreased from thirteen to eleven in the four-year interval. There remain some sixteen female associate vice-presidents. Together, women in the vice-presidential corps account for just over one-quarter of the total. In contrast, the total body of women in the Canadian cadre of academic administrators has reached about 490, or 12 percent of the total.[41]

Although these data reflect a real increase in the number of women in academic administration in Canada, they are still far from the reasonable target of 52 percent. Perhaps even more disturbing is the fact that entire universities and colleges are without female academic leaders. In others whole faculties, and sometimes more than one, are bereft of women among the deans, associate deans, chairs of departments and leaders of analogous units, i.e., the academic unit cells of academe.

SUMMARY AND PERSPECTIVES

The particular role for women in academic administration and in the academy is to validate the reality of women as more than half of the intellectual talent pool of humankind. It is to bear witness to the reality of the sexual difference in humankind so that gender inclusive knowledge will be understood as an imperative of academic excellence in every and all dimensions. It is to ensure that the realities of women will be forever embraced in the ongoing search for truth and knowledge; that they will never again be marginalized and excluded from the warmth and nurturing fires of creative human endeavour; that women in academic administration may serve as a reflecting mirror for one-half of humanity; and that, by their exemplary existence, they may attest to the "en-gender-ing" of knowledge. It is to empower women in all walks of life, but especially in academe, to aspire to fulfill their potential, whatever that may be. It is to say to female staff, students and faculty in academe "lift up thine eyes unto the mountains."[42]

NOTES

*   This paper is derived from one initially delivered at the "Symposium on the Impact of Feminism on the Academy," January 22, 1993, at the McGill Centre for Research and Teaching on Women.
1. Collins 1992; Signs 1987; Selin 1991.
2. Eichler 1988; Miller and Treitel 1991.
3. Sheinin 1991; Tuana 1993.
4. Keller 1985; Lindberg and Westmen 1990.
5. Hanks 1986.
6. Geiger 1986; Reingold 1987.
7. McCormack 1991; Winders 1991.
8. Little, Fowler and Coulson 1956.
9. Reingold 1987.
10. Allen 1985; Sheinin 1991: 3.
11. Keller 1985; Lindberg and Westmen 1990; Allen 1985; Sheinin 1991: 3.
12. Klapisch-Zuber 1992; Pantel 1992.
13. Cook and Mitchison 1976; Noble 1992.
14. Landes 1988: 3, 8, 9, 10; Marshall 1989.
15. Bacon, cited in Burtt 1967: 67–69; Keller 1985.
16. Dawson 1884; Gillett 1981; Trott 1984.
17. De La Cour and Sheinin 1986: 73–77; Ford 1984.
18. Koblitz 1984; Rossiter 1982; Stock 1978.
19. Beecher 1842; Innis 1970; Prentice and Danylewycz 1984.
20. Dembski 1985; Faragher and Howe 1988; Rossiter 1982: 15; Stowe-Gullen 1898.
21. Backhouse et al. 1989; Looker 1990; Perry 1989; Association of Universities and Colleges of Canada 1990; Sandler and Hall 1986.
22. Sheinin 1989.
23. Aiken et al. 1988; Cott 1984; Dubois et al. 1992; Minnich et al. 1988: 1.
24. Aiken et al. 1988; Cott 1984; Dubois et al. 1992; Minnich et al. 1988: 1.
25. Aiken et al. 1988; Cott 1984; Dubois et al. 1992; Minnich et al. 1988: 1.
26. Backhouse and Flaherty 1992; Lauter and Howe 1978; Rowbotham 1992; Thompson 1962.
27. Backhouse and Flaherty 1992; Lauter and Howe 1978; Rowbotham 1992; Thompson 1962.
28. Goggin 1992.
29. Borins and Feldberg 1992; Hamilton 1985; Palca 1990.
30. Plasse and Simard 1989; Sen 1992.
31. McKeen and Burke 1991; Mikalachki et al. 1992; Tancred 1992.
32. E.M. Fulton 1991; Offerman and Beil 1992; Rosener 1990.
33. *Collective Agreement Between Concordia University and the Concordia University Faculty Association.* Article 16.01. (In effect until May 31, 1992).
34. American Council on Education 1985; Cross 1992; Hartman 1986.
35. Hartman 1986: 9; Labarge 1986; Monson 1992; Newman 1988.
36. Adamson 1988; Echols 1989; Flexner 1976; Rendall 1984.
37. Buechler 1990; Darsigny 1990.
38. Darsigny 1990: 24; Sen 1992: 25.
39. Baines 1980; Pay Equity Act, R.S.O. 1990, Chap. p7; Government of Canada 1960; Government of Canada 1977.

40. *Canadian Charter of Rights and Freedoms, Part II.* 1982. Schedule B of the Constitution Act 1982, U.K. c 11; *Québec Charter of Human Rights and Freedoms / Chartre Québecoise de droits et des libertes de la personne.* 1960. RSQ 1960 C. C-12.
41. These data, which are derived from the following, are approximate: Gill 1992; Statistics Canada 1991.
42. Psalm 131; A Song of Degrees.

Hiring of Women at Canadian Universities: The Subversion of Equity

Anne Innis Dagg

Discrimination against academic women has always existed at Canadian universities.[1] Initially it was overt, with the few women hired being paid less than the men because they did not have dependent families.[2] As recently as 1972 a dean of science stated that he would never give a married woman tenure because she had a husband to support her.[3]

In the past decade, sexual discrimination has become more covert because, thanks to pressure from the women's movement, policies and laws have been drawn up and passed to combat it. One way it now seems to operate is against feminists rather than against women *per se*—feminists being defined, for the purpose of this paper, as women who work openly to improve the status of university women; those who belong to university women's groups formed for the same purpose are also here considered feminists.

The kind of women hired as professors makes a difference:

- If feminists are hired and given tenure at a university, they will push for more women professors and for changes on campus that benefit women. Feminists working to create a less "chilly climate" for women in the Department of Political Science at the University of Victoria have caused great consternation within the previously all-male department.[4]
- If apolitical non-feminists are hired, their perspective will be similar to that of most men in their department, which is how they have been taught to address academic matters. They will nudge the gender statistics in the right direction, but do little to challenge the dominant male ethos in course content and academic style. However, some of these women may eventually become politicized into feminism by their experience as professors, particularly if they teach in women's studies.[5]
- If activist anti-feminists are hired, they will be a boon to misogynist men because they will do their work for them, speaking out against positive changes for women and against women's studies. At the University of

Alberta, at least three such women attack women's studies and feminists in general.[6] They can do incalculable damage to the cause of women both on campus and off, because media love to interview them for their controversial views. Camille Paglia is one such publicized anti-feminist.

University departments are well aware of the political ramifications of hiring women who are, or are not, politicized about equal rights. If they hire feminists, they can expect disruption and pressure for change in systems that have been devised by men and suit them well. If they hire women who are not feminists, they can improve their female:male ratio without such disruption. If they hire anti-feminists, they may be criticized by feminists for this, but they have the bonus of improving their position in the battle against change.

The hypothesis of this article is that a widespread university practice is to hire women who are non-feminists and anti-feminists in preference to those who, as feminists, are seen to have a political agenda. No statistics whereby one could prove this hypothesis will ever be available, but strong anecdotal evidence supports it. In addition, if one considers the overwhelming desire of people and institutions to maximize their options, it is not surprising that universities, all male-dominated, should elect to hire those women who will cause them the least disruption. By doing so they follow the letter of equity policies and laws but not the spirit, which should in principle be hostile to any form of discrimination. I do not argue that non-feminists or anti-feminists should never be hired, but that hiring should be based on a person's academic abilities, and not on political beliefs. If two women of opposing political views about women are said to be equally qualified, I believe the feminist rather than the anti-feminist should be hired as the feminist will presumably (by the definition I am using) work for a more balanced professoriate. At present, feminists are rare at universities; Eichler estimates that possible feminist supervisors for students comprise only about 2 percent of all professors in Canada.[7]

Recently-credentialed scholars are being hired to replace the large number of professors now approaching retirement age. If the female fraction of this incoming group is composed largely of non-feminists and anti-feminists, the cause of equality for women will be undermined for another generation; the universities will have complied with equity considerations only in formal, not substantive, terms.

THE HISTORY OF HIRING ACADEMIC WOMEN
Women became a significant part of university faculties after the First World War; by 1931, 19 percent of full-time university teachers were women,[8] almost as many as there are today. In the pre-expansion period there was no great competition for jobs because university teachers were poorly paid.[9] In addition, women teachers were routinely paid less than men. Constance Beresford-Howe,[10] who taught English at McGill University, noted that around 1950

women professors, usually single, were assumed to be more or less temporary staff who would eventually marry and resign. Their salary was kept particularly low because they could live inexpensively at home or, in her case, supplement her earnings by writing.

Between the two world wars, when the women's movement was in low profile, women professors seem not to have categorized themselves as feminists. Their reminiscences focus not on fighting for women's right to be professors, but on their experiences teaching and doing research, complete with anecdotes detailing various (and often horrendous) incidents of discrimination they overcame to enable them to achieve their success. In spite of relatively large numbers of women faculty, many university departments at that time, and subsequently, refused to hire a single university professor who was a woman.[11]

The proportion of women teachers dipped slightly in the depression years, when married women were urged to resign if their husbands had a job, and decreased much further during the 1950s when society decided that women's place was in the home. By 1960, only 11 percent of professors were women.[12] Canadian universities expanded greatly in the 1960s, but women scholars benefitted little—by 1970 they comprised only 13 percent of professors.[13] The salaries offered during the decade were much greater than in the past, so that many men competed for openings and there was little need to hire women. Controversy over hiring bias focussed exclusively on the Americanization issue (the hiring of American academics).

In the 1960s, before the rejuvenation of the women's movement, gender bias in university hiring was neither remarked upon nor criticized. If there were few women professors, this was assumed to be because few women wanted and trained to be academics. The problem of qualified women who were unable to find positions was assumed to be personal rather than systemic. When sociologist Jessie Bernard published her definitive book, *Academic Women*, in 1964, the lack of women professors did not bother her. She wrote that she didn't think the contribution of such women "is necessarily any better or more socially useful in every case than their contribution as wives, mothers, and community leaders."[14] She did not believe at that time that discrimination against women was important, if indeed it existed; she claimed that she herself had been an academic ("man and boy," to quote her words) for forty years without ever experiencing sexual discrimination in her profession.[15] Rather, she discussed the various ways in which women were different from men, to the women's disadvantage since men were the norm: women had more family cares, produced fewer research publications and were, perhaps, too nurturant with their graduate students because some were retained who might better have been dropped from their programs.

From about 1970 on, women began to talk about their personal experiences of discrimination in universities and to realize that the problem was not an individual but a systemic one. They spearheaded over one hundred reports on the status of women at universities across the country, documenting problem areas for women and insisting that women's concerns be taken seriously.[16] The impetus arising from their initiatives has meant that more women are being hired than in the past. However, the rate has been glacial until the recent introduction of employment equity schemes, and somewhat less slow since then. Researchers have found that female professors are not interchangeable with male professors, so that it is not only the lack of opportunity for academic women to have a career that is at stake when few are hired. We know now that women professors are needed to give women students role models and mentors, to elicit discussion among women in the classroom, to counteract male bias in the curriculum and in research and to show women as authority figures.

Although on average only 20 percent of Canadian professors are women (with far fewer in engineering, mathematics and science and somewhat more in the humanities), there is already a strong backlash in many departments against the hiring of more faculty women, especially when openings are few because of cutbacks in university funding. A continuing anger is also seen against women's studies programs which, among other things, critique university curricula for male bias.[17] If the backlash can be contained, hiring equity should improve women's status considerably, since 32 percent of those obtaining PhDs, and therefore potential members of the hiring pool, are now women.[18] If in the future significant numbers of women are to be hired as professors, so that qualified women have equity with qualified men, feminists or women working for change must be present to apply pressure.[19] And experience shows that the number of feminists needed to elicit change must reach a "critical mass" to be effective.[20]

The current backlash against feminists in the universities, the employment equity regulations and the anecdotal evidence of hiring and tenure decisions against women, apparently because they are feminists, all affect the concept of critical mass in this context.

BACKLASH AGAINST FEMINISTS

As early as the late 1970s, feminists were experiencing a backlash in academia. Between 1978 and 1982, when affirmative action plans to encourage the hiring and retention of women, Blacks and Hispanics were in vogue in the United States, Boston University School of Theology refused to hire, or fired, three feminists, all of whom had outstanding qualifications.[21] Such discrimination continues at Canadian universities, even though they pride themselves on their belief in academic freedom.[22] The negative comments often received from their male students and sometimes even death threats for women who teach as feminists are well documented. Women's studies programs are a special target for anger because they teach that women and their accomplishments have been, and are, downgraded in universities just as they are in Western society. Women's studies programs, which form a base for feminists at university, are poorly funded and too often staffed by part-time academics who lack tenure.

Students who raise feminist concerns in the classroom, or who dare to critique male bias in the curriculum and on campus, are likely to be harassed and derided by their peers and sometimes by their professors. They may receive death threats which, in Canada, carry special menace because of the trauma of the 1989 Montréal massacre in which fourteen university women were murdered because an insane gunman believed them to be feminists.

EMPLOYMENT EQUITY

For the past few years, pressure from the women's movement has at last made university departments realize that they must hire more women as professors if they are to retain credibility. The federal Employment Equity Act (1985), the Federal Contractors Program (1986) and provincial employment equity legislation send the same message. If university departments wholeheartedly believed that women had as much to contribute as men to higher education and to society, they would be anxious to hire well-qualified feminists so that they, too, could help bring equality to universities as quickly as possible. The evidence indicates, however, that some professors are not anxious for such a change; indeed many professors appear to be against affirmative action or employment equity schemes, realizing that they cast a shadow on their past integrity in hiring. These professors argue that they have always hired and continue to hire the best people available to be professors; it follows from their logic that, if academics must be hired from specified groups, these will likely not be the best qualified. These new recruits will therefore lower the standards of the university.

Some professors feel so strongly about this issue that they have formed the national Society for Academic Freedom and Scholarship to fight against efforts to hire more women and minority men as professors. It has solicited memberships in university newspapers—twenty dollars for faculty and ten dollars for students. At the University of Waterloo, over 200 professors, one-quarter of the professoriate (and not all professors had an opportunity to express their solidarity), sent a petition to the former NDP Ontario government to protest against the hiring of scholars whom they believed would be unqualified, even though these sometimes had better teaching and research records than the professors doing the protesting. A similar "Merit Only" group was organized at the University of Alberta to lobby against the hiring of unacceptable individuals.[23] This became in 1992 the Association for Concerned Academics, with a membership of about 100 out of 2,000 faculty. Such professors are adamant that they alone know who should be professors, and it seems that these professors should think and act and be very like themselves—usually white, middle-class, heterosexual and male.

The scholars who do not fit this stereotypical description believe that hiring criteria should be far more open. A wealth of research has shown that women and minority men have been far less likely in the past to be hired as professors than have white men; instead, these marginalized academics have suffered extensive discrimination. They feel they have been excluded from universities and hope that employment equity will provide a level playing field so that in the future they will have as fair a chance of being hired as anyone.

As there clearly is significant opposition in universities to employment equity schemes, as strikingly evidenced by the open opposition of nearly one-quarter of the faculty of the University of Waterloo, it logically follows that universities will encounter internal dissent when they try to implement such schemes. More generally, since universities like other institutions have their own interests, it would be surprising if university authorities did not often apply new policies and laws in ways most compatible with the universities' historic goals, thus minimizing radical changes in the status quo.

Examples of university authorities applying rules in a self-interested fashion are so widespread that they almost fall into the category of normal conduct. Undoubtedly, if laws forced universities to hire more non-white professors, the likely benefactors would be Japanese or Chinese academics who are highly assimilated into Canadian culture.[24] The subjects of new rules also tend to modify their behaviour, even their identity, to maximize their gains. In the Olympics, for example, a few men have pretended to be women so they have more chance of winning a medal in sports requiring great physical strength; women contestants therefore have had to take a chromosome test to show that they have XX rather than XY chromosomes. As another example, in New York City white police officers have asked to have their racial classification switched to Black or Hispanic so they can qualify for promotion under a racial quota system.[25] The historic example in society of Blacks passing for white to obtain white privilege illustrates the same phenomenon. Similarly, if tax laws are changed, business practices will also certainly change to ensure that companies pay as little tax as possible.

ANECDOTAL EVIDENCE
One will probably never prove that many departmental hiring committees prefer to hire women who are non-feminists or anti-feminists rather than feminists because departments are unlikely to admit to this aim, which may in fact not even be recognized by the individuals concerned. But anecdotal instances quoted here indicate that it happens all too often. Some of these cases have appeared in published sources as cited. Others have been described in personal letters to me; to preserve these authors' anonymity, the names of the academics and universities involved are withheld.

At Queen's University, an Iranian woman was refused a three-year posting in political studies in 1992.[26] She complained about her treatment and her grievance was upheld, with the university admitting it had discriminated against her on anti-feminist, sexist and racist grounds.

When several scholars are being interviewed for the same position, a feminist often loses even though she is the most qualified. Recently, when the

Department of Sociology at the University of Waterloo had only two women professors, a woman was interviewed for a vacancy. A male dissident of the department noted that "she devoted her seminar presentation to uncovering male bias in the conduct of Canadian demography. It was not because she was a woman that the job went instead to a man. It was because of the kind of woman she turned out to be."[27] She seemed too much of a feminist.

In another example, two women were interviewed for one faculty position at the University of Western Ontario. A respondent to a survey noted that one had good credentials, gave an excellent lecture and handled questions well. The other was less competent and less confident, but much prettier and dressed in a feminine manner. This second woman, who seemed less of a feminist, was hired. The respondent remarked, "I think she was chosen because she was less threatening to the men in the department."[28]

At another Ontario university, a department agreed, according to equity rules, to hire three women, i.e., one-third of the permanent department positions. The first hired was very anti-feminist and completely opposed to employment equity, although she herself had benefitted by an equity position. The second hired was a non-feminist; and only the third hired, after some controversy, was a feminist. One male professor, backed by the vice-president academic, went to great lengths to block this feminist appointment but was eventually thwarted because of the presence of university equity policies.

Another department of this same university, which was forced to hire women, chose the candidate perceived to be the most non-feminist or anti-feminist available. One woman, who had not completed her PhD and who made no mention of being feminist during her interview, was hired over another, who had a completed PhD and publications but who gave her interview lecture on feminist theology. An anti-feminist woman graduate student in the department was asked for her opinion of the lecture (which was a negative opinion), but a feminist professor was not consulted.[29]

A later hiring centred on another two women, both of whom the same department tried to reject. One had written a thesis on women while the second, strongly non-feminist in her views, had not even begun to write her thesis. The dean insisted one of the women be hired unless the department wanted to lose the position. The department tried to choose the non-feminist who lacked a degree but it was overruled by the dean. Most men in this department remain hostile to women and to any effort to introduce feminist courses.

Their feminist perspective helps to explain why most women's studies programs have low budgets and low-status teachers compared to other disciplines.[30] Feminists may be hired to teach women's studies courses but few win tenure and therefore a career.[31]

Women known to be lesbians also often seem to be feminists. Four lesbian academics interviewed by Jeri Dawn Wine all believed they would not have obtained tenure and thus a permanent career had they been doing research that reflected a lesbian or even, in some cases, a feminist bias.[32] Several lesbian professors have sexual orientation clauses in their contracts so they cannot be sanctioned for their sexual orientation.[33] In cases from the University of Western Ontario and from a northern Ontario university, administrators have been documented as warning those at other universities not to hire certain women because they were lesbians.[34] Some lesbians at the National Women's Studies Association in the United States in 1981 formed a Fired Lesbian Caucus to address their concerns.[35]

"Queen Bee" feminists is a name given to power-hungry women who claim to be feminists, but who do not support other women. At one Ontario university, an "official feminist" has been designated—a woman so labelled by the university and by herself, who spends much of her time approving policy. This person "actively opposed all but *one* strong female job candidate in five years of such candidates. She did, however, occasionally push female candidates with no publications and feeble teaching evaluations."[36] Other self-styled feminists with tenure have even routed feminists with less power from a women's studies program.[37]

Many women are hired as professors, then lose their jobs because they are denied further contracts or tenure if they are too feminist. There are three main reasons for this. First, woman's feminist research, often carried out on a topic of interest to women and from a woman's perspective, will be judged by a predominantly male tenure committee that is unfamiliar with such research and often antagonistic toward it. Second, the content of her courses and her teaching may be criticized, and even her use of gender-neutral language queried, by some of her students. The anti-feminist students will give her poor teaching evaluations. Third, she may be asked to sit on a number of committees to provide a woman's perspective; this is important work, but it will eat into time that she should be spending on research if she is to win tenure.

One woman seeking tenure from an Ontario university found that her career was jeopardized in part because the committee refused to consider that the teaching evaluations of women are generally lower than of men,[38] just as the same research paper is judged inferior by students if it is thought to be by a woman rather than a man.[39] As well, her evaluations for her women's studies course were considered irrelevant in the committee's deliberations.[40] Other women have had their research trivialized because their topic is deemed too women-centred, or too qualitative and interdisciplinary, and also because it may be political and useful rather than theoretical and abstract.

A newly hired professor in an Ontario university has documented attempts to intimidate or control tenure-track feminists, such as herself: "the department has a history of denying tenure to women who make trouble."[41] She has had her proposed courses cancelled or belittled and has been verbally abused by colleagues. Two of these men have told their classes that the department had to hire "two unqualified women," which was untrue.

Feminists who have won or are about to win tenure at a university may be too disheartened by their experience to want to remain and help to improve the status of women there. Several such women have told me that the "hostile environment" and "intolerable atmosphere" in which they have to function is unacceptable. They plan to look for jobs elsewhere.

CRITICAL MASS

How many women are needed in a department to ensure changes that will improve conditions for women? What is the required critical mass? A critical mass has been defined as that amount of a substance or group that will make a difference, whether it is the quantity of fissile material required to trigger a nuclear reaction or the number of monkeys (said to be one hundred) that, upon learning something new, will transmit this new finding to the entire monkey population.[42] The proportion is variable to some extent; Gerd Engman, a feminist politician in Sweden, believes that at 20 percent participation, the level of women on committees is still only tokenism; at 30 percent, women start to have a voice; but only when they reach 40 percent are they really able to bring about change.[43] Rosabeth Kanter believes that change in a corporation can occur if more than a third of a group are women.[44] Peta Tancred agrees that in management, as women become more than one-third of a work group, previously accentuated resistance to their presence starts to diminish.[45] She does not know if universities operate in the same way. Patricia Aburdene and John Naisbitt[46] claim so many people now support the women's movement that it has reached a "critical mass," never to be turned back. In both American and Canadian universities, the presence of a campus women's group, exerting internal and external pressure has been a major factor in making affirmative action programs effective.[47]

The evidence of what might comprise a critical mass of women professors to create change favourable to women at universities is complex. In some university departments in the past, any women professors were perceived as too many by department heads and other professors. Victoria College and the zoology department at the University of Toronto vetoed women as professors into the 1930s and 1940s; at University College in the University of Toronto, women were refused tenure-stream appointments in English until 1965.[48] In 1973, the University of Waterloo had no women professors in seventeen of their departments, some of which were in the humanities where many qualified women sought positions.[49]

When there are so few women in a group that they are regarded merely as tokens, their presence may trigger no political reaction from men. They are not seen as threatening male power. This may be why, in the past, so many academic women have commented on the fair way in which they were treated (although their rosy memories may also be a result of their unraised consciousness about women's status both then and now). Helen MacGill Hughes notes that she herself, as well as other pioneering women, reported civil relationships at work.[50] It was only when their number increased that discriminatory treatment might become common. She wonders what the number is that triggers a response of prejudice rather than of tolerance.

Women rarely work on women's issues if they are a small minority in male-dominated disciplines such as engineering or economics;[51] they seem reluctant to call attention to their sex. However, if the women are strong feminists and their male peers complaisant, two women may be enough to make changes. In 1976, feminists Karen Messing and Donna Mergler were the only full-time women faculty members in the biology department at the Université de Québec à Montréal.[52] Together they lobbied for more women to be hired. They were so effective that now women constitute one-third of the full-time faculty of forty-six.

In general, the more women there are, the more changes there will be to benefit women. Women's groups seeking an improvement in the status of women in their discipline were formed very early during the second wave of feminism in sociology, modern languages and psychology, where women comprised 20 to 30 percent of association memberships.[53]

Paradoxically, however, if a discipline is dominated by women, such as home economics or nursing, it is not in the best position to demand equality for women as one might suppose. Rather, it is perceived by the university in general as being academically weak and may be phased out entirely.[54] This has happened before at Canadian universities,[55] and continues to happen. In 1996, the University of Waterloo saved money by closing the department of dance, the only department on campus that had a completely female faculty and catered almost entirely to women students.[56]

CONCLUSION

Feminists bring new ideas and a feminist worldview, which are often lacking in university disciplines. They should therefore be actively sought as professors rather than discriminated against (although a woman should never be hired solely because of her political beliefs). Their acquisition can best be achieved by having at least several feminists already on a department faculty, and a minimum of anti-feminists who work against equality for women. Fairness in process is essential to ensure that the best qualified women are hired for university positions.

NOTES
1. Dagg and Thompson 1988.
2. Beresford-Howe 1984.
3. Personal conversation.
4. Andrews 1993.
5. Eichler and Tite 1990.
6. Byfield 1991; Gruhn 1992.
7. Eichler 1989.

8. Vickers and Adam 1977: 114.
9. Johns 1981: 246, 248; Logan 1958: 216.
10. Beresford-Howe 1984: 37.
11. Pacer 1973; Ford 1985.
12. Dagg and Thompson 1988: 65.
13. Vickers and Adam 1977: 114.
14. Bernard 1964: viii, ix.
15. Bernard 1964: vii, ix.
16. Lougheed 1993: 10.
17. Dagg 1992: 89–92.
18. Statistics Canada 1992a: 189.
19. Chamberlain 1988: 16.
20. Kirby 1992: 9.
21. Heins 1987: 1, 23, 65.
22. Dagg 1992.
23. Williamson 1990: 40.
24. Winn 1985.
25. Urofsky 1991.
26. *Kitchener-Waterloo Record* 1993.
27. Westhues 1989.
28. Backhouse et al. 1989.
29. Letter to Anne Innis Dagg, dated Jan. 6, 1993.
30. Dagg 1992.
31. Fulton and Pujol 1991: 31–36.
32. Wine 1990: 161.
33. Wine 1983: 9–11.
34. Backhouse et al. 1989; personal communication December 11, 1989.
35. Cruikshank 1982: ix–xviii.
36. Letter to Anne Innis Dagg, dated November 3, 1992.
37. Nemiroff 1984.
38. Basow and Silberg 1987.
39. Goldberg 1969.
40. Letter to Anne Innis Dagg, dated January 10, 1993.
41. Letter to Anne Innis Dagg, dated January 11, 1993.
42. Keyes 1982.
43. Kirby 1992.
44. Kanter 1977.
45. Tancred 1990: 17–20.
46. Aburdene and Naisbitt 1992.
47. Drakich 1991; Stewart 1991: 28; Weitzman 1975: 80.
48. Ford 1985: 59–60.
49. Pacer 1973.
50. Hughes 1977.
51. Klotzburger 1973.
52. Kranias 1990.
53. Klotzburger 1973.
54. Beach 1975.
55. Dagg and Thompson 1988: 42.
56. Hudgins 1993.

The Revolving Door:
Faculty Women Who Exit Academia

Peta Tancred and Susan Hook Czarnocki

Colleges and universities are classic examples of male-dominated institutional settings. The ever increasing numbers of women earning PhDs are only slowly being reflected in the proportions of women on their full-time teaching staffs. Recently the phrase "chilly climate" has come to symbolize those aspects of the academic setting that tend to make women feel unwelcome, out-of-step, marginalized.[1] It seems reasonable to suggest that an institution that generates such a characterization may be sending many women PhDs through the "revolving door" rather than onto the tenure track. Rothblum mentions a study of Smith College faculty appointments, which documents that 19 percent of the women faculty resigned voluntarily before or after the first reappointment.[2] Thus, research is needed into the career decisions of women who achieve high-level academic credentials but who eventually exit from the standard academic career paths.

Unfortunately, "job exit" is a very difficult topic to research, whether at academic institutions or in the broader labour market. Studies of the labour force can draw samples from existing records, but minimal information is available for those who exit. Thus the current literature tends to focus on the experiences of women in academic life, but generally does not consider whether these experiences affect their rate of exit.

Through indepth interviews with former academics, this study begins to pass beyond speculation and to look at why women exit from academic research and teaching environments.[3]

WOMEN'S EXIT FROM ACADEMIA
We have quite a few descriptive studies of women's presence in and experience of academic life. In Canada alone, the range of studies includes Bannerji et. al. 1991; Dagg and Thompson 1988; Smith 1975; and Symons and Page 1984.[4] But we don't know why women leave academia. A survey of the literature has turned up three studies of this topic:

1. Rothblum (1987) cites a number of possible reasons but she has very little evidence, other than from the aforementioned Smith College report. The Smith women mentioned barriers to conducting research, such as heavy workloads and unsympathetic environments; heavy teaching demands; psychological factors, such as stress on junior faculty; and social and family life concerns. On the basis of this evidence, Rothblum can only suggest institutional, psychological and interpersonal factors that "*may* help account for the rates of voluntary resignation by women from academic positions."[5]

2. Aisenberg and Harrington had a unique chance to raise the question in an ideal setting.[6] As part of the "Alliance of Independent Scholars," a group of highly educated women who were without academic jobs and who were based in the Cambridge, Massachusetts area in the early 1980s, they interviewed thirty-seven women without academic jobs as well as twenty-five women with tenure-track positions.[7] However, because of what they cite as "less difference than commonality in the stories of tenured and deflected women," they carry out a general analysis of the interviews of women both within and outside academia.[8] Thus, one again gets a description of women's experience with academia rather than an analysis of why some have left.

3. Finally, Martin and Irvine undertook a study of women (and men) radio astronomers in Great Britain, in which they argue that the lack of "career success" (yet another unfortunate term) of the women is due to social factors within the family.[9] In fact, in the women's early careers, they achieved a higher proportion of publications and citations than their presence within the studied population would suggest, and they were very successful in obtaining their first jobs. However, after this stage, the demands of husbands' careers shaped their own careers, and 44 percent of them cite husbands' moves and family commitments as reasons for their own job moves. The authors hypothesize that the move to less satisfactory jobs and their dissatisfaction with such positions would be unlikely to encourage high research performance.

Thus, a range of factors has been suggested, with family reasons playing an important role in studies on two continents, but the major question remains unanswered: why do academic women exit from academia? In an attempt to begin to answer this question, this study focuses on the micro-level context of the career decisions of women who achieved high-level academic credentials and teaching positions but did not end up pursuing a "standard" career in a university, i.e., doctoral studies followed by entry status, tenure and eventual promotion to associate or full professor.

CREATING A SAMPLE

Tracing those who have left an organization is always a delicate matter. The organization tends to be discreet on this topic, and there is no other central location from which these individuals can be traced. In its earliest formulation, the focus of this project was to be on women leaving full-time tenure-track positions. This turned out to be a naive assumption for more than one reason. For one thing, as we learned, women exit from occupations in a variety of ways; as opposed to the "voluntary resignation" which we had anticipated, women take "early retirement"; their post-doctoral fellowships do not lead to permanent appointments as would be true of the usual career; they switch areas of employment; they decide to take another graduate degree; and so forth. Secondly, as we should have known, very few women start off in tenure-track positions. Thus, the few women we would be able to trace would not necessarily have started with such a privileged status. In fact, the term "exit" turned out to be a fortuitous one, for it committed us to no specific interpretation of the term and we learned to insert a variety of content into the expression.

But even to put together a comprehensive list of persons exiting from a university did not turn out to be a simple matter. In the university from which most respondents were drawn, no provision had been made in the employee information database to retrieve information on persons exiting from academic employment. Although it would be possible to construct such a retrieval system, this would require the consent of the central administration—with all the complications that obtaining such access would require.

For a low-budget pilot study, some economical strategy was needed to develop a set of potential subjects. Information in university telephone directories is public record, and its use could have few negative repercussions. By using the phone listings at two different dates (1985 and 1991), it was possible to obtain some idea of who had left and who remained, though the employment status and gender of the discrepant individuals were not always clear. Through contacts with departments, we could then acquire some information on employment status, verify that these individuals had indeed left, and attempt to obtain a current address.

The following tables provide a summary of data obtained in this way:

Faculty listed in 1985, but not in 1991
Total[10]	276
Clearly male	153
Clearly female	51
Unclear	72

Breakdown of 51 women
Died	7
Had not left (error)	9

Moved to new academic post	5
Left academia	12
"Retired" in Montréal	14
"Retired"/moved out of Montréal	4

We were left with a list of twelve persons who had clearly "exited" from academia. We also contacted local people who had retired, as there were indications that "early retirement" was another form of exit that might merit inclusion. While we had originally hoped for ten interviews, it was extremely difficult to obtain this number. There was a high proportion of refusals, mainly due to the pain of the experience that we were asking respondents to discuss. As one woman said: "It's just too painful to talk about it; I guess I'm not altruistic enough." Another stated categorically: "I'm not interested in discussing my years at X university for any purpose." Another, reflecting on her busy schedule, commented: "I have committed just about every waking hour between now and July," and she invited us to return in four months time! One person was so fearful of even the initial contact that she phoned back to ask how we had obtained her name, and to remind us that we were liable to legal action if we had obtained private information on her. We finally obtained six interviews locally, plus one additional interview on an out-of-town visit. The interviews were open-ended, starting with a one-page questionnaire outlining the person's career; we then focussed the major part of the interview on why the person decided on a specific reorientation of her career. In the following section, we analyze the reasons for such exits from academic life.

EXIT FROM ACADEMIA
Our group of seven respondents is drawn from a wide spectrum of disciplines, ranging from women's professional schools through the humanities to the traditional sciences. If we had been able to select the respondents, we could not have done better. The nature of their exit from academia took on three main forms: from the university to the non-university sector, from one discipline to another or from the academic to the administrative sector within the university. In all cases, the respondents had graduate degrees appropriate to university teaching in their fields, and they had all held some form of university appointment—as post-doctoral fellows or in part-time or full-time teaching positions. Clearly, we are not in a position to judge the extent of their competence within their specialized field, but we have no reason to question such competence. This judgement is supported both by the extensive *curriculae vitarum* spontaneously offered by a couple of women and also by the achievements of all subjects in their subsequent fields of employment. Thus, we had no impression of subjects who left academia because of inadequate qualifications or competence.

At the time of the interview, two women were married (with no children), one was married with a stepchild, two were divorced (they were also single parents), one was single and one was widowed. In effect, other than the woman with a stepchild, no respondent had domestic responsibilities towards *both* a husband and children but rather one or the other, though obviously several women had carried this dual responsibility during their careers. Most of the women were in their 40s, a couple were in their 30s and one was in her 60s. One interesting fact that came up spontaneously during the interviews is that at least three of the women came from working-class backgrounds, which may be a sheer matter of chance but appears to be a high proportion in a group of ex-academics.

Before analyzing the interview data, we should underline that for all interviewers, including our research assistant, the interview experience was profound. We have among us considerable experience of academia, of talking to colleagues in academia and of writing about academia. When we separated for interviews, those who had *exited* from the academy, the themes that emerged were in some ways familiar to the women who remained in academia.[11] The experiences, however, were so forceful, so overwhelming for us, that the interview experience was extremely poignant. One woman broke down and wept during the interview and, as we have already indicated, several women immediately refused to speak to us because of the pain involved. Thus, we would argue that the experiences of those who exit an occupation differ significantly from the experiences of those who do not exit; familiar themes are brutally underlined by exits and new themes are introduced.

If we were obliged to summarize the main reasons for the exit of our seven respondents, we would say that three described workplaces that were intolerable for patriarchal or harassment reasons; two spoke of discrimination within academia and the pull of new workplaces, which had much to offer them; and two gave the competition between family and academic obligations as their main reason.[12] Obviously, the categories are not mutually exclusive and nearly all the women gave secondary explanations based on one or more of the following categories.

Patriarchal Mechanisms
If we define the mechanisms of patriarchy as the means whereby men in positions of power ensure their continuing domination over women, nearly all respondents spoke of being subjected to patriarchal experiences while in the university. These experiences took various forms, including the devaluing or denigration of women. This was mentioned by over half the respondents: "The place was so unhappy. . . . I felt 'what do I need to be here for,' you know? Why do I need to be spurned or—he didn't even bother to spurn me—ignored?" (Respondent 1).[13] This woman went on to say that she felt that no attention was paid to her ideas, including specific suggestions she made about possible actions within the department.

Another respondent talked about the problems of "growing up in the

THE ILLUSION OF INCLUSION

system," i.e., of continuing to work in a department and university where she had started as a research assistant, such that she was always regarded as junior. Her attempt to free herself of this student status by reorienting to another discipline was not very successful:

> I didn't really realize what it was like to be a woman until I went to Law School . . . how women had been put into a certain inferior position; also because I felt that women were treated differently than men. . . . You hear this all the time, but it was true, that women were not taken as seriously when they spoke in class and I think it was really very marked. And I'd never seen anything like that before. (Respondent 2)

Another woman talked about being rendered literally invisible in a project proposal:

> And every place where my name had been mentioned previously—I was out. And even when they put me in as field coordinator, they didn't put my name. Everybody else's name was mentioned, but it was like, field coordinator—6 months—but I didn't have a name. (Respondent 3).

Finally, a respondent talked about her time in graduate school as "a really terrible," "disgusting" experience. As the fourth university she had attended, it was the worst: "I was shocked, devastated. . . .They treated students like dogs. . . . You had to go around begging for someone to supervise you" (Respondent 5).

An infrequently acknowledged mechanism of patriarchy is the devaluing of qualifications. Interestingly, the women did not identify this mechanism as patriarchal, for several of them were completely convinced that if only they had additional/alternative qualifications, their situation within academia would have been improved if not solved. The woman who suffered from eternal junior status in her department, talked about the difficulty of working in a clinical area without a medical degree; she underlined that the PhD had much lower status than a MD and that this was not a gender-related issue. However, she did take an alternative qualification—a law degree, since she felt that she was too old to enter medical school—only to find that the additional qualification was no panacea. Her gender identity succeeded in diminishing even her new qualification, for on applying for a position that required just her combination of qualifications (science and law), it was her husband (with scientific qualifications only) who was appointed rather than herself—and "me who was not getting paid and he who was getting megabucks—and he asked me questions [about law and ethics], which I refused to answer" (Respondent 2).

Another respondent in a professional school felt insecure about the type of degree she had, and was convinced that she needed additional qualifications in order to accomplish the level of research and publications required for tenure. She registered for a doctoral program with the conviction that, as she put it, "the PhD would allow her to compete on an even playing field in the future in academe" (Respondent 4).

One woman wished that she had qualified in another discipline—specifically biology: "Biology is so magical. . . . It opens up all the wonders of creation. . . . There are more jobs. . . . It is more marketable. You can do other things than teach" (Respondent 5). And a final respondent, who had qualifications in physical chemistry, said that she was made to feel a misfit in her university appointment because she did not have a pure *bio*chemistry background (Respondent 6). In general, the qualifications of these women were defined so negatively by the male establishment that the women themselves came to believe that there was something wrong with their qualifications.

Despite this denigration of women's qualifications, there was little encouragement towards additional professional study (in contrast to encouragement towards the basic qualifications for academia, for which certain women received considerable encouragement).[14] Respondent 1 mentioned that she had wanted to undertake further study and received no encouragement from her superior: "I didn't expect him to be the author of my motivation, but it was hard enough to do it, that when he said, well, 'What do you want to do that for?' You know. . . . "

Once the additional qualifications are acquired, there is still little encouragement. Respondent 2 indicated that after her reorientation to law, she expected some guidance or possibly an invitation to play a role within the university. She was invited out to lunch by her former boss and thought: "Oh good, we're going to discuss things." But her possible future role was never mentioned; she was "stymied," "shocked." Another respondent mentions the minimal technical support for research within academia, no discussion of the issue in faculty meetings and no mentors—yet research was increasingly emphasized for tenure (Respondent 4). Respondent 6 contrasted this situation with her private sector job where she is "appreciated," "respected" and "recognized," such that she has "bloomed."

Finally, as a patriarchal mechanism, many of the respondents talked of being isolated or marginalized. Respondent 2 talked of being excluded or "fringed" at the university; she was never asked to be on any committees and she "didn't really feel part of it." She now works out of her home and, while she likes the independence and autonomy, she has the feeling that it is "non-work" (i.e., the greatest form of marginalization) and she wishes that she could change her mentality to think of it as "work." Respondent 5 talked of the absolute isolation of her graduate student days when she spent two hours on a bus to come in for interviews with professors who did not show up. She was so isolated that she did not know how others were treated and every time she was "counted out" she took it personally ("I must be 'dumb'"). (Interview 5).

Respondent 3 talked of her field work where she was "fringed" on her research project. Despite the fact that she went ahead of the directors of the project to prepare the way, when they arrived she was edged out: "Because it literally was a body thing where we would be in a group and then somehow I would be elbowed out. I would end up in the back. . . ." She also talked of camp experiences where she could not participate in the male talk; she subscribed to magazines to have the necessary words for communication with her male colleagues but, when she was accused of sleeping with her boss, this isolated her even further.

Another form of marginalization is to teach "in the field." One respondent found this very stressful; she talked about the extensive workload and being physically scattered around the city (Respondent 4). On the other hand, Respondent 1 found field work her "happy period"; there was no top-down teaching relationship, she was able to remain distant from department politics, relations were cordial and more distant, she had more autonomy as her "own boss," and she was working mainly with women in her outside instruction—in effect, she was happiest when she was furthest from the university. On the other hand, when within the university, she felt the marginalizing effects of male language:

> I couldn't get the male language and the female language to really meet. . . . I'm referring a lot to the words and the way the words are put together, as well as what those words and the way they are put together reflect. . . . I just feel that it was people who were able to think in a more masculine way [who] did better in those meetings. . . .

> [What is the masculine way?] It's tidier . . . it's organized . . . it's as if there were no context often. . . . I mean, don't misunderstand me, I can arrange it [her thoughts] but, in its spontaneous form, it is not very arranged . . . and I know that, and that's partly why I keep quiet until it's arranged, heh? Because I know this is a meeting for arranged thoughts so (laughs) better to keep quiet. . . . When it was ready . . . it didn't come out explosively female, but it came out arranged.

Harassment—Atmosphere and quid pro quo

While harassment could easily be included under patriarchal mechanisms, it has become such an important aspect of workplace relations that it is being dealt with separately for purposes of this analysis. The literature now describes two forms of harassment: a) atmosphere harassment where women, usually in non-traditional[15] occupations, find their position rendered intolerable through a constant emphasis on the masculine atmosphere of the workplace; and b) *quid pro quo* harassment where, as the term suggests, certain organizational advantages are offered in return for sexual favours.[16] In our interviews, we found evidence of both forms of harassment, sometimes in horrifying examples.

Respondent 2, suffering from eternal junior status within her department, described the situation within her profession:

> For example, I would to go meetings and I would be an invited speaker. My husband would be in the audience, and people would ask him questions about my work. It really happened. . . . Luckily he didn't know so much about my work to be able to answer, which was perhaps fortunate.

She also talked about her time in law school and of the constant "sexist" and "jock-oriented" atmosphere; the exams always had "jock" questions, for example on hockey, and she mentioned a moot court where the case dealt with the selling of "bull balls." However, when she was asked whether she had ever felt harassed, she gave a negative response, explaining that it wasn't that she wasn't harassed but that she ignored it or "didn't even notice it at the time."

Respondent 3, who had worked in the field in her initial discipline and who had also undertaken some field work abroad when she changed disciplines, gave us unending examples of harassment in both arenas. She talked about a camp setting where the men wanted to get rid of another woman; they claimed that she wasn't tough enough because she "wore bows." They were "trying to break her" by cutting down her work and by placing her in the most unpleasant types of jobs. She also talked of graduate student experiences where professors inserted naked women into their slide shows during lectures and where, when she tried to prevent a "trick photography" slide show from taking place because of its sexist overtones, she was completely isolated, "fringed" by both faculty and her peers. Her worst examples came from her field work abroad where her attempts to obtain suitable accommodation were always accompanied by attempts from her so-called male "patrons" to obtain a set of keys to the accommodation: "I have never experienced such intense sexual harassment."

One woman spoke very eloquently about the sexism of the workplace. When asked to define the form of sexism (which she linked to "ageism") she said: "A certain amount of flirtatiousness with younger, attractive females. . . . He [her superior] was really not nice to women. . . . He was using women to feel better about himself" (Respondent 1). Not surprisingly, these are the three women who cite an intolerable workplace as their main reason for "exiting" academia.

Discrimination
Those who don't cite harassment give examples of discrimination during their experience in academe. For example, Respondent 5, who found graduate work a terrible experience, first denied that this was discrimination against women:

"It was not a special problem because I was a woman; the guys don't want to supervise." But then she reflected: "I do think that if I had been a guy, they would have been more concerned about my future and they would have, you know, helped me find a job or given me more guidance. . . ."

Respondent 6 talked about the main incident that propelled her departure from academia. A tenure-track position was advertised and when she enquired whether she could or should apply, she was basically told that she was not "qualified" since someone with *bio*chemistry qualifications was required. However, she found out later that they did hire an American male with essentially the same qualifications as hers. She found this "much too similar for me to swallow" and she was "hurt." Despite this reaction, she never considered gender to be a factor in the decision. This fits with her general "humanist" rather than "feminist" stance, a person who is "capable of fighting my own battles" and one of the attractions, for her, of non-academic employment is that she feels that she "was not hired for being a woman; here I don't think they notice if you have a skirt or pants on. . . . Gender doesn't enter here."

Respondent 7 recounted a similar experience of applying for a position as a university research fellow when the Department told her: "my research was too closely related to a person already on staff. We both studied the same group of birds, but he studied physiology and I was studying ecology and behaviour. . . ." However, as a comment on the practice within this department of "hiring its own," she adds: "One of the two they supported had a MA and PhD from [the same university] and was in the same area as the prof he was working with. . . . I was quite perturbed." In contrast, she felt that there was never any discrimination while she was a graduate student, such that it was a shock on entering the "real world" of employment.

Respondent 2 who talked about obtaining additional qualifications—only to find that her husband, with more restricted qualifications, was given priority over her—was obviously also giving an example of discrimination. In effect, over half the respondents had very specific examples to cite on this topic. Taken together, patriarchal mechanisms, harassment and discrimination were part of the experience of *all* respondents—sometimes in combinations, which made the academic workplace impossible to envisage for continuing employment.

Family Influences
Family responsibilities did play a major part in the decision of two women to leave academia, but several other respondents also spoke of the pull between family and workplace obligations. Respondent 1, with three children, said: "There were times when it was nearly impossible." She mentioned feelings of guilt and self-blame, "tension times" in family life that were quite difficult to manage, as well as the lack of acknowledgement of these types of strain within academia:

And there wasn't much acknowledgement of that. Women faculty members—we would commiserate with each other. But we had this image of ourselves: that we are supposed to do this and not let these strains show. You can get us to a meeting where we'll talk about it officially, but day to day, we're supposed to be able to cope with this, you know.

And obtaining family help was not a self-evident route, as she tried to cope with a child with school phobia: "It took another group [of women] to tell me to ask my husband to take his turn dragging the kid to school."

Respondent 2 talked of the influence of her husband's career on her own, particularly when they had both moved to a new university where she felt she had escaped her "daughter" status and she had obtained an academic position that she greatly enjoyed. But her husband was less contented with his position and they returned to their original university. She called this a "joint decision," confirmed by a refusal of the pay raise she had requested at the new university and which she felt was justified. But her husband's career clearly influenced her own in geographical terms. Respondent 6 talked of a "supportive" husband, but said that she would not have hesitated to move if he had done so. On the other hand, at the time of the interview, she was considering a promotion that would move her geographically and it would be mainly family reasons—her husband's career and her mother—that would make her hesitate.

Our final interview was with Respondent 7, who had no children. In exploring that topic, she put very graphically the limits on her capacities: "I think I can do two things well: have a good relationship with my husband and do very well in my career, but I can't see having all three. . . . Very few women have all three working well." As indicated earlier, none of the respondents "had all three working well" at the time of the interview, and either childlessness or divorce reduced the triple burden.

Even a double burden can be very onerous, as both single parents indicated. They talked at some length about their responsibilities to their children as affecting their academic trajectory. Respondent 5, apart from "trailing around" after her husband while doing her graduate work (which became "no planning at all"), felt that she could not uproot her children from their home city because of their need to see their father. Instead, she took a job outside the city and not in academia. She said she felt guilty for having left the children and for not always being around during her doctoral studies; to this day, her ex-husband feeds her this "crap" about her "lost" youngest son, i.e., he has not embarked on a career. She said very quietly, so that it is hardly audible on the tape: "I deserve that; I feel that way too."

Respondent 4 talked about having been attracted to academia because the schedule could be helpful for her children. She also talked about waiting until her children were old enough before she could reorient to another discipline with "peace of mind," and she talks at some length of "minimum family obligations." Tenure is difficult, she adds, for those who will not sacrifice their health or family life: "I do want a balance between what I do as work and what I do as living. I don't consider work equals life."

Do finances matter in family terms? "On occasion," two respondents indicated. Respondent 1 talked about "coming in" to academia from a field position, which she preferred purely for economic reasons. She was an "unwilling academic" who still had fairly major responsibilities at home: "I wasn't at a risk-taking place in my life." Respondent 5 talked of her post-divorce period: "I was very broke for a very long time after the divorce, even though and at least my ex paid child support on time; there was great urgency to find a job—any job" and academia was not the easiest market.

But in some cases, money had little importance in family terms. Respondent 4 indicated that she had a generous basic living allowance from her former husband and was able to have live-in help. Respondent 2 had few financial obligations, with an employed husband and no children. She talked a great deal about finances, saying, "I like the money [but also] "It's the prestige. My self-esteem is so low that I would like to have the public acknowledgement."

HOW DO WOMEN MANAGE?

One of the themes emerging from these few interviews is that the women interviewed had certain ways of managing their lives that released the pressure in some ways. Mention has already been made of channelling themselves towards "doing two things well," i.e., work and husband *or* children. Another strategy was much more hidden but, when we became conscious of it, it drew together the experiences of many of the women; they tended towards the creation of a women's environment wherever they were. This could take on a number of forms. One respondent worked part-time in an all-female clinic where she could be open and where she had no male-dominated hierarchy with whom to deal. She also valued field instruction, which brought her mainly into contact with women. Another respondent, when asked about contacts with her male colleagues, revealed to us that she worked only with women. All her research assistants and associates were women and she negotiated with the male hierarchy through a female administrative assistant, though she had not been conscious of this until we posed the question. Another respondent talked of the great relief of finding a female supervisor in graduate school where she could enjoy "women's culture": "We were always going from the interpersonal to the global . . . instead of always staying at the global all the time" (Respondent 3).

Respondent 5 talked of "feeling great" on finding a female work group, after years of isolation, where the women welcomed her, invited her out to lunch and were very supportive. A respondent in science was surprised, on checking her list, to find that nearly half of her colleagues were women—and this within a very obviously male-dominated discipline. One woman moved to secondary school teaching which was obviously more female-dominated than the university. Finally, six of the seven respondents used this strategy; seeking a higher level of comfort in a female-dominated workplace. This result fits with Jacobs' macro-level statistical observation that 8 out of 10 women who left non-traditional jobs moved to a female-dominated occupation.[17]

CONCLUSION

Clearly, this is a very preliminary analysis of some limited data gathered in a pilot project,[18] but it points to certain possibilities for future research. One of these includes an exploration of the intertwining of gender and class. Based on the fact that three of the respondents were from working-class backgrounds, one is encouraged to reflect upon the possibility that two devalued statuses—being of blue-collar origins and female—are more than the academy can include. In fact, if atmosphere harassment is a response to a perceived threat, perhaps the stance of the upwardly mobile woman is even more threatening to male domination. The hypothesis at least needs to be explored and it could operate in a wide range of non-traditional domains.

Secondly, it is clear that we can only suggest conclusions on the basis of a pilot study. However, it is of the greatest importance that a significant proportion of the respondents were citing the nature of the workplace[19] as their main reason for exiting from academia. Clearly, this hypothesis needs to be explored in other non-traditional settings and it should have significant policy implications, but the emphasis on family responsibilities as the main explanation for women's workplace behaviour is not supported by this research.

Finally, the women firmly stated through their actions that triple responsibilities—work, husband/partner and children—are beyond realistic expectations, and this prompts one to ask whether the nature of the work responsibilities, rather than personal responsibilities, could not be modified. In the academic setting, many respondents felt they could handle *either* the teaching or the research responsibilities but, in conjunction with domestic obligations, they could not cope with both. Many respondents expressed a great dedication to students and were clearly gifted teachers with good evaluations and/or teaching awards. One respondent preferred research and felt that she would be unable to do a lot of teaching at the same time (it was "demanding," "exhausting"). But with the present structure of academia, these women had no choice; if they wished to work full-time (and *none* of them even mentioned the part-time option), they had to take on a workload equivalent to that of their male colleagues. If academia, but also other non-traditional workplaces, does not wish to lose valuable women candidates, the modification of the expected work responsibilities deserves considerable thought. The options should be open to both women and men, and both options must be accorded equal salary and standing. Otherwise, the "revolving door" will continue to operate and post-secondary educational institutions will fail to reap the full benefits of women's talents.

NOTES

1. The term "chilly climate" was introduced in 1982 by Hall and Sandler. The Department of Equity Services at the University of Western Ontario prepared a "video-based educational package" entitled "The Chilly Climate for Women in Colleges and Universities." See also *University Affairs* 1993.

2. Rothblum 1988: 14–17.

3. We thank Darcie Olijnek, our very helpful research assistant on this project.

4. Bannerji et al. 1991; Dagg and Thompson 1988; Smith 1975: 4; Symons and Page 1984.

5. Rothblum 1988: 16.

6. Aisenberg and Harrington 1988.

7. Whom they sadly describe as being "off the normal career track."

8. Aisenberg and Harrington 1988: xii.

9. Martin and Irvine 1982.

10. We did not take the time to count the total number of phone-listed faculty by gender. However, of those who were not listed by the latter date and who can be clearly identified by gender (a total of 204 individuals), 25 percent are women. Given that, as of 1990, women in this university were only 16.9 percent of faculty, women are significantly overrepresented in the non-listed group on the basis of these approximate statistics. Obviously, more precise data would be desirable on this subject.

11. As noted by Aisenberg and Harrington 1988. The choice of the term "deflected" is another unfortunate formulation of these women's choices.

12. Not surprisingly, these categories are coherent with the reasons, already mentioned, which emerge from our survey of the literature.

13. Because of the possibility of identifying respondents in such a small group, no more details can be given on each respondent other than the respondent number.

14. We make the distinction between encouragement of graduate students, whose accomplishments can reflect on their supervisors, and encouragement of colleagues, who may become a threat.

15. Definitions of non-traditional work for women vary from a specific focus on manual occupations to a broader definition, which includes managerial or other higher-level occupations that have traditionally been associated with men. For the purposes of this paper, the term "non-traditional" is used interchangeably with the term "male-dominated occupations," i.e., an occupation where 70 percent or more of the position occupants are currently male. See Jacobs 1989: 68.

16. Crull 1987; MacKinnon 1979.

17. Jacobs 1989.

18. For the development of the theme of women's exit from non-traditional occupations, see the subsequent research, particularly that on women architects and engineers, which has been carried out by Tancred et al. 1997; and Adams and Tancred, forthcoming.

19. This, of course, would coincide with Feldberg and Glenn's (1979) argument that job models (i.e., motivation from on-the-job factors) are as applicable to women as to men and that women are not only motivated by off-the-job or family reasons.

Part 4
Policies and Practices: More Illusion

Ensuring Our "Vocal Presence" in the Classroom: Considerations of a Complex Task

Patricia Hughes

When we think about extending education to the women and men of traditionally excluded communities, we cannot talk about their mere physical "presence" in the school or in the classroom. Rather, we must talk of their "*vocal* presence."[1] Hence the first part of my title: *ensuring our vocal presence.*

Since I am stressing "vocal" in my comments, however, I want to make clear that we should not assume that speaking is always the way to communicate. Silence may be significant: this has been called "the importance of context."[2] Silence may be a choice; the student may be "speaking, perhaps more loudly, with silence."[3] Once we have learned to "hear" it as a deliberate choice, we must learn to respect this silence as much as we must learn to respect the vocal assertions.

Women and men of traditionally excluded groups have not had their experience treated sufficiently seriously in the classroom. As students they have not been respected: they have been ignored; their contributions have been ridiculed; their persons have been insulted. Their lives also have been ignored: in selecting or devising fact situations or examples to encourage students to think about and discuss a particular topic, teachers have often been insensitive to or careless about the experience of the members of excluded groups, both by what they have included and by what they have not thought to include. In particular, this "silencing," as it is often called, takes two forms: the *content* of what is said, such as derogatory comments about or to male and female persons of Asian or Black heritage, aboriginal persons, gays and lesbians, or white women, as well as the lack of *affirming* content about traditionally excluded groups; and the *amount* of what is said by members of dominating groups as compared to how much is said by members of marginalized groups. Sexism and racism in the classroom have been described as "poison[ing] the atmosphere for learning."[4] They constitute a powerful message about the "proper place" of excluded groups in education and in society generally, and they provide a salient cue about what "matters" in the learning process.

The culprits have been both students and professors—the latter not only by their own comments or conduct but also by a refusal or reluctance to deal with the inappropriate comments or behaviour of students. Thus, professors have either been active accomplices in the silencing or have been complicit by not speaking out against the hostility of the oppressing groups. On the other hand, female professors may be subject to verbal attack by students and, in these cases, female students are hardly reassured about their own position.[5]

Many of us teaching in post-secondary environments have struggled to ensure the vocal presence of members of traditionally excluded communities who are entering our institutions; some of us are trying at the same time to ensure our own vocal presence as teachers. We know that this is an ongoing process and one that is far from completed. But as we work our way through this process, most of us have had to face a concomitant question: as we ensure the vocal presence of some in the classroom, how do we respond to those who have traditionally enjoyed a virtual monopoly on a vocal presence?

It is this question that I wish to explore. While I am speaking from the law school context, because that is where I actually struggle with this question, I believe that most of what I have to say is transferable to other contexts. Our endeavours must balance a number of different realities about ourselves, our students, our responsibilities as teachers and, not least, the "outside world" (to the extent that is different from ourselves and our students). In short, as suggested in the title, we are indeed struggling to carry out a complex task.

THE COMPLEXITIES

Starting at the Beginning: Exactly What are We Talking About?
Even the way we define the issue reveals its complexity and has implications for how we approach it. Some teachers talk about "making space" for women, for students of Black heritage or for aboriginal students; others think about "free speech in the classroom." The idea of "making space" is appealing and one that I have found useful, but it does carry connotations of limitation: space is a limited resource, after all. If one thinks of the discussion as having been dominated by specific members of the class, this metaphor implies that their participation must be reduced in kind or extent in order to enhance the opportunity for others to speak. And, indeed, I have heard teachers who use that terminology say that they are not troubled about the implications of preventing members of dominant groups from speaking: it is their turn to face restriction. There is no question that some students, who are used to their viewpoint being taken for granted (so much so that it did not need to be made explicit either by their teachers or by them) or their voices filling the room, will consider the participation of others an invasion of their territory. In this, as in so many other ways, the classroom resembles the outside world.

On the other hand, characterizing the issue as one of "free speech" (and thus phrasing the issue as "can we limit speech in the classroom and if so, how?") presumes an entitlement to speak, but by whom and for what purpose? Put bluntly, this is a "right" that has effectively been enjoyed by the majority group and that is now claimed by others. One response by those seeking to enhance the participation of marginalized communities has been to accept the right of the latter to speak, while denying the right to the traditionally powerful group. But the use of free speech terminology requires a justification of the denial of the right to some members of the class. The "free speech" approach merely plays into the hands of the dominant group; they can easily complain about "censorship" and force consideration of the issue to an "us" and "them" level, which masks the complexity inherent in the transition in the classroom from relations of oppression/subordination to full and equitable participation by all members. The all too easy response that one should not be concerned about the denial of the "right" to those who have been the oppressors simply evades the difficulty of identifying the oppressor among those who might superficially resemble him, and assumes that those who now are encouraged to speak will not at times transmit their own biases.

A variant of the free speech approach tries to reduce the significance of derogatory comments by referring to many of them as "jokes." One effect of this, of course, is to place the responsibility on the subject of the joke, blaming him or her for not having a sense of humour. Furthermore, as has been pointed out in the context of orientation week "pranks," "referring to these sexist, racist or homophobic activities as 'jokes' undermines the level of intimidation or actual danger these activities pose for other students [and] . . . effects a rhetorical denial of the sexist and racist ideology to which the jokes tacitly refer."[6] Rather, many of the verbal or written attacks on students and professors (for example, graffiti in the washroom) are best characterized as part of "*a practice of inequality enforced through violence and hatred*," that is, as a reflection of sexist and racist practices in society at large.[7]

Framing this issue as one of "free speech" assumes that we have as our goal a free exchange of ideas, a rational discourse out of which "truth" will emerge. This is unrealistic; it equates all persons in the classroom as if they have "equal weight and legitimacy" inside and outside the classroom, whereas this has not been and is not now the case.[8]

There are advantages to avoiding both of these approaches. Instead, I should like to try to describe the issue around the underlying interests represented: *what are the various "groups" involved trying to gain, enhance or protect?*

Women who are making the claim to a vocal presence are concerned about gaining full recognition in the classroom and about having oppression eliminated. Some members of the class will not be hesitant in their efforts to prevent that recognition; their goal is to maintain their power and to deny effective inclusion of women in the classroom. Members of yet another group would identify their interest as developing a knowledge base and understanding about the issues that arise in the particular discipline involved; they may not immediately see the relevance of these "other" questions and complain about the raising of them, since these people are, as they might say, just interested in "getting an education." Others will confess to confusion about how they are to behave or what they are to say; and their very expression of those doubts may seem questionable (at the least) by those who are impatient at the lack of progress in their status.

This article is premised on the legitimacy of the claim to inclusion in the educational process. In my view, the second interest, that of maintaining power and denying effective inclusion, is not one that we can treat as meritorious. The third and fourth groups, however, pose the issue that I am addressing. It is our responsibility as teachers to help the third group to understand that their education is incomplete without an appreciation of the extent to which the discipline involved meets or satisfies the claims of previously or currently excluded groups. We cannot do that without also involving them in the shifting social/political dynamic represented in the classroom. The fourth group will say things we do not wish to hear in our classrooms. But I believe that I am obligated to consider their questions even when I otherwise might speak out against the views they express.

It is difficult to identify the kinds of issues that fall into the second category; two examples might provide a flavour. Teresa Scassa refers to an incident in which a woman commented on what she considered derogatory views expressed about women in the context of a criminal law class on rape; a male student told her to shut up—she was "just jealous because [she was] too ugly to be raped."[9] In one of my classes, a student referred to the way in which aboriginal people have been "named" and have named themselves: as Indians, as native people(s), as aboriginal people(s), as First Nations peoples. Another student pointed out that the word "Indian" has connotations of "drunken, lazy (etc.) Indians," while the term 'First Nations' reflects a sense of pride. "But," he said, "most native people *are* drunks, lazy (etc.)."

These kinds of comment clearly fall outside the ambit of acceptability: they are personal (even if the subject is not present) and derogatory, with no purpose other than to be derogatory. Quite often, perhaps most often, a quick and firm response is the most appropriate way to deal with the type of comments typified in these examples. They should not be allowed to divert the class from the serious business of learning what they are there to learn; and the culprit should not be reinforced by the attention anything more would provide. (I leave open here the possibility that the object of the remark might wish to "respond" on his or her own initiative; I suspect that a lengthy encounter would not help anyone.)

As an example of the kind of comment made by someone in the fourth group, consider questions about whether pornography is really hate literature against women or whether restrictions on it interfere with free expression. My own answers to those questions would be in the affirmative and negative, respectively. Yet I do not believe I should prevent a discussion on those issues; on the contrary, they serve as a catalyst to exploring why pornography is harmful to women. I also would not prevent a male student from arguing that "men suffer violence too," during a discussion on violence against women, even though a female student has told me that it was upsetting to her to hear it. I would try to show why violence against men and violence against women are different.

I admit that my reasons for searching for a different way of framing the issue are in part related to the much maligned "freedom of speech" issue; I have some concerns about the degree of certainty teachers must have in the rightness of their own views to dictate to their students what they may discuss. But my major reason is the very practical question of the effect a strict approach may have on students who might have been hesitant about speaking. I believe that one of our goals as teachers is to encourage students to articulate their views on issues, to raise problems they may be having with a particular topic and generally to learn how to interact with each other. Many students have not developed an ease with speaking in the classroom, not only because of the factors discussed here, but for quite separate reasons that arise out of their own personalities and background. Although we may be reluctant to do so, we must also realize that many students have not developed either a particularly sophisticated understanding about what are appropriate and inappropriate comments or skills in how to phrase their questions and concerns. Some of these students may have difficulty identifying the line between those comments that we, as teachers, are prepared to discuss and those we have decided are inappropriate for discussion. They may not be sure that they will not be treated in the way we have treated other students whose comments have been deemed offensive and out of bounds and therefore they may be reluctant to speak. We need, therefore, to be careful of how broadly we define the category of forbidden comment.

Are There Any Simple Answers that are Worthwhile?
There are, of course, no simple answers. In substitute, I propose some considerations that might assist in developing a response for a particular situation.

Fundamental to ensuring women's vocal presence is acceptance of where the responsibility for silencing lies. One commentator has forcefully argued that we must reject the explanation that women are "alienated" from the law school environment and that making the law school "a more hospitable environment for women" will solve the problem.[10] Using the notion of alienation "turns attention away from the behaviour of the men within the law school environment" and "focuses the attention on women and their 'difference'"; in short, "[i]t blames the victim by not blaming the perpetrator."[11] The concept of "alienation" is perhaps better understood as an articulation of women's distance from our own identity and our own ability to name our experiences because of having to function in male-defined and male-dominated environments, including the educational environment. "Making the [educational context] a more hospitable environment for women" is another way of saying that women's experiences, as defined by women, must help in forming or building the environment itself.

In this sense, it is not enough that women be "allowed" to talk about the subjects that have been traditionally considered "important" in a particular discipline. Women must also determine what subjects form part of a curriculum and, within that curriculum, what issues are considered significant enough in a particular course to form part of the discussion in the classroom. One of the items on the agenda of more extensive, inclusive discourse is identification of whomever has the power to decide what is appropriate and what is inappropriate speech.[12] In fact, we cannot avoid the fact that the teacher makes that determination but, in making those decisions, we must be conscious of and take into account what members of the "marginalized" group consider appropriate.

One of the most obvious things we know about ourselves, but one of the hardest to recognize in others, is that people are not at the same place during their lives or at only one place; most of us have multiple identities, which do not always smoothly fit together. Our alliances shift and there is rarely a distinct dichotomy between "us" and "them" in the classroom.[13] As Elizabeth Ellsworth found in a class dealing with racism and self-consciously devoted to ending silence:

> Things were not being said for a number of reasons. These included fear of being misunderstood and/or disclosing too much and becoming too vulnerable; memories of bad experiences in other contexts of speaking out; resentment that other oppressions . . . were being marginalized in the name of addressing racism—and guilt for feeling such resentment; confusion about levels of trust and commitment surrounding those who were allies to another group's struggles; resentment by some students of color for feeling that they were expected to disclose "more" and once again take the burden of doing the pedagogic work of educating White students/professor about the consequences of White middle-class privilege; and resentment by White students for feeling that they had to prove they were not the enemy.[14]

Above all, and aside from the temptations driven by our desire to do "the right thing," we must remember that we are dealing with *individuals*. People may or may not claim identity based on their affiliation with particular marginalized or dominant groups, but, in any event, we are never only our colour, our sex, our physical and mental abilities. As teachers, we would be unwise (and even insulting) to assume that we know from particular characteristics how a person feels, why the person is acting as she or he is, what the person wants or needs. It is perhaps these intersecting realities about each of us that form the most "complex dynamics" in the classroom.

Finally, we have to tread that fine line between taking on another's burden and speaking for her. Nevertheless, we cannot expect students to speak up for themselves.[15] If male students begin to shout slurs at female students, the professor should not depend on the women to respond and should not ask them to respond. Encouraging self-assertion is, in my view, desirable but it is fundamentally wrong in expecting a woman to "defend" herself against a remark such as "you're too ugly to be raped." It is our responsibility to reveal the hatred inherent in that abuse. Similarly, we also should not assume that it is the job of the marginalized to educate those who have oppressed them.[16]

Setting the Atmosphere, and Knowing We Can't Have it All Our Way
In my course outline for my Feminist Legal Theories course, I wrote the following:

> This is a seminar class. . . . Everyone in the group brings a different experience and perspective and I hope we are all able to benefit from our combined experiences and perspectives. . . . I am not concerned whether you agree or disagree with me or with anyone else in the class; I *am* concerned that we are all open to and respectful of each other and of different views put forward by our colleagues in the group.

I also invited anyone who was reluctant to speak to feel free to come and discuss this with me.

At one level, this kind of statement simply makes a commitment to polite discourse. It does not preclude passionate discussion, but it does preclude, as do the "rules" of civility, personal attacks, slurs, interruptions, especially for the purpose of "shouting down" to prevent traditionally unpopular views from being expressed, and so on. It perhaps goes further because it really is a statement that everyone has a place in the classroom, as long as each is respectful of the other. It is a failure to respect that brings opprobrium, not the articulation of ideas, although I acknowledge that some "ideas" are inherently disrespectful of other people and therefore beyond the pale.

A short discussion about the need to respect each other's entitlement to be in the classroom and to participate in discussion can be used to give students "ownership" of the process and therefore a greater propensity to accept it. This enables everyone to think about the general framework for discussion in class. It may well have the effect of encouraging those who disapprove of comments indicating that disapproval. Both professor and students have then contributed to establishing the proper atmosphere.

The atmosphere can be maintained or reinforced in a number of ways while establishing the outer parameters of the dialogue. It is not unusual for any professor to curtail discussion of matters that are not *relevant* to the subject matter of the class, although there are certainly times when that practice is loosely applied. Nevertheless, the guideline is vital if the subject is going to be communicated to the class. There is no need to make an exception for inappropriate comments that are impeachable on another ground as well as lack of relevance, for fear of being criticized for censorship or for imposing one's own views.

Some of the most impeachable comments or conduct are intended to undermine the professor's authority or have the goal of disrupting the class. Sometimes this motive is clear through form (shouting or constant interruption) and sometimes through content (ongoing criticism no matter what is said by other students or the professor) and, of course, often through both. This is similar to lack of relevance (and often will be one and the same) and should be treated accordingly. It cannot be treated as having any merit; the entitlement of other members of the class to an environment that enhances the learning process requires that disruptive conduct be stopped. On the other hand, when someone takes an unpopular view and seems at odds with the general tenor of the class in making comments that some people might not want said, but (and one must make a judgement about this) appears to be trying to address the matter sincerely, it is preferable to deal with the comments on their merits. In this category, for example, I would put questions about whether pornography is protected by freedom of speech or even whether particular portrayals constitute pornography.

On the other side, we should not forget that there will always be students who are not sure how to behave. Opportunities to show appropriate conduct should be taken. In my class, one of the female students, of Asian heritage, did that by commenting favourably on language I had used; under the circumstances, her interjection was confirming for me and instructive for other students.

I do not forget that, as a practical matter, an approach that serves well for one class will not for another. The size of the class, the rapport between students and professor and the length of time the class has been together will be factors to be taken into account in deciding the most effective approach.

Why Do We Teach: To Advance Understanding or to Set the World Right?

The simple answer is "a bit of both." Rather naively and optimistically perhaps, I shall describe a professor as someone who attempts to transmit "knowledge" and to inculcate the kinds of outlooks and skills that enhance people's abilities to find "knowledge" themselves. Professors come equipped with all manner of points of view. It is inevitable and desirable that teaching has a "political" dimension (although admittedly, a professor's anti-Semitic or misogynist outlook is not a "desirable" political dimension). As a feminist, and in the context of my own discipline, it seems to me incumbent on a professor of law to show how the law has excluded marginalized groups, including but not limited to diverse women, and also to show how the law must change to include the experience of those groups. Prior to going into law, I taught political science and, in that context, it seems to me imperative that the teaching of political theory acknowledge that much of theory has failed to understand the political dynamic of the private sphere or that what is not talked about in theory is as important as what is. As a feminist, I suggest that teaching practice and content are intertwined or, in short, *how* we teach cannot be separated from *what* we teach.

To what extent does this mean imposing one's own views on the students? Clearly, the hierarchical relationship that exists between professor and students (notwithstanding the well-intentioned efforts of some faculty members to diminish it, professors still give marks and students receive them) carries with it the danger that students will think they must "toe the party line" and, worse, that professors will expect them to do so. Even under the best of circumstances, it is difficult to convey to students that they should develop their own ways of thinking. Professors who claim to be neutral are denying their own humanity and, indeed, have not taken advantage of the opportunities that the academy offers to develop understandings of phenomena that cannot realistically or appropriately be separated from taking a normative position on that understanding. But professors are irresponsible, in my view, if they fail to acknowledge that the world is a complicated place and that they do not have all the answers, and if, as a result, they discourage questioning and searching.

Recognizing that we are not "neutral" or without views and commitments about the way the world should look and that we have an obligation to our students to enhance their ability to assess the world in a critical fashion, I suggest that our task as professors is rather more complicated than "censoring" comments we have deemed inappropriate. Rather, I believe we should take the comments and use them in the educational process. This is particularly so if we maintain that men have a responsibility to unlearn their own sexism; we cannot, as professors, cut off their opportunity to do that.[17] This is, however, different from focusing on men's concerns about women's claims.

As Teachers, We Are Only Human Beings
As teachers, we must acknowledge our status as human beings, with the frailties and imagination that entails, and also our status as members of a "society" that is structured in a particular way. None of us is immune from saying the "wrong thing" even, for the sake of argument, giving us all the credit in the world for openness and good intentions. While it would be a mistake to assume that all inappropriate remarks are made inadvertently or out of ignorance or thoughtlessness and that a bit of education is all that is required, many comments of which we might disapprove may well arise in that way and, at times, they may be made by us.

Few of us are immune from prejudice in some form and, for some of us, it lies too closely to the surface to assume it will not be revealed. We must examine ourselves; we cannot hope to be "pure" and should not act as if we were, but we can be aware of our own limitations and be seen to attempt to transcend them. As professors, we must show that we are amenable to being told that our comments are not appropriate. We need to make an explicit statement about this vulnerability and be open to our students' coming forward.

We must continue to question our own actions. One law professor "wonder[s] if [she's] fuelling racism or sexism by the stories [she] tell[s] to try to educate or provoke discussion," including the racist remarks of a judge.[18] Yet we cannot ignore these stories; they are part of what our students face in the future. Telling the stories as carefully and as sensitively as we can helps us to prepare students for "real life" after their formal education and may even help to move our world towards change.

We need to maintain our own perspective, as well, to give ourselves a "pause," to not expect too much all the time. We are attempting a difficult and sometimes frustrating task when we take responsibility for a safe classroom environment. It is not always clear what we should do and not always clear that what we do will work anyway. We can easily empathize with a law professor who is reconsidering her commitment to "trying to be fair all the time"; she may stop worrying about that because "the confrontation comes anyway. I know I am a fair person and I'm tired of proving I'm fair."[19] We need to maintain contact with our own identity, our own core being.

The Classroom: Just a Little Part of the World

The classroom is somewhat artificial on the one hand, and a microcosm of the outside world on the other. The way in which women are treated in the classroom and the way in which they experience that treatment cannot be separated from their treatment and experience in the wider society. They enter the classroom with that knowledge and too often find it reinforced there. Women do not change what they are when they enter the classroom. Thus, for example, they remain "caretakers" of men and therefore may take on men's concerns—to worry if we are too critical of men or if men are "uncomfortable" with what is being said.[20] Part of our task will be helping our female students to resist subsuming their own interests in those of men, even while we remain committed to that which is positive in caring for others.

The limitations of the classroom also require us to be realistic about what we can accomplish: "an attempt to recognize the power differentials present and to understand how they impinge upon what is sayable and doable in that specific context."[21]

The emphasis in this article is on what individual professors can do to ensure vocal presence. But we need institutional support if we are to be successful, or if we are to be successful without an enormous emotional toll.

INSTITUTIONAL COMMITMENT: HOW CAN IT BE SHOWN?

At the very least, institutional support helps us to succeed in our own individual efforts, but the need goes beyond that. It is necessary to the recognition of the entitlement of "a vocal presence" of all those in the institution, and of those who may be joining it, that it be a place that respects that entitlement. This kind of commitment must come from the highest levels of the institution in the same way that, for example, sexual harassment policies must; they must then be replicated through the various levels of authority (such as the dean of a faculty or head of a department).

The faculty or department can hold workshops directed at professors' own conduct to educate us about what is appropriate. These may be best conducted by someone outside the workplace (for example, I spoke at another university about sexual harassment; I would not be likely to do the same thing at my own university, but would more likely bring in a visitor to do so). The visitor can come in, read the riot act and leave.

The other kind of workshop which a faculty or department can hold teaches professors about the practices of traditionally excluded groups, as well as about discrimination generally. These workshops assist us in teaching subject matter with which we may not be familiar, as well as in developing new pedagogic tools. The authorities must use as much pressure as they can to ensure attendance at both types of workshops.

We should try to ensure a vocal presence not only because it is "just" to do so for the members of the excluded groups, but because it is likely that we are not teaching our courses properly if we do not include in the curriculum the claims made by members of marginalized groups. This should be part of "good pedagogy" as defined by the institution and should be considered in assessing and rewarding teaching.

With respect to students, these issues should be dealt with as part of the normal orientation sessions held at the beginning of term; if no orientation is normally held, one should be instituted for this purpose.

CONCLUSION

In short, this not an easy matter. We will make mistakes. We will be misunderstood. We will reveal our own failings. But we have a responsibility to make hard choices. While it may seem easier to take a broad approach to what is not acceptable and a challenging approach to everything falling within those parameters, I believe that our task is a rather more complex one. We must balance our obligation to encourage our students to think and to question with our obligation to enhance an appropriate learning environment; that environment must include respect for all the students in the room. This means, in practice, that we must decide which comments are ill-intentioned, meant to be harmful or meant to be disruptive, and which are said out of an attempt to expand the inquiry or which represent an honest attempt to deal with the issues in a constructive manner. We must learn to distinguish the questioning or the confused student from the bigot, those who are open to learning and change (even if not exactly as *we* would like in *our* ideal world) from those whose closed minds and hearts are an impediment to learning. Above all, we have an obligation as teachers to be as harsh with our own failings as we feel we have a right to be with the failings of others.

NOTES

1. Scassa 1992.
2. Orner 1992.
3. Orner 1992: 81.
4. Abell 1991.
5. McIntyre 1987–88.
6. Wayne and Ulster 1991.
7. Gochnauer 1992.
8. Ellsworth 1992: 94.
9. Scassa 1992: 813.
10. Scassa 1992.
11. Scassa 1992: 822.
12. Luke 1992.
13. Orner 1992.
14. Ellsworth 1992: 107–08
15. Abell 1991.
16. Ellsworth 1992.
17. Lewis 1992.
18. Abell 1991: 388.
19. Abell 1991: 389.
20. Lewis 1992: 174–75.
21. Orner 1992: 81.

Women and Post-Secondary Science Education: A Case for Curriculum Transformation

Peggy Tripp-Knowles

The science classroom in Canadian colleges and universities still retains an atmosphere more comfortable for men than for women, as evidenced by the proportions by gender of faculty and registered students. Statistics provided by Labour Canada, Statistics Canada, and the Ontario Ministry of Colleges and Universities indicate that, in 1991, the majority of Canadian undergraduate degrees in the sciences and engineering combined were awarded to men; the majority of science graduate degrees were awarded to men; and the vast majority of science instructors at Ontario colleges and universities were men. Why does this imbalance persist? It is commonly believed that the mere passage of time will shift societal attitudes to encourage more women to consider science-related careers. Is it just a matter of time? Or is there something more stubborn about the connection between science and a masculine perspective that resists our attempts to bring gender equity to the classroom?

For well over a decade, I have instructed biology courses in diploma, science undergraduate, professional undergraduate and master's programs at a Canadian university. Simultaneously, I have conducted a nationally-funded scientific research program in genetics and worked with a group of academics to establish a women's studies program at my institution. Reflections concerning social and environmental responsibility have recently motivated me to reevaluate my research program, with the decision to close it down entirely. Furthermore, a variety of recent opportunities have enabled me to reflect on the interface of gender and science as it relates to both research and teaching. These opportunities included the following: (1) attendance at recent conferences targetting women, science and education;[1] (2) a six-month research associateship at the Five Colleges Women's Studies Research Institute at Mount Holyoke College in Massachusetts;[2] (3) discussions with collaborators at a Canadian Association of University Teachers' Status of Women Conference;[3] (4) readings in the feminist science literature and the feminist pedagogy literature; and

(5) the experience of being the sole woman faculty member for a decade, with thirty male departmental colleagues. It is the culmination of these reflections on the topic of post-secondary science education that I present here.

In my view, curriculum transformation is a crucial strategy for bringing gender balance into science. In other words, I propose that we must reconsider *what* we teach in post-secondary science classes, not just *how* we teach. Many educators and scientists react to such a suggestion with the exclamation, "But science is science, how can you change that?" My response is that there is not only room for but a need for improving science itself as well as for the development of more personal, experiential ties between science and students of science. Transforming the science curriculum would attract more women to the study of science and ultimately provide more balance to science as a discipline.

Several models in the literature on feminist pedagogy have focussed on curriculum transformations. For example, Peggy McIntosh describes five phases in the process of altering the curriculum and uses examples from science disciplines in her analysis. The first phase of the model is best described as the traditional curriculum where scientific principles and male scientists' contributions are emphasized.[4] The next phase incorporates women scientists (for example, women Nobel Laureates) into the curriculum without altering the basic framework. As a third phase women scientists and women's experiences with science are actually addressed but from the viewpoint of being aberrant or anomalous, deviating from the norm. Next, the fourth phase actually focusses on women and minorities as categories of analysis providing important contributions to science, which is redefined as a multidimensional approach to reality to incorporate these perspectives. Finally, the fifth phase presents a completely transformed curriculum that includes all of these analyses from the previous phase, an inclusive curriculum that reflects the diversity of experiences in science and thus appeals to the diversity of students of science.

How can we approach this inclusive curriculum? Of paramount importance is the support and extension of research focussing on scientific contributions by women and about women, as many women's studies programs in science have developed. Next, of course, these findings need synthesis and integration into mainstream science curriculum. This is a very difficult task, indeed. Any post-secondary curriculum transformation is a formidable exercise and this one has the added problem of strong resistance. With this goal in mind, however, smaller steps can be taken to alter what is taught in post-secondary science curriculum so as to increase the compatibility between women students and science.

First, I recommend the incorporation of more topics concerning science and society issues into the mainstream post-secondary science curriculum. Secondary education often has entire courses devoted to such topics. However, at the post-secondary level, much less emphasis tends to be placed on the relationship of scientific endeavours and societal concerns. From my perspective, this misleads first-year college and university students into thinking that they have just stepped into "real" science. Initiating more separate courses on "science and society" topics would be advantageous but not as valuable as incorporating such issues directly into mainstream science courses. Such inclusion of science-related societal issues into the post-secondary curriculum would attract more women students who, on average, may bring with them a socialization experience with more of an emphasis on societal connections, relationships and concern, as compared to competition and individualized achievement.

A related issue is the incorporation of ethics as a topic into the post-secondary science curriculum. Again, such topics are rarely examined in a systematic manner in science curriculum; values and science have traditionally been considered separate realms. But are they really separate? The feminist science literature has contributed to this question by uncovering many biases inherent in science as they are in all human endeavours. For example, Elizabeth Fee analyzes "objectivity" in science and finds it misrepresented in many instances.[5] The deliberate and systematic inclusion of bias as a topic of study would better represent the realities of science as a discipline, as well as appeal to students, particularly women students, who have generally been found to have a more contextual approach to ethical dilemmas.[6]

The presentation of science as a human endeavour by focussing on scientists' lives and motivations is similarly conspicuous for its absence in the traditional post-secondary science curriculum. This would be easily accomplished by highlighting contributions of selected scientists, including their personal life experiences and motivations as well as the cultural milieu and popular acceptance of their contributions during their era. Such a diversion into the history or the "humanities" component of science would, in my opinion, accomplish just that: incorporate more humanity into science.

I am not suggesting that the presentation of scientific principles be completely replaced by human-related issues, but rather that content presentation be slightly reduced or reorganized to allow for presentation of the issues described. Such a suggestion is often met with skepticism: "Isn't this tantamount to watering down science, or to lowering the quality or standards?" My response is an adamant "Au contraire!" If such a human-oriented science results in attracting and retaining more women in science, as I believe it will, then this approach will eventually influence science as an endeavour. Perhaps more women in science may influence what questions are asked and how national scientific monies are distributed, or have an impact on international scientific policies. I am not suggesting that there are particular changes that women would make in science. What I am suggesting is that whatever develops as "science," as an endeavour practised by a more balanced representation of men and women, would truly be a *human* endeavour, representing human interests and not a masculine endeavour as it is practised now.

Ironically, this objective of encouraging more women into scientific careers corresponds to policies designed by national science funding agencies to maximize Canada's "brain power" and, thereby, optimize our competitive role in the international scientific community. In spite of this laudable policy, I beg to differ with the stated purpose. Rather than maximizing our competitive edge, Canadian science would be intrinsically improved by reflecting the motivations, goals, enthusiasm and work styles of its men *and* its women.

From a focus on *what* is taught in science classrooms, or curriculum issues, I will now shift my attention to science teaching procedures or techniques. By this I mean *how* science topics are presented, or teaching methods that may increase women's participation and success in post-secondary education independent of science content.

Illustrative of the significance of pedagogical techniques for teaching science to women is the work by Mary Belenky, Blythe Clinchy, Nancy Goldberger and Jill Tarule, who analyzed "women's ways of knowing."[7] They describe "five different perspectives from which women view reality and draw conclusions about truth, knowledge, and authority."[8] In particular, science exemplifies what they call separate, procedural knowledge. "Separate" refers to the separation of the knower and the object of study, and "procedural knowledge" is described as "a position in which [a person] is invested in learning and applying objective procedures for obtaining and communicating knowledge."[9] Is there a difference between men and women in their compatibility with this scientific "way of knowing"?

Sue Rosser has considered this question and points out that the manner in which science is conducted and taught is less compatible with the "way of knowing" of many women compared with that of men.[10] Furthermore, Sue Rosser explores the different ways in which many women scientists actually practise science in their disciplines. The women scientists in her examination strictly adhere to the traditional scientific method but, according to Rosser's documentation, they exhibit subtle but significant differences in their choice of problems, formulation of hypotheses, focus of attention in the observational stage, methods of data collection and drawing of conclusions. These differences contrast to the traditional manner in which male scientists approach their tasks. With this evidence that women's "ways of knowing" are on average less compatible with science as well as the indication that women scientists *do* science slightly differently, we can reasonably conclude that women's ways of learning science might well be different.

A recurrent theme in the literature about how to teach science to women students is the notion that women learn well when their subjective experience is integrated with learning. For example, Fran Davis and Arlene Steiger have helped to alter physics instruction with this integration in mind.[11] Similarly, Anne Fausto-Sterling echos this idea when she recommends that "more thought needs to be given to teaching about science as a part of daily life."[12] The exploration of science and society topics as well as ethical issues in science

149

offers excellent opportunities for such integrative approaches.

Another common thread offered by many specialists in feminist teaching is the successful teaching of new cognitive skills through emotional pathways. For example, Anne Fausto-Sterling "encouraged students to move beyond a recounting of 'the facts,' trying to get them to talk about their emotional reactions to what they read.[13] "Related to this is the strategy of trying to reduce the distance between the student and the object being studied, or between the knower and the known. Feminist scientists such as Evelyn Fox Keller have highlighted the traditional masculine emphasis of objectivity in science as uncomfortable for women.[14] Any classroom techniques that can connect the knower with the known, such as describing scientists' passion for their study organisms, would help to appeal to women students.

Another component of teaching methodology that may have a differential impact on women and men students is the interdisciplinary approach to science presentation. Sue Rosser notes that "women students will be more attracted to science and its methods when they perceive its usefulness in other disciplines."[15] She attributes this to women's interest in relationships and connections and proceeds to document several interdisciplinary college programs that successfully attract women students. As an example, I would propose a class exploration of a general concept such as continental drift by examining the different scientific principles across disciplines (chemistry, physics, biology and geology) that pertain to understanding the issue. This interdisciplinary approach, although untraditional at the post-secondary level, has powerful potential for teaching science.

A related teaching and learning method for attracting and retaining more women into science is the incorporation of collaborative learning into the science classroom. Such a model would include dividing the students into small working groups, each of which would be responsible for solving a problem or becoming familiar with a scientific concept. Individual mastery of the learning assignment is only one of the tasks of the group; students would then be encouraged to help other group members to understand the material. This emphasis on sharing a goal through cooperative learning has the potential of appealing to women students, many of whom may be uncomfortable (or unfamiliar through socialization) with the more individual and competitive teaching and learning methods characteristic of our present post-secondary science education.

Finally, teaching style has, in my view, much to do with the retention and success of women in studying post-secondary science. By teaching style, I am referring to neither content nor teaching techniques but rather to subtle gender sensitivities in the classroom. Many of my suggestions will seem obvious to primary and secondary educators but they remain problematic in many post-secondary settings.

First is using examples for scientific concepts that are either gender-free or at least alternating examples that are meaningful for women students with the more common ones that are traditionally meaningful to men. As an example of examples, I have always been surprised at the lack of textile-related analogies in the presentation of scientific concepts. In the discipline of forest ecology, terms such as "food chain" predominate in the presentation of ecological interactions; the term "weaving" is conspicuous for its absence in this context.

As another example, the use of gender-neutral language when referring to students, scientists and scientific professionals remains yet an aspiration. As early as 1978, Wendy Martyna showed the negative effects on girls and women when generic terms such as "he" and "man" are used.[16] Most primary education textbooks have been purged of stereotypical language and illustrations and, concomitantly, teachers have developed sensitivity to the importance of avoiding discriminatory language. However, many post-secondary educators, particularly in the sciences and science-related professions, have not been exposed to a milieu of gender sensitivity. Thus, it is not at all uncommon to hear post-secondary instructors refer to students and scientists in the masculine gender. Correcting this language discrepancy is a crucial step.

Next, instructor awareness of gender differences in classroom dynamics plays an important role in the success of women students. Research on gender differences in group interactions indicates that, on average, men more often interrupt in discussions and often contribute more assertively to discussions.[17] I was suddenly reminded of these research findings in one of my own classes of graduate students, composed of one woman and five men. I had just responded to the woman student's question with a short answer and directed an extended query exploring the implications of this question to two of the men students. The realization that I had been neglecting the woman student shocked me into an appreciation that even I, a woman instructor, had assimilated the accepted "style" of teaching. Awareness of these issues with teaching style adjustment would improve the comfort level of women students in higher education.

The importance of women role models for post-secondary women students of science cannot be over-emphasized. Why would young women seek a science-related career if they had rarely seen women in such a career before? Do you know many women scientists? I certainly did not and still do not. How many young women today are foregoing a satisfying career in science or a science-related discipline because it is beyond reality to even imagine it?

A critical issue concerning this lack of women role models in science is the confusion many young women report about combining marriage, a family and a scientific career. Karen Arnold's study of high school graduates indicated striking differences in career choices between young men and women and these were directly related to young women's concerns about marriage and family.[18] My experience with young women science students has emphasized to me that this is a crucial issue in the minds of these students. Without role models, mentors and a forum for discussing these issues, untold numbers of women are redirecting their career aspirations away from science.

As a final suggestion concerning teaching styles that encourage women in post-secondary education, I would propose exactly that: offering active and constant academic encouragement to young women in the sciences. This entails spending time and attention on women science students and their academic concerns. This is not, of course, a revolutionary suggestion. All students tend to improve academically with direct attention and guidance; however, I propose this suggestion with a deeper meaning in this context. As indicated in my recommendations about curriculum transformation, I believe that women in particular would be more attracted to and comfortable with science if it were presented in more of a social, cultural and ethical context. A teaching style of personal contact and encouragement acts as a microcosm of this model.

I personally attempt to emphasize interactions with women students on a one-to-one basis before and after class, during office hours or during happenstance encounters. I often initiate questions about an individual student's career goals and am pleased to respond to more personal queries about my thoughts on combining a personal life with a scientific career. Research on science and gender in secondary schools confirms that young women who have an opportunity for discussing their concerns about the implications of an untraditional career on the rest of their lives tend to have a more positive attitude towards pursuing such untraditional career goals.

This concept of discussing concerns with women science students forms the foundation of my conclusion. For too long we have viewed science as an immutable enterprise, unchangeable and immoveable. We have tried to effect change in societal attitudes and to mould women students into appreciating the challenges and rewards inherent in studying science. Without abandoning those tactics, I suggest an additional objective. We need to listen to women's concerns in science, including young women studying science as well as women scientists, and be willing to consider making changes in science, both as it is instructed and as it is practised. Without more women in science, can it ever truly be representative of all of humanity?

NOTES

1. The Sixth and Seventh International Conferences on Gender and Science and Technology (GASAT), held in Melbourne, Australia in 1991 and Waterloo, Canada in 1993, and the conference on "Teaching and Learning Liberation: Feminist Pedagogies" held in Saskatoon, Canada in 1993.
2. I am grateful to the Five Colleges Women's Studies Research Institute for their space, support and encouragement.
3. CAUT Status of Women Conference, Halifax, October 16–18, 1992. Many of the ideas presented here result from discussions at that conference with Mary Frances Richardson of Brock University in Ontario and Hilda Taylor of Acadia University in Nova Scotia. I am grateful for their input.
4. McIntosh 1983.

5. Fee 1982.
6. Gilligan 1982.
7. Belenky et al. 1986.
8. Belenky et al. 1986: 3.
9. Belenky et al. 1986: 15.
10. Rosser 1990.
11. Davis and Steiger 1991.
12. Fausto-Sterling 1985.
13. Fausto-Sterling 1986.
14. Keller 1985.
15. Rosser 1990: 64.
16. Martyna 1978.
17. Spender 1980.
18. Cited in Rosser 1990.

Women Don't Count in Our Classrooms

Beth Rubin and Christine L. Cooper

Attitudes and behaviours frequently found within universities limit the opportunities for women to participate and perform well as university students. We begin with a true vignette that depicts the events of a faculty teaching workshop which the authors, both assistant professors, attended in the role of students. We use the vignette to illustrate 1) how sexist attitudes are manifested in behaviours that constitute barriers to women's effective performance at university, and 2) how the barriers are compounded when others deem the issue to be unimportant. We conclude with recommendations for university actions that can reduce and eventually eliminate the barriers to women's participation in and performance at universities.[1]

CASE IN POINT: A TEACHING WORKSHOP FOR PROFESSORS
Our management faculty is concerned about providing our students with high quality instruction in the classroom. In an effort to promote such quality, our dean and associate dean arranged a faculty workshop on "Teaching with Cases." They hired two national, case-method experts to prepare and conduct a two-day workshop. The workshop was designed to provide both a general overview of the objectives and processes of teaching with cases (for those who were largely unfamiliar with the case method) as well as discussions and exercises to aid those faculty who already use cases in improving the teaching skills particular to this pedagogy. All professors in the faculty were offered the opportunity to attend, without fee. Approximately forty interested faculty members and instructors from local accounting firms attended the workshop.

Participants were each sent a textbook to read before the workshop. About three-fourths of the text contained descriptions of experiences and ideas of university teachers; the vast majority of the teachers described were male. The experiences and ideas of female teachers were limited primarily to the "Special Considerations" chapter of the text. In addition, the language of the text was not inclusive, i.e., sensitive to including different groups of people. For instance, the textbook included casual references to "the girl in the back row" or "the person with the beard in the front row," or "students" who bring their "wives" or "girlfriends" to dinners or parties.

At the start of the workshop, the two instructors distributed additional materials, including exercises and several example cases, all of which portrayed the case decision-makers as males with Anglo or European surnames. The workshop began, simply, with a discussion of what the case method of teaching is and how it is superior to other teaching techniques. Early in this discussion, one of the presenters told a joke: "It's like the one about the man who's married to a woman who nags constantly. You know, nag! nag! nag! Finally, at long last, they get divorced. And what does he do? He goes out and gets married again! It's the triumph of hope over reason!"

Despite this questionable icebreaker, the discussion progressed and three major points emerged: 1) that the case method is different from all other teaching techniques in that it brings into the classroom a "real-world" problem, one with which a manager or executive actually wrestled; 2) that when a problem is brought intact into the classroom, the students are intrigued by its "real-worldliness" and are motivated to give the case their best shot and then to compare their solution to the one actually implemented by the manager/ executive in the case; and 3) that the students must come to identify personally with managers/executives in the cases, to put themselves in the managers' shoes and vicariously experience the problems, in order to maximize their motivation and learning.

Following the discussion, the instructors directed our attention to the first exercise, which was based on the first example case in our workshop materials. The case involved one "Mr. Alex Jones," a vice-president of Canadian operations for an international hotel chain. During the discussion of this case, one of the authors asked whether attaching a name to the decision-maker in the case was really necessary. "Mightn't naming the decision-maker 'Alex Jones,' or any other name, inhibit certain groups of students from identifying with the decision-maker? Couldn't an instructor facilitate student identification with the decision-maker more readily by just having the case say 'You are the vice-president of Canadian operations . . . '"? The workshop instructors answered "no," argued that student motivation and learning stem from the "real-worldliness" of a case (as opposed to the aforementioned student identi-fication with the decision-maker), and concluded, therefore, that changing the decision-maker's name would not be advisable since it sacrificed the objective of bringing the data intact from the "real world" into the classroom.

Another female faculty participant refocussed the question: "Which would be more important for effective learning: conveying the case data exactly as it occurred in the "real world" or facilitating student identification with the decision-maker, even if that entailed making changes in the 'real world' data?" At this point, a male faculty participant suggested that "bringing data intact into the classroom probably meant holding up examples of white, male decision-makers that could reinforce systemic barriers to women and other minorities in business." We discussed these issues for ten or fifteen minutes before the workshop instructors brought our discussion to a close. They reiterated their original position, and added further arguments that 1) removing the decision-maker's name would actually make student identification with the decision-maker more difficult, and 2) changing the gender of the decision-maker would constitute a gross deviation from the actual "real world" events of the case. The instructors concluded that any or all of these efforts would ultimately compromise the students' motivation and learning.

The discussion was clearly focussed on how to maximize student learning using the case method. The questions regarding the implied gender of named decision-makers raised the concern that women may be less able to identify with the named decision-makers and, thus, may learn less from the pedagogical technique. Nonetheless, many of the workshop participants hastily concurred with the speakers and belittled the issues raised by saying that these issues were really peripheral to the topic of using the case method of teaching. They said things like "This is stupid. The point is to describe what really happened in the case," and "We do this all the time in accounting. No one complains about not being able to identify with the decision-maker." Other participants actively ridiculed the concern, with comments like "Well, if this is such a concern, perhaps we should make the manager a female, diabetic Nigerian."

After the lunch break, several of the female faculty participants did not return for the workshop's afternoon session due to previous commitments. The "scuttlebutt" among the returning participants was that the women who did not return were obviously upset at not having their views supported that morning. During the afternoon session, several participants commented to one of the authors that the morning discussion was inappropriate. They claimed that, if those concerns needed to be raised at all, they should have been raised at another time and place; such a "special interest" issue should not have taken valuable workshop time from those who were there to learn about teaching with the case method.

One author decided not to return to the workshop after that afternoon. The other author (having missed the afternoon session) rejoined the workshop that evening. However, she remained as a passive observer, one who was not comfortable offering ideas or raising issues. She, too, decided not to return to the workshop the following day.

BARRIERS TO WOMEN IN THE UNIVERSITY: TEACHING MATERIALS AND CLASSROOM COMMUNICATION THAT COUNT WOMEN "OUT"
This vignette illustrates several factors that made the faculty workshop far less accessible to many of the female participants than to the male participants. These factors include the sexist images and language used in written teaching materials and the demeaning messages implicit in the formal and informal communication between and among the instructor and students in the class-

room. Each of these factors constitutes a different mode of communicating non-inclusionary, sexist views. And while no single factor was extraordinarily harmful in and of itself, the cumulative effect of the factors was to alienate several female professors from the workshop.

This outcome reflects the findings of a great deal of research on the "chilly climate" in universities, findings that document the systemic barriers often faced by women in academia.[2] The research shows that each problem or slight a woman experiences is likely to be minor, but the frequency and pervasiveness of such encounters create a major problem: a climate in which women feel that they are not important, do not have the right to take up others' time and should not raise concerns or issues that men don't share. Despite the thorough documentation of these problems, it is the authors' experiences that the majority of university faculty members fail to recognize such phenomena.[3]

Therefore, we will systematically consider each of the above factors. We will 1) provide at least one example of each factor, based on our experiences in the role of students during the faculty workshop described above; 2) provide other examples of each factor that we have observed and/or encountered; and 3) document the effect that each factor had on us during the faculty workshop and is likely to have on other women students in universities.

TEACHING MATERIALS
One potential barrier to women's effective performance in universities is the verbal and pictorial images portrayed in many written teaching materials: textbooks, cases, readings, exercises, etc. These teaching materials frequently incorporate images that reflect the current state of society and societal views. However, many university teaching materials have failed to keep pace with the recent and rapid changes in the role of women in society.

Recall, for example, the textbook used in the faculty workshop described in the vignette. The experiences and ideas described in the text were largely those of male university teachers; the experiences and ideas of female teachers were limited primarily to the chapter of the text about "Special Considerations." Furthermore, not one of the example cases used in the workshop portrayed a woman in the role of decision-maker.

This exclusion of women from significant roles is common within university teaching materials. Even though women comprise 52 percent of the Canadian population, over 40 percent of the Canadian labour force, over 30 percent of entrepreneurs and over 32 percent of all managers and administrators,[4] most textbook examples of workers, leaders, and decision-makers are men.[5] Similarly, when women are presented in cases, they are often portrayed in the role of the person who is encountering or even causing the problem. The decision-maker who must identify and solve the problem is typically a male with a western European name.

The differential importance of men and women as portrayed in the verbal images is also likely to be supported by gendered language in the textbook and other teaching materials. This gendered language may be manifest in several ways: using a masculine pronoun to refer to all people (e.g., "go up to the customer and ask him . . ."); using terms for roles that imply the people who hold them will be or, even worse, should be male (e.g., fireman); using masculine pronouns to refer to incumbents of jobs that are stereotyped as being male, and feminine pronouns to refer to incumbents of jobs that are stereotyped as being female (e.g., referring to a manager as he and to his secretary as she); referring to females with terms that imply youth, unimportance or subordination (e.g., comparing girls with men or people); and assuming that the people who are important in a mixed-sex group are the men (e.g., "the members of the tribe fled, leaving behind all their property and their women and children").[6]

Finally, the differential importance of men and women is also evident in the pictorial images portrayed in the materials. When textbooks, cases, readings and exercises are illustrated, the overwhelming majority of pictures, particularly those of decision-makers, are of men. When women are depicted, they are most often shown in roles and jobs that have been historically dominated by women and that have little social status, such as homemakers, secretaries and food servers.[7]

Thus, the verbal and pictorial images in many teaching materials foster traditional stereotypes of men and women. The images encourage both male and female students to continue stereotyping men and women into historically traditional roles. And the underlying messages behind such stereotyping are that women are less-than-legitimate in certain roles and that, in most work-related situations, the people who really matter are likely to be men. These messages effectively inhibit women's pursuing traditionally "masculine" opportunities and occupations, and thereby maintain and foster access discrimination in women's careers.

CLASSROOM COMMUNICATION

In addition to the language and imagery in teaching materials, another potential barrier to women's effective performance in universities comes in the form of demeaning oral communication in the classroom. This communication can come from the professor during lectures and discussions and/or from other students during class discussions and small group interactions. During these processes, both professors and students comment not only on the issues being taught, but also on the participation of the students, on the university and faculty in which they study, and on a host of other topics. Often jokes are told. Subtle sexism is regularly evident in these types of classroom communications,[8] which some would consider the quintessential aspect of university teaching.

Perhaps the most important source of gender stereotypes is the communication of professors. Because of the authority inherent in a professor's position in the classroom, students often come to view professors as the intellectual and social leaders of a class. As a result, students frequently assume that the information presented by a professor is unequivocally "correct," if not in a "real world" sense, then at least in the sense that it must be relayed as such in an exam. Therefore, the attitudes and behaviours expressed by a professor (and assumed to be "correct" by the students) can have a strong influence on both the students' immediate feelings about being in the class and their more enduring expectations regarding appropriate behaviour in the professional world.

Recall, for example, the joke told by one of the presenters at the faculty workshop: the one about the man who's married to a woman who nags constantly. The joke assumes that 1) we are all familiar with the annoying, nagging behaviour of many women; 2) a reasonable man would not get married again, due to the strong likelihood that his new wife also would be a nag; and 3) some idealistic men nevertheless maintain hope that they'll find that one-in-a-million woman who won't nag—thus, we see "the triumph of hope over reason." The assumptions implicit in this joke are neither explicitly stated nor analytically critiqued aloud. Nonetheless, they are the assumptions one must hold in order to understand the humour in the joke, and to find it funny. They are the assumptions the instructor assumed the workshop audience held when he told the joke. However, several workshop participants did not hold these assumptions, did not find the joke to be funny and, therefore, experienced alienation from the group of participants who did find the joke to be humorous.

Similar experiences of alienation may also come from sexist messages inherent in professors' comments that imply that female students are less well prepared, less bright, less articulate or have fewer analytical or quantitative skills than their male counterparts. Such messages, whether couched in humour or not, are based on assumptions that are demeaning and derogatory towards women and convey the idea that women students are not the students who matter. When professors express humour at women's expense, women quickly come to understand the message that they are of less importance than men in the classroom.[9] Many women students seem to take this message to heart. As in other settings, women are less vocal in the classroom (i.e., less likely to ask questions, answer questions and/or offer points of discussion)[10] and, therefore, may earn lower scores for classroom participation. Women are also less likely to go to the professor for help with problems. Overall then, the attitudes and behaviours expressed by professors have a strong influence on women students' mental and emotional involvement in the university process, which may result in lower levels of learning.

Professors' expressed attitudes and behaviours can also have a strong influence on students' enduring expectations regarding proper behaviour in the world of work. In many disciplines, professors act as role models for students, showing them what professionals in their chosen fields are "like." Sexist language by a professor teaches both male and female students that such language is acceptable in the field and sexist jokes teach students that this kind of humour on the job is not only appropriate, but perhaps even admirable. In addition, sexist, stereotypic remarks towards students (e.g., "I would have asked Jane, but I wouldn't want her to cry") teach students the way that some professionals view the appropriate roles for men and women in today's society. And here again, the comments espoused by the professor, which are assumed to be acceptable professional behaviour, devalue (however subtly) the group being ridiculed or insulted.

Sexist ideas also may be evident within the communication among students during class discussions or small group interactions. Jokes and comments based on sexist assumptions regularly arise. These remarks are frequently made by males, either directly or by implication, to the other men in the audience. While the sender obviously understands that there are women in attendance, and that they are probably listening, his comments are not addressed to them. This omission, of course, belittles the women in the group. And while professors may not explicitly make such remarks, they may allow students to express them without comment or disagreement, and some students will likely interpret such a reaction as implied consent. In any event, the relative worth of men versus women in the university is again being communicated. While women are allowed to be at university, they are not really welcome there. The casual, off-colour and "fun" comments in the classroom are made by and for the people who matter (the men) at the expense of those who are less important (the women). The women don't really count.[11]

In summary, sexist ideas are often reflected in communications that occur in a university classroom. They are implicit in jokes and comments that assume or imply that women are in some way lesser (e.g., stupid, unorganized), inherently negative (e.g., manipulative, gossipy) or nothing more than sexual creatures.[12] These remarks may be made by professors or by students, either male or female.

While such comments often yield laughter and the apparent general approval from the class, they ultimately serve to undermine university students by teaching and/or reinforcing sexist attitudes that will make their pursuit of success in the work world more difficult. Again, this is true for both male and female students. Increasingly, the business world contains both men and women in all occupations. Women who have had traditional stereotypes reinforced through certain university learning experiences will likely have a more difficult time pursuing a managerial role, supervising men, and helping and being helped by women peers. Men who have had traditional stereotypes reinforced through university experiences will likely have a more difficult time being supervised by women, helping and being helped by women peers, and supervising women subordinates when the supervisors' performance depends on the performance of their subordinates. These are particularly poor lessons to be teaching in a time when Canada's global competitiveness depends, at least in part, on effective cooperation among an increasingly diverse and educated labour force.

COMPOUNDING BARRIERS:
DEEMING GENDER EQUITY A "SPECIAL INTEREST" TOPIC

The described barriers to women's effective performance in university are compounded when others deem the issues to be unimportant. For example, recall the issue raised during the case teaching workshop in the vignette (i.e., what effect did naming a case decision-maker have on different students' ability to identify themselves as the person in that role?) and some of the participants' responses to the issue: "This is stupid. The point is to describe what really happened in the case," "We do this all the time in accounting [and] no one complains . . . ," and "Well, if this is such a concern, perhaps we should make the manager a female, diabetic Nigerian." Remember, too, that several participants later commented that the discussion around the issue had been an inappropriate use of workshop time.

All of these comments conveyed the message that the gender issue raised was neither central nor important. At best, the issue was seen as one that is peripherally related to the "real" issues of teaching: mastery of the teaching technique (e.g., group work, teaching with cases), mastery of arcane sub fields within an academic area, mastery of designing perfect tests, and mastery of new computer programs that make compiling grades easier. According to the majority of workshop participants, gender issues are tangential to the process and outcome of education and, therefore, should be addressed only as a special interest topic, if at all.

Women students are likely to hear similar remarks in the classroom. When these students raise or address gender-related concerns, the reaction from professors and from fellow students is often negative. Common reactions include ridicule, dismissing the issue, and/or labelling the women as overly sensitive or unrealistic. If professors do not openly take such a position, they often allow other students to express these positions without comment or disagreement. Such reactions effectively define classroom topics as either "central" or "peripheral" (some would say "legitimate" or "illegitimate") on the basis of whether the majority (and especially the professor) is comfortable hearing them, rather than on the basis of their importance or effect on education.

All of these problems and their negative effects on women, and to a lesser extent on men, have been explored and documented for years. University students, particularly female students, are able to describe such problems in detail. Nonetheless, the prevailing attitude among many academics is to continue to regard the sexism of pedagogical materials, and of instructors' classroom conduct (especially oral communication), as peripheral to the topic of effective teaching. Rather, these issues are viewed as ancillary topics, which are of interest only to special interest groups. Therefore, when women at university do identify or raise gender-related concerns, they are likely to be penalized (e.g., ridiculed or dismissed) for doing so. They are also likely to be marginalized as being members of a special interest group, and therefore biased. Consequently, even if women are well-versed in the issues raised, their audience is likely to discount their arguments as inaccurate, given their personal bias toward advancing their own interests. Once marginalization has occurred, anything women say about gender issues is easily discounted.

Many women are afraid to be, or simply choose not to be, so marginalized. Therefore, both professors and students learn to share ideas, raise issues and discuss strengths and weaknesses related to just about any issue except gender equity. And through such self-censorship, women actively contribute to the maintenance of the view that gender issues are peripheral, illegitimate and special interest topics.

Numerous university practices further support this view. For example, we noted that gender sensitivity is often not considered a relevant criterion to use when selecting textbooks, cases or other course materials. Furthermore, when universities offer teaching instruction, either for graduate students who wish to enter academia or for professors who wish to increase their knowledge and skills, gender inclusiveness and gender equity are rarely discussed. Very few graduate students who are learning how to teach are explicitly trained in avoiding sexism when teaching or when developing written teaching materials. In fact, many graduate students learn the opposite when they witness and model respected and otherwise knowledgeable experts who display sexism in the ways previously described. Similarly, very few current professors have been trained or are being trained in avoiding sexism in the classroom. As the opening vignette shows, even the currently fashionable teaching techniques maintain the likelihood of sexism in classrooms. Finally, gender issues are not considered relevant criteria to consider when selecting guest speakers, workshop educators, conference presenters or other educational leaders.[13]

All of these practices work to maintain the view that gender equity in the classroom constitutes a special interest topic, one that is not of concern to most professors. We find this view to be disturbing. It denies the reality that over half of undergraduates and about a third of graduate students are women.[14] Given these statistics, we believe that sexism within teaching materials or an instructor's style in the classroom is likely to have three detrimental effects. These effects include making learning more difficult for nearly half the students; failing to prepare the students for the sizeable proportion of female peers, subordinates and supervisors they will encounter in the workplace; and reinforcing student attitudes and behaviours that will likely inhibit their job performance and make it more difficult for them to succeed. This should be of grave concern to all educators.

WHAT CAN UNIVERSITIES AND COLLEGES DO?
We recommend that university administrators interested in overcoming gender inequity in the classroom pursue two endeavours. In the short term, administrators need to publicly and financially support gender sensitivity in the teaching

pedagogy used by the faculty. This would likely entail training professors in the importance of gender-neutral pedagogy; establishing criteria to be used in evaluating different pedagogical methods; training professors in how to identify problems with pedagogy from a student's point of view; and funding and rewarding faculty time taken to evaluate and change pedagogy in support of diversity. Over the long run, administrators need to include sensitivity to gender differences as an explicit criterion for selecting personnel for administrative, regular faculty, staff, visiting faculty and guest speakers. This would involve openly informing applicants that gender sensitivity is a priority among the faculty, training selection committees in applying established criteria to be used in assessing applicants, and rigorously screening applicants to find those who are supportive of the idea of a gender-neutral faculty culture.

We recognize that pursuit of these recommended endeavours would basically constitute systematically changing the organizational cultures of many faculties or universities. We further recognize the substantial investment of both time and money required by such a pursuit. Nevertheless, we believe that the benefits to the students, to the university and to society from providing truly equal opportunities for women students in university, will far outweigh the costs.

NOTES

1. The authors wish to acknowledge that, while the issues presented in this paper are couched exclusively in terms of gender, the vast majority of our arguments are equally applicable to the issue of race.

2. Both women instructors and students face a "chilly climate," as described by Constance Backhouse 1988 and Backhouse et al. 1989. Many published and unpublished analyses of university climates as experienced by women (e.g., analyses by the Council of Ontario Universities, the University of Toronto, York University, the Canadian Association of University Teachers (CAUT) and others) have also found systemic barriers.

3. These problems have been documented at all educational levels, from elementary school through to university. Research by Sadker and Sadker 1985, Serbin and O'Leary 1979, and Guttentag and Bray 1977 identified significant gender discrimination in primary and secondary grades, including calling more on boys, providing boys with more feedback and giving boys more attention. Selma Greenberg's work (1988) indicates that these actions can produce passivity and learned helplessness within girls. Research at university levels, such as Fleming's (1984) analysis of male and female students, Aisenberg and Harrington's (1988) study of women academics, and many unpublished internal studies, have found that women students perceive unfair treatment, and over their university years show lower confidence, assertiveness and achievement motivational levels. Tidball (1973) also conducted research that strongly supports the widespread nature and effects of gender discrimination. He found that women who have achieved at high levels, such that they are listed in *Who's Who of American Women*, are twice as likely to have attended all-female universities and colleges than coeducational ones.

4. These statistics are drawn from Judge Rosalie Abella's (1984) report on the women and other disadvantaged groups in Canadian society and Anderson's (1991)

comparative study of the status of women in twelve countries.

5. For example, Carole Hahn et al. (1988) showed that social science textbooks are far less likely to depict women in high level and leadership positions than men, present women in stereotypical professions, have far fewer biographies of women than they do of men, etc. Unpublished research conducted by students at the University of Manitoba show similar findings for textbooks in management. Morgen and Moran's (1990) paper on changing curriculum materials in one discipline highlights some common and interesting examples.

6. The characteristics of gendered language, and the problems in communication clarity and images of women and women's roles that result, have been thoroughly documented by Miller and Swift 1988, 1991; Spender 1980; and Eichler and Lapointe, 1985.

7. Unpublished research by University of Manitoba students and by Beth Rubin has shown this. A perusal through virtually any illustrated textbook in management, science, literature, psychology and a host of other fields demonstrates this, as would most journals in those fields.

8. Virtually all of the university assessments of the "climate" faced by women reflect the damage done by such informal communication processes. See descriptions in Backhouse 1988; Backhouse et al. 1989; Aisenberg and Harrington 1988; Spender 1989; Fox-Keller 1977; and Weisstein 1977.

9. Barreca (1991) presents an incisive analysis of gender and humour, particularly describing the messages underlying such humour and the effects on its targets. She also provides several interesting examples of the use of humour in academic settings by male professors towards female students or peers.

10. Both of Spender's (1980, 1989) books document the fact that women generally speak far less than men, particularly in academic settings. Aisenberg and Harrington's (1988) interviews with female academics and Fox-Keller's (1977) and Weisstein's (1977) descriptions of their graduate training also paint a graphic picture of the silencing of women in universities.

11. See Barreca (1991) for a detailed analysis.

12. A Canadian university is currently conducting an investigation into one professor who allegedly remarked to his class, regarding a female student, "We know she has a vagina, but does she have a brain?"

13. Sadker and Sadker's (1988) article shows that most education of teachers fails to address the issue of sexism. However, some universities are making concerted efforts to change their practices. Volume 18 of the journal *Women's Studies Quarterly* (1990), a special issue on curricular and institutional change, describes many attempts to deal with this problem. Beck et al. (1990) describe a program of broad changes at the University of Maryland; Spector (1990) describes a similar large-scale program at the University of Minnesota; Crawley and Ecker (1990) describe efforts in a particular discipline; and Cannon (1990) describes specific pedagogical techniques for use in individual classes. Most of these authors describe opposition to the movement towards gender-neutral pedagogy from both within and outside their departments, faculties and universities. These programs are still extremely rare and, as Backhouse (1988) reports, often are implemented more in name than in substance.

14. Cited from *Women in the Labour Force* (1986) and the CAUT's (1993a) report on the status of women in Canadian universities.

For Her Own Good? Women and Safety at Post-Secondary Institutions

Nancy Johnston

Perhaps the most disturbing barrier for women in post-secondary education is the uncomfortable and too often hostile campus environment. [1]

Students can make a difference. Real progress has been made in the last fifteen years towards creating safer and more equitable post-secondary campuses. Women students across Canada have committed time and creativity to supporting advocacy offices and sexual harassment centres, raising funds for and often running self-defense courses and publicly voicing their concern about women's safety.

Changes, even small ones, have been hard won. Many feminist students involved in campus safety issues, whether lobbying for better parking lot lighting, campaigning to raise awareness on date rape or speaking as members on university safety committees, have helped to change attitudes and policies. But the commitment of energy to longer projects, especially to reorganizing existing safety services, is particularly difficult for graduate and undergraduate women. Often our political energies are directed toward (or divided by) important and immediate campus concerns. The personal and academic costs for such commitment also are high. Concerned professors, supervisors and family remind us of our other academic and professional work and the fact that we must eventually graduate. Nevertheless, the anger, frustration, fear and hope of fellow students and our common concerns about physical safety lead many of us to advocate for more control over security services on campus.

In the fall of 1991, we began research on safety and security practices and provisions at our own institution, York University, a large Ontario university of approximately 45,000 students.[2] As graduate women teaching and studying at York, we were interested in how existing security practices and provisions did, or did not, address the safety needs of graduate women students. In the course of our research, we became aware not only of the need for change to concrete practices and provisions for the York campus security, but also of the general approach to and analysis of safety that organizes and mobilizes York Security.

Our original report[3] for the York University Task Force on the Status of Graduate Women focussed on our own specific university site and the safety of graduate women who study *and* work on that campus. The purpose of this article is to expand our study of York University and to encourage similar work on women's safety on other Canadian campuses. As many feminist activists and researchers have pointed out, issues of violence against women and the safety of women students have for too long been ignored.

While graduate women may face certain risks that other women on campus do not, most campus safety issues—such as poor lighting—affect all women (and men) at most post-secondary institutions. Other recent studies concerned with women's physical safety on Canadian campuses, such as the final report from the Canadian Panel on Violence Against Women (1993), confirm this finding. At the same time, the assumption that graduate women, or all women students, share identical safety concerns smoothes over differences between these women and their security needs, and concerns related to other issues such as their race, sexual preference, religious and political orientation, etc. To address this, we tried to highlight and suggest remedies for some problems of particular concern to graduate women of minority groups, such as women with disabilities, lesbians and women of colour. This study and similar reports on other campuses recommend that all security employees undergo education aimed at sensitizing them to the various safety problems of women and other minority groups, and encourage them to work with advocacy groups on campus and other knowledgeable organizations to devise effective solutions to these problems.

RESULTS OF TWO YORK SAFETY STUDIES
Over a two-year period, we collected data in two open-ended surveys of graduate women and examined additional data from a union survey of 272 women graduate students working as teaching assistants.[4] This survey was produced by Canadian Union of Educational Workers (CUEW),[5] representing contract employees and teaching assistants at York University. Perhaps the most significant finding overall is the enormous amount of fear women have for their safety. At York, more than 85 percent of graduate women respondents to the CUEW union survey stated that they feel unsafe on campus; this sentiment also was confirmed by the other surveys and discussions. Many women (71.4 percent) indicated that they avoid the campus at night for safety reasons. Women stated that they are fearful in nearly every building on campus, in all parking lots, at public transit stops, in the library and even in their own offices and classes. With the increased enrolments of students in Ontario, overcrowding of facilities and offices has become a common feature of the university and college campus. Many women students believed that campus overcrowding had made the campus progressively more dangerous for women. Their perception of danger therefore forces women into making extensive accommodations to remain physically safe.

FOR HER OWN GOOD?

One woman wrote: "I have established a routine that works on the premise that York is unsafe. Therefore, I avoid the campus at night. I ensure that when I am on campus at night I leave with someone." Other respondents to the union survey noted that they try to organize their time so that they work and study on campus only during the day. If forced to be on campus at night, they ensure that they never have to walk alone. One respondent even stated that she brings her dog to protect her at night, "a personal solution to a public problem." Many women also pointed out that they never socialize on campus alone and would never consider doing so. As might be expected, women's fear for their safety escalated after the Montréal Massacre. This tragedy brought home for many women the fact that their fears were neither exaggerated nor unjustified, as might have been previously suggested.

The degree of fear expressed by women is of serious concern. Among other things, it is a clear indication that colleges and universities do not meet their obligation to provide women graduate students with an adequate learning and working environment. It is not enough, however, to report on this fear; we must also attempt to account for it. One reason women say they feel insecure on campus is that provisions to ensure safety from physical violence are often sorely inadequate.

One campus provision that was the subject of great dissatisfaction in the surveys was the availability of emergency phones, that is, phones connecting directly with York University Security, and general-use phones enabling one to dial out. Repeated complaints pointed out that no emergency phones were available in particularly dangerous and isolated places such as building basements, tunnels, labs, bus stops, change rooms in the athletic centre and laundry rooms in campus housing. In addition to requests for more emergency phones, the majority of women emphasized the importance of having regular telephones, especially in their offices or in shared study space such as laboratories. Many women reported feeling at risk without a phone in their offices. According to one respondent: "I have, on two occasions, felt trapped in my office when I detected someone's presence outside my door. With no phone, I couldn't report the suspicious behaviour." Of the graduate women who have office space, 61.3 percent said they would use it more frequently if there was a phone in their office. Any telephone would ensure that these women had direct links with security in the event of safety or health emergencies. A further 81.2 percent wanted a phone in their offices purely for safety reasons. Since our original study, representatives from student federations, unions and campus advocacy groups have lobbied the university for more emergency phones and many have been installed in parking lots, in residence lobbies and in laundry rooms. Women students, however, still emphasize the need for further safety provisions. For women students who want to study or work late on campus, emergency and other telephones are a means of controlling, for themselves, their personal safety.

Another inadequate safety was campus signage in individual buildings, building complexes and on the campus in general. Nearly half of the women surveyed found directional signs in buildings to be inadequate and an even greater 70.7 percent felt lost in campus buildings. They found that their personal sense of safety was undermined by difficulties in locating elevators, finding alternative routes around campus construction sites and negotiating their way through the campus tunnel system. The lack of directional signs accommodating persons with disabilities also was mentioned by respondents. The scarcity of large print maps, braille signs, enlarged floor plans and colour directional arrows remains an issue on many Canadian campuses.

Inadequate campus lighting has long been a concern for women advocating better safety. In campus safety audits, in guides on college or university campuses and in city planning, lighting is usually the first safety issue mentioned in community efforts to enhance safety and security in public space. Insufficient lighting has a substantial impact on the degree of fear expressed by all students. At York University, good lighting in tunnels between buildings, parking lots, around construction sites and wooded areas was said to be particularly important. The same was said about the lighting on the busiest foot paths between buildings and in and around bus stops and shelters.

As well as these security provisions, several services of great importance to women at York were found to be inadequate. One such security-run service has been York's Escort Service. Many other Canadian campuses, among them Carleton, Dalhousie and Western, have launched successful student initiatives and volunteer programs to ensure late night escorts for students, staff and faculty. York's Escort Service is operated solely by security officers and trained personnel. At present, York University Security claims to be the first Canadian university to offer a combined foot and van escort service run by paid security personnel. Women, persons with disabilities and people travelling on campus alone are given priority for escorts. Unfortunately, although the service is a popular one, poor communication between security personnel and the York community has meant that the escort service's policy, mandate and operational procedures are often not well-publicized. During our first survey of the graduate women who did use the service, 36 percent stated that waiting periods, reportedly up to 45 minutes per escort, were far too long. Moreover, 26.6 percent reported having to wait at unsafe spots outside campus buildings, which left them feeling even more at risk than had they simply walked to their destination alone. For this reason, some women stopped using the service and opted to take their chances. Beyond these problems, women reported feeling uncomfortable and even harassed by escorts who were described as insensitive and patronizing to women's concerns. Other kinds of inappropriate behaviour carried on in escort vans and/or condoned by escorts also were reported. One woman confided, "One of my experiences in the escort vans involved dropping off a bunch of male students at the edge of campus. . . . they were heading to the strip joint just across the street and joking about it. I find this very disturbing." In a recent move to address some of the student concerns and to streamline the on-call escort service in a climate of budget constraints, York Student Security implemented controversial changes to the escort service. It now provides a complementary Escort Service Program consisting of a call-in and scheduled shuttle service. York Student Security has also demonstrated its willingness to work with campus advocacy groups to improve the sensitivity of escorts through retraining.

A second service with which graduate women are dissatisfied is security patrols. York campus has two large security departments with regular security patrols and a call-in emergency line. However, many women felt that patrols were too infrequent in the areas where women studied and worked, particularly in building basements, near labs, in tunnels, in parking lots, at bus stops and around the campus in general. Communication between security personnel and those on campus at night was also felt to be inadequate. Respondents wanted more knowledge about patrol operations as well as input into patrol schedules. As in the case of the escort service, women felt that patrollers lacked sensitivity to women's issues and were not flexible enough to the needs of women students.

Women students did not separate issues of accessibility from issues of safety. Respondents noted that the lack of ramps, convenient access to well-signed elevators and graded entrances made many buildings inaccessible to mobility-impaired women as well as to women with small children and strollers. Accessibility to buildings was also limited by inconsistent and unpublicized lock-up schedules for buildings. These problems constitute a real safety risk. Women reported having felt at risk either because they were locked in or out of buildings or because they were forced to find alternate access to and from buildings when doors that they expected to be open and/or accessible were not.

Although we had expected that women working in isolated laboratories or offices would complain about their safety, we were surprised by the number of complaints about the library. Graduate women indicated that campus libraries, on our and other Ontario campuses, were unsafe study spaces. Women said that libraries were not adequately equipped with security provisions such as emergency phones and patrols. Budget restraints have limited the number of security officers patrolling and monitoring the libraries. Theft and indecent flashings in libraries are problems reported in many universities. Some women also expressed their discontent with library closing procedures, which did not accommodate the needs of hard-of-hearing persons or persons with other disabilities. This resulted, in at least one case, in a woman with a hearing impairment finding herself locked in the library overnight.

Additional locations of concern to graduate women are campus parking lots. In our surveys, every lot on campus was cited as a potential danger area. Women stated that parking lots were poorly lit and poorly marked. Their chief concern, however, was the inadequate monitoring of lots, either by security patrols or by parking lot attendants, without which even improved lighting and numbering would ultimately be ineffective. Respondents also indicated that the high cost of parking lot tickets and permits forced them to park in more distant, and thus more dangerous, lots. Of those graduate women polled, 71 percent agreed that, in order to make them safer, women who work at night should be granted parking permits that allow them to park in reserved lots close to the buildings in which they work. At York, women who have parking stickers are currently able to move into reserved parking lots after five o'clock; however, this privilege is not extended to women who pay for parking each time they use it.

Two final locations where women have concerns for their safety are campus residences and athletic facilities. In terms of the former, women reported that intercoms, if existent, were often out of service, that elevators were improperly maintained, and that security locks were often faulty. Telephones or intercoms were also requested in isolated basement laundry rooms. Since our report, members of a joint safety committee addressed this specific problem by citing the installation of emergency phones and/or pay phones in residence laundry rooms as one priority in their application for new provincial grants to fund safety provisions for women. As to the athletic centre, respondents stated that, although women had lobbied successfuly for new security locks into women's change rooms, these doors were continuously left open by staff and patrons. This, coupled with the lack of emergency phones in these change rooms, left women particularly vulnerable to potential intruders.

Finally, there were indications of a significant degree of stress-related illness on the part of female students. This illness is due in part to stress caused by anxiety about safety on campus and by women's attempts to organize their lives in order to avoid the campus on off-hours. It is also due to stresses caused by lack of institutional support for women, such as recognition of and allowances for women's family responsibilities, lack of funding for female graduate students and many other problems that are addressed in greater detail in various other reports of the York task force. Unfortunately, the situation on other Canadian campuses is not much different than at York. A related report on unwanted sexual experiences among students of the University of New Brunswick and St. Thomas University found that women who had been the victims of unwanted sexual aggression and assault, whether within or outside their relationships at university, were less likely to become involved in university community activities and had difficulty concentrating on studies.[6] Another final contributor to women's stress-related illness is the anxiety caused by the "chilly climate" in the university: the general sense that women are unwanted guests or intruders who are, at best, tolerated in an essentially male academic institution.

Both in our surveys and our meetings with graduate women students, the chilly climate generated considerable discussion. Aspects of the climate that women students found disturbing moved along a continuum that involved being excluded from course material, from class discussions and from decisions about course scheduling; being trivialized, for example, when bringing up feminist issues or critiques; being subtly harassed through sexist jokes, racist graffiti and homophobic remarks; being overtly harassed; receiving promise of reward or punishment if they did or did not comply with sexually-oriented requests; and being physically threatened. The Canadian Federation of Students offers graphic examples of sexism experienced by female students from across Canada and suggests that even more incidents go unreported.[7] In addition to causing women serious discomfort and pain, these situations often left women feeling powerless and unsure of how best to respond. Some women reported that they refrained from resisting both subtle and blatant harassment for fear that their attempts would meet with denial, ridicule or intensified hostility. And although some women reported successful resolutions of their situations, more often than not, those who did resist noted that their attempts met with precisely the reactions they feared and produced other negative personal and professional repercussions.

Although the issue of the chilly climate is not generally included in discussions of safety and security, it is highly relevant as it constitutes a security risk to all women in at least three respects. First, as noted above, aspects of York's climate have caused graduate women considerable stress that may in turn threaten both their mental and physical health. Indeed, we heard of at least one case where a woman was forced to take a year's leave of absence due to stress caused by harassment. Second, there is an intimate connection between women's being unwelcome in the university and the physical violence perpetrated against them. Events on other Canadian campuses more than illustrate the relationship between inequality and violence. In November 1990, "No means kick her in the teeth" and "No Means Dyke" were responses displayed by male students to the "No Means No" anti-rape campaign at Queen's University in Kingston, Ontario.[8] In October 1990, at the University of British Columbia, 300 written threats, including "We'll crush your cervix to oblivion" and "You're a fat cow, but I'll fuck you anyways," were distributed to women students sleeping in their dorm rooms.[9] At Humber College in Toronto, a woman was sexually assaulted during daylight hours within sight of witnesses and her dormitory.[10]

A chilly climate affects campus security and prevents women from feeling safe at York in the larger sense of being comfortable and at ease. Post-secondary institutions can also provide an environment that enables women to express and develop themselves fully and freely. The chilly climate prevents this as it leaves women feeling constantly open to attack—personal, professional and physical. The chilly climate is a form of low intensity violence against women that keeps them feeling vulnerable and limited while at the same time contributing additional risks to their mental and physical well-being.

FOR HER OWN GOOD?
RETHINKING SECURITY MEASURES FOR WOMEN'S SAFETY
Security provisions and services aimed at protecting women from physical violence at York, while comprehensive in scope, are generally found to be inadequate in both quantitative and qualitative terms. There are not nearly enough emergency phones, regular phones, signage and lighting on campuses, campus buildings and facilities. In addition, grounds are not adequately maintained, supervised or patrolled. Provisions and services are also often delivered in an unwise and insensitive manner. For example, the emergency phones that do exist on campus are poorly distributed (particularly in especially unsafe places), and escorts may not only make women uncomfortable, but may also put them at risk by making them wait for unreasonably long periods of time in unsafe places.

The comments made by graduate women in our surveys and discussions, often corroborated by other campus women, suggest that many security officers and student escort workers tend to see women, whether graduate or undergraduate, faculty or staff, primarily as potential victims of violence rather than as full members of the university who have the right to learn and to work in a safe place. This tendency often leads to a paternalistic, insensitive and disempowering treatment of women and their safety concerns. Many respondents indicated that safety services and provisions for women seem to be regarded by the university as a costly extra for which women should be grateful, no matter how flawed and/or inconvenient they are. This attitude leaves women feeling frustrated, resentful and unable to take control of their own safety. Security departments must vie for limited resources and compete for provincial and federal grants that demand that safety issues be prioritized. The implementation of progressive change to campus environments is being expedited by the pressure of student governments and women's groups who now lobby governing boards directly or with the support of security departments. At York, the union representing graduate women working as teaching assistants was directed by its membership to include safety issues in collective bargaining. The result was the installation of additional telephones in all isolated or basement offices, laboratories and computer rooms.

A third problem with security and safety for women is that it seems to be understood and addressed primarily in its most narrow form, namely as protection from the threat of physical violence. The vast majority of safety resources are dedicated to protecting women from physical violence, and few if any resources are put into protecting women from other threats to their physical and mental well-being or into making the campus a place where women feel safe in the larger sense of being comfortable and at ease.

The "charity model" of providing safety services and the limited conception of women's safety relate to the implicit assumption that security workers are the only people responsible for and capable of keeping women safe. This assumption, shared in the past by many security workers, university administrators and students, stems in part from administrative mandates that designate authority to security departments to act on all issues of safety and security. It is also reinforced by the specialized training that all security workers undergo. This assumption therefore discourages security departments from educating and mobilizing all members of the university community around safety issues and practices of relevance to women and minority groups. They also have neither the time nor the resources to do so and are discouraged from soliciting the input of campus members into safety matters and from setting up effective mechanisms of accountability to the community which they serve. This unintentionally exclusionary approach to women's security serves to fragment and privatize what should be treated as a community issue. As opposed to encouraging all women and other members of the university community to become involved in and to take responsibility for their own and other women's safety, this approach leaves many students indifferent to or ignorant of women's safety issues and practices and leaves many women feeling highly dependent, isolated and fearful.

Rather than simply accepting it as a fact of life, violence against women must be understood as both a cause and a result of women's inequality in society. Violence against women is produced, among other things, by women's subordination in the university and is, at the same time, a reaction to women's attempts to resist and combat male dominance in this institution. If violence is both a cause and a result of women's inequality, a vital precondition for making the university safe for women is to secure for themselves a truly equal place within it. In other words, women's equality in the university must be understood as a security issue, and transforming the university in such a way as to make women equal should be a long-term goal that informs all security practices.

In order to facilitate the provision of services that are responsive to graduate women's needs, university and college security departments must engage in more frequent consultation with graduate women and the organizations that represent them. They must also improve and expand mechanisms of accountability to the graduate, and other, women they serve.

Consultation with graduate women and their organizations should help security personnel to identify ways to make universities more hospitable places for graduate and other women. Security offices should consult and cooperate with various advocacy groups on campus, such as sexual harassment centres, centres for persons with disabilities, race relations offices, employment equity offices, as well as other relevant campus groups such as faculty associations, unions and student associations, in their effort to make campuses places where women are not only free from harm but also free to express and to develop themselves fully.

The security department must rethink its relationship with the rest of the university. It must recognize that it cannot possibly make campuses a safe place for women on its own. Security personnel need the active participation of all campus members to make their institution a place where all women are both comfortable and secure.

People can participate in making the campus safe for women by opposing sexist pedagogical practices, racist jokes, homophobic graffiti and other threats to women's comfort in the university. Women's organizations and advocacy groups, such as sexual harassment centres and undergraduate women's centres, have taken the lead in advocating funding for comprehensive education programs, Wen-do and self-defense programs for women and improved security practices. In general, student federations and unions have supported these measures and argued for representation of constituency groups on safety advisory committees. Participation from the wider campus community can be encouraged by informing, educating and mobilizing the campus around safety issues.

While such a transformation will be neither easily achieved nor the perfect solution to ensuring graduate and other women's safety, we feel that the general strategy we have proposed is superior to the piecemeal reforms to security that have been made to date. Such a transformation of the security department's practice and operations will improve the quality of security services in both the short and the long term. It will also enhance their effectiveness, as people will be more aware of safety issues and more inclined to use safety services and provisions. Perhaps most importantly, this transformation will allow security personnel to contribute to a larger transformation of York and other universities into places where women truly are equal. In so doing, they will be attacking the problem of violence of all kinds against women, as opposed to simply managing the problem as they have done up until now.

The proposed transformation of security departments has other benefits for post-secondary institutions. For example, educating and mobilizing members of the university around safety issues may help to foster some sense of community, which is often lacking on many campuses, and improve the reputation of urban campuses when it comes to women's safety. It may also encourage women to stay and work on campus on off-hours, thus enhancing their own productivity as well as the general intellectual climate. Finally, implementing the proposed strategy will prove to graduate women, to all students and to the larger academic community that universities and colleges take seriously the issues of women's equality and safety and that they understand the connection between the two. At a time when resistance to women in the university and the accompanying violence against them is on the rise, colleges and universities need to adopt safety and security strategies that will be a positive step forward.

WORKING PROPOSALS FOR IMPROVING SAFETY FOR WOMEN
In the comprehensive Canadian report on violence against women, *Changing the Landscape: Ending Violence—Achieving Equality*[11], participants were

FOR HER OWN GOOD?

concerned with the physical and social environments of schools, colleges and universities as a site of inequality and danger for young girls and women. They recommended "zero tolerance actions for all organizations and individuals in the education sector."[12] The report emphasizes many of the same issues outlined in the following recommendations: the reallocation of education resources; implementation of safety audits of all educational facilities; and the appropriate use of human resources through sensitivity training, employment equity strategies and consultation with women's organizations like community groups and women's teachers' federations.

An alternative approach to university women's safety must be adopted. The following recommendations are organized so that the more global, enabling ones come first, and the more concrete and specific recommendations follow. Those responsible for implementing these recommendations are urged to resist the temptation to implement only the more specific recommendations as they can only be effective as part of a larger, comprehensive change to security. The limitations of some these recommendations is acknowledged; due to constraints of time and space, all recommendations in the major report could not be included. Finally, more studies on the issue are not required because the implementation of the initial global recommendations lays the groundwork for enhanced and continuous community input and involvement in campus security, which is ultimately the best means of improving it.

To improve campus safety at post-secondary institutions, the following actions are recommended:

- All administrations will provide adequate funds, support and other resources necessary to ensure that security departments and advocacy groups can implement their security procedures and ongoing education programs.
- All members of security departments will undergo immediate, mandatory education aimed at sensitizing them to the safety needs of women and minority groups. This education should be provided by campus advocacy groups as well as other relevant organizations in the surrounding communities. In addition to immediate education, ongoing education should also be provided to all security workers.
- Campus groups representing women, visible minorities, gays and lesbians, persons with disabilities and any other groups that face particular security risks will be consulted and included in the process of security policy-making.
- Security departments, in cooperation with other relevant groups on campus, will fund and oversee the provisions of voluntary and mandatory educational workshops on safety issues relevant to women and other minority groups, for administrators, faculty, teaching assistants, support staff and students.

175

THE ILLUSION OF INCLUSION

- After the second recommendation is completed, colleges and universities will develop and implement, in conjunction with the relevant advocacy groups on campus, a university-wide, comprehensive publicity campaign dedicated to making the university or college safer for and more hospitable to women and minority groups. This campaign will be broadly informative on all issues of physical safety on campus. It will also educate campus members about the nature of sexual as well as other kinds of discrimination and harassment, other aspects of the chilly climate and their connection to violence against women. In addition to heightening awareness of safety risks to women and minority groups, this campaign will encourage all campus members to take responsibility for making the institution a safe and hospitable place for all attendees.

- Security departments will improve both their communication with and accountability to the broader community. Among other things, security personnel can do this by holding open meetings to discuss issues of concern, such as proposed changes to security services or new safety initiatives; by making more frequent and improved use of safety reports and bulletins; and by providing the community, particularly new students, with more detailed information about security practices and provisions. The security department also will more actively encourage community input and feedback with respect to its performance.

- Community initiatives aimed at enhancing the safety of women and minority groups and organized by campus groups such as women's centres and advisory boards will be encouraged, supported and funded either by the security department or directly by administration.

- Colleges and universities will support financially and in principle women's counselling and crisis centres in the surrounding community, as these centres provide important services to women students.

- All safety and security services and emergency procedures will be made accessible to persons with disabilities. Immediate improvements will include making all emergency exits accessible with ramps or graded exits and ensuring that all procedures for closing and evacuating buildings make provisions for persons with disabilities, for example, using an alternate warning system of flashing lights for deaf and hard-of-hearing persons.

- Regular and varied health and safety and emergency training sessions, including self-defense courses, will be made available to all teaching personnel. Such training should take place on paid work time, be mandatory for all new employees and be strongly encouraged on an ongoing basis for all personnel. Further, university and college administrations should provide the funding for similar courses for all students.

• Combatting the chilly climate will be identified as an integral part of any security mandate, and the security department will consult and cooperate with other concerned campus groups to develop effective means and mechanisms to deal with the interrelated aspects of violence and thereby to provide safety and security for all members of academe.

POSTSCRIPT

Although most of the students involved in the surveys have since graduated or moved on, some positive results have occurred at York in the last few years as a direct result of student political action and involvement on safety committees. In 1994, graduate women students, working through the new teaching assistant union (CUPE 3903), negotiated a contractual obligation for the university administration to improve workplace safety and install office telephones. Additional lighting, patrols and emergency telephones also have been installed across campus and an expansion of the escort service has been implemented. Similarly, York's Security Advisory Council, composed of students, faculty members and both union and security representatives, has addressed the recommendations of the original task force report (1992). According to their forthcoming 1998 report, the task force committee states that Safety and Security Services and its members should be commended. The committee does, however, encourage communication with the university community.

Communication alone will not ensure women's safety and security. Cuts in funding and services on campuses across Canada have already had a direct effect on campus safety. At York, many practical safety improvements, such as installing $5,000 automatic accessible doors and emergency telephones, were made possible because of large provincial grants earmarked for women's safety concerns. With changes in government, shrinking budgets and pressure to cut services, we must continue to have a voice on security committees and decision-making bodies where we can make a positive difference.

NOTES

1. Canadian Federation of Students 1991.
2. This article is based on an earlier report conducted jointly with Claire Polster. Due to her input in the research, I have chosen to use "we" to emphasize her part in the earlier study. The new extended analysis is my own work. Other sources consulted in this study include Gilmore 1991; Lougheed 1993: 10; Wekerle and City of Toronto Planning and Development 1992.
3. Johnston and Polster 1992.
4. All statistics are based on the findings of the *Canadian Union of Educational Workers (CUEW) Safety and Security Study* (Morris 1991). The comments of individual graduate women were recorded in open-ended questions on our two surveys and in the CUEW study. Claire Polster and I were also involved in the development and deployment of the CUEW study.
5. Morris 1991.

6. Finkelman 1992.
7. Canadian Federation of Students 1991: 1–6.
8. Canadian Federation of Students 1991: 3.
9. Canadian Panel on Violence Against Women 1993: 260.
10. Canadian Panel on Violence Against Women 1993: 260.
11. Canadian Panel on Violence Against Women 1993.
12. Canadian Panel on Violence Against Women 1993: 69–70.

Part 5
Warming the Climate: Towards Inclusion

Balancing Child Care and Work: The Need for a "Woman-Friendly" University

Jennie M. Hornosty

Unless you support women in their role as mother,
you will never get equality of opportunity.[1]

A major problem for women professors, librarians, administrators, staff and students in universities today is captured in the above quotation. The gendered division of labour in our society is such that women, not men, must continually strive to find ways of juggling home and work, of balancing the desire to nurture with the desire to achieve. While women with children are generally responsible for finding adequate child care arrangements, the specific sorts of problems this poses for women in university depends on their positions. For example, female faculty with children must balance child care arrangements with scheduling office hours, classes, time for research and meetings with colleagues, whereas a major difficulty for students may be the cost and the limited hours during which child care is available. Although the problem is not new, universities have, by and large, failed to adequately address this form of systemic discrimination against women.

Canadian universities first came under attack for their inequitable treatment of women in the 1970s. Allegations that female faculty and students often faced a discriminatory and hostile environment at the time prompted many institutions to establish internal committees to examine the situation. In their 1984 report, *Some Questions of Balance*,[2] which was commissioned by the Association of Universities and Colleges of Canada (AUCC), Symons and Page examined the status of women in Canadian academic life and stated in no uncertain terms that women were victims of discriminatory attitudes and practices in many areas of higher education and research.[3] Like the various internal university committees established earlier, they made a number of important recommendations for improving the conditions for women on campus.

Also in 1984, Judge Rosalie Abella submitted the findings of her Royal Commission, which had been mandated to inquire into ways of promoting equity in employment opportunities for four designated groups, one of which was women.[4] She argued that equality in employment necessitated identifying and removing barriers and discriminatory disadvantages, which were the consequence of systemic discrimination.[5] Her findings and recommendations were to have a direct effect on Canadian universities through the establishment of the Federal Contractors' Program.[6]

Given the number of reports and recommendations made over the last twenty years, have things actually changed for women in universities? On the surface at least, an argument can be made that a great deal has changed. A snapshot of campus life today compared with one taken in the 1960s would show a number of interesting differences. For example, significantly more women, especially students, are on university campuses today. As well, a larger proportion of these women have young children. The majority of Canadian universities now have employment equity programs, maternity leave policies, sexual harassment policies and a significant number have child care facilities on campus. More courses are available, especially at the undergraduate level, which focus on women's experiences and issues of concern to women. Feminist pedagogy,[7] while still rejected by some, is increasingly gaining legitimacy as a necessary corrective to mainstream scholarship.

One might be tempted to conclude that women have finally taken their rightful and equal place in the academic community. Unfortunately, this semblance of equality is only part of the picture. Despite the changes, there remain some important systemic and institutional barriers to women's full and equal participation in university life. Women's primary responsibility for child care, coupled with inadequate child care facilities at an institutional level, set limits to equality for women, as shown by the current situation of women faculty and students in the academic community.

GENDER IMBALANCE PERSISTS

In the last thirty years, the number of women teaching full-time in Canadian universities has grown dramatically from fewer than 750 in 1960 to just under 6000 in 1985, an increase of 713 percent. In the same period, the number of male faculty increased by only 410 percent.[8] Between 1985 and 1989, over 1200 more women were hired compared to just under 500 men.[9] Despite both this absolute and proportional increase in the number of female university teachers, women faculty remain a minority in many disciplines and in the profession as a whole. Female academics tend to be concentrated in the lower ranks, are more likely to be employed part-time and tend to be paid less than men. This pattern of gender imbalance has not changed significantly in the last thirty years. For example, in 1989–90 the percentage of women teaching full-time in Canadian universities was 19.5 percent, only an 8.5 percent increase from 1958–59 when female academics comprised 11 percent of university teachers in this country.[10]

A further indication of gender imbalance is that women faculty are still "ghettoized" in certain academic disciplines. Despite changing attitudes towards women in non-traditional fields and proactive attempts to recruit women, female faculty remain greatly underrepresented in traditionally male fields such as engineering and the applied sciences. At the same time, they are disproportionately found in traditionally female-dominated areas like education and health. While there are a number of possible explanations for this, one contributing factor is the ease with which one can combine particular careers with a possible future role as wife and mother. Teaching and nursing, both associated with women's traditional roles as nurturers and caregivers, have always been viewed as suitable for women; they are perceived to be occupations from which one can "take time out to raise children" without great penalty. By contrast, a career in science or engineering, especially if one is interested in research, demands uninterrupted devotion. Success in such disciplines is determined by the number and amount of research grants one receives, which in turn is dependent on one's productivity as measured by research papers and conference presentations. Taking time out for any reason can potentially jeopardize one's career. For women who want children, this is a real dilemma.

The number of female students in university at both the undergraduate and graduate levels has also grown dramatically over the last thirty years. In 1960–61, female students earned 25.8 percent of the undergraduate degrees awarded in Canadian universities.[11] By 1990, more than half (56 percent) of all bachelor's and first professional degrees were granted to women.[12] Similarly, at the graduate level, women's participation rate has increased substantially. In 1960–61, only 15.9 percent of the master's degrees and 8.8 percent of the doctoral degrees awarded were given to women.[13] By 1992, women earned 48 percent of the master's degrees and 32 percent of the doctoral degrees.[14]

Although this increase in the number of female students is a sign of greater gender equality, the large numbers also mask the degree of inequity that remains. As with faculty, female students tend to be concentrated in traditionally female disciplines and greatly underrepresented in disciplines such as engineering, mathematics and the physical sciences. For example, in 1990, the top three fields in which men earned doctorates were mathematics, physical sciences and engineering, whereas the top three fields in which women earned doctorates were the social sciences, education and the humanities.[15]

◊ A recent survey by history graduate students, which highlighted some of the difficulties women students in particular face, provides a further example of how gender inequity manifests itself. Almost half of the women respondents without children stated that their involvement in graduate work had affected their decisions regarding childbearing. Lack of money and time required for graduate work were cited as major reasons for either postponing or abandoning plans to have children. A number also commented that they felt that they would not be viewed as serious academics if they were to have children. Female graduate students with children spoke of the stress and exhaustion they faced in trying to combine their responsibilities as graduate students with those of mothering. Other structural constraints mentioned were the lack of maternity leave provisions, the loss of funding and various university privileges if they took time out to have children, and the time limits set on how many years one can take to complete a degree. In addition to these institutional constraints, female students encountered overt sexism, sexual harassment and an unwillingness to recognize the academic legitimacy of courses in women's history. The authors concluded, quite correctly, that "[t]he male model of the single, unencumbered student who devotes all waking hours and resources to academic work remains alive and well in departments across Canada."[16]

Universities, like other institutions, reflect the structure and values of our society. The barriers to gender and educational equity are based in deeply entrenched stereotypic assumptions about appropriate roles for men and women, particularly as seen in the imbalance of work roles and family responsibilities. One way of understanding the implications of this for women is through the concept of systemic discrimination.

SYSTEMIC DISCRIMINATION

Systemic discrimination has been defined by the federal government as "indirect, impersonal and unintentional discrimination that is the result of inappropriate standards which have been built into the employment systems over the years."[17] The problem is not that of isolated instances of unequal treatment of a few individuals, but rather that of a social system premised upon narrow and limiting concepts of who women are and what they are capable of achieving. To eliminate systemic discrimination, one must focus on the institutional base of the inequities. In the words of Judge Rosalie Abella, "[s]ystemic discrimination requires systemic remedies. . . . The effect of the system on the individual or group, rather than its attitudinal sources, governs whether or not a remedy is justified."[18] To remove structural barriers one must determine whether any institutional practices and policies, which may appear to be gender-neutral, actually impede the full participation of women.

According to Abella, equality in employment for women means, among other things, "acknowledging and accommodating the changing role of women in the care of the family." This includes "the active recruitment of women into the fullest range of employment opportunities, . . . accessible childcare of adequate quality, [and] paid parental leaves for either parent. . . ."[19] No matter what else women do, the division of labour in our society is such that it is women who bear children and, for the most part, are still the ones primarily responsible for child care, family care and domestic work.[20] Under such circumstances, we can only treat men and women equally by acknowledging and accommodating their differences. Universities, unfortunately, have been slow to recognize this principle of equality.

INSTITUTIONAL BARRIERS

For a number of reasons, universities have been slow to change. One important reason lies in the monastic tradition from which universities emerged. The model of a single scholar, who is able to devote all *his* time and energy to academic pursuits epitomizes this tradition. While historically this possibility was open only to males, more recently females who were able to fit into this model were given an opportunity to compete on the same terms as men. However, academic women who do not fit into this model, that is those with children and family responsibilities, pose a challenge to the system. Their presence, according to Chaviva Hosek, means that the "transcendent" image of the university is called into question by the demands for adequate childbirth leave, parental leave, child care facilities and policies on sexual harassment. "These bring into the university the world of contingency, necessity and frail human biology—just the traits which women have symbolized to our patriarchal society and which it has a long history of wishing to deny."[21]

For too long, the underrepresentation of women among faculty, administrative and student ranks has been explained as the choices individual women made. This has led to victim-blaming rather than a focus on structural barriers, both in the university and society at large, which place serious limits on the opportunities available to women.

Feminist academic Dorothy Smith has pointed out that women historically have been excluded "from the making of ideology, of knowledge, and of culture . . . women have been deprived of the means to participate in creating forms of thought relevant or adequate to express their own experience or to define and raise social consciousness about their situation and concerns."[22] In our universities, men were and, for the most part, still are the "gatekeepers," both in terms of defining the criteria of academic suitability and influencing the structures and policies by which universities operate. The higher one goes up the university hierarchy, the smaller the proportion of women; very few, for example, are found in senior administrative positions. And even in those cases where women are in positions of power, their concerns are often marginalized and they are seldom able to implement the sorts of structural changes that would make the university a more equitable place.

In a system that has traditionally excluded women from the production of knowledge, women's work is often judged to be inadequate and non-academic. As well, women who question the prevailing assumptions of the university can be labelled "troublemakers" or dismissed as not being serious academics. The assumption is that what happens in the university is determined by gender-blind criteria. In fact, though, the institutional structure and its policies have evolved in particular ways which suited and perpetuated a particular model of a proper academic. "[F]or more than ten centuries, those who judge excellence in academics have continued to use standards which were defined exclusively by a very select group of men, to accommodate those whom they continued to select."[23] Despite a rhetoric of fairness, we know that perceptual bias, however unintentional, does exist.[24]

Perceptual bias and the male definition of "reality" means that women are often perceived as less serious and their scholarship is undervalued. The perceptual bias also helps to explain why women, who make up less than 20 percent of full-time university faculty (1992), account for approximately 40 percent of the cases that come to the Academic Freedom and Tenure Committee of the Canadian Association of University Teachers (CAUT).[25] If one considers only those cases that involve "early career decisions"—appointment, renewal, tenure and first promotion—one finds that the percentage of complaints from women is closer to 65 percent.[26] Subjective values, often shaped by stereotypical assumptions prejudicial to women, influence how women in the university are evaluated and perceived; until these are changed women will remain marginalized at all levels of academic life.

FAMILY RESPONSIBILITIES:
A MAJOR OBSTACLE TO AN ACADEMIC CAREER
Various difficulties are experienced by female faculty, librarians, students and administrators with children when they attempt to combine a career with their family responsibilities. These include negative attitudes and behaviour as well as the practical problems of finding adequate, affordable and flexible child care. The roots of these stereotypical attitudes prejudicial to women can be traced back to the traditional sexual division of labour in society, which assigns women primary responsibility for the home and family. This means that women who decide to have a family and pursue a career find that they carry a double responsibility. Time budget studies reveal that, despite some changes, women continue to do a disproportionate share of domestic chores, and employed mothers more often than fathers participate in primary child care activities.[27]

When conflicts arise between the two, women generally accommodate themselves to the needs of their family; men, on the other hand, seldom do so.[28] As a result, academic women have often paid a high personal cost for their decisions in terms of interrupted careers, fewer promotions, less pay, denial of tenure, greater stress, less academic recognition and feelings of inadequacy.

Despite some changes, the academic workplace remains structured on an assumption that faculty are men with someone at home to look after family needs while they engage in their research and other scholarly activities. The hierarchical and highly competitive nature of the academic world demands an extraordinary commitment of time and energy. For the female academic with children, such expectations create difficulties and barriers. Because of family responsibilities, women may take longer to obtain their degrees or to develop a research program; they have difficulty finding adequate time for research and writing or obtaining the necessary qualifications for tenure and promotion. Consequently, their opportunity to succeed within the academic world is limited.

185

Issues of family responsibility and child care also impinge on the sorts of career choices academic women make. A biology professor at the University of New Brunswick mentioned that she has had several gifted female students with little ambition beyond getting PhDs and becoming instructors, for they didn't want to get into the "rat race" of applying for research grants and publishing; "most women don't find that compatible with family life."[29] Similarly, a former faculty member in business administration said: "It comes down to a question of values: which is more important, working every night, weekend and summer to get ahead in your career or spending time with your family?"[30] The above dilemmas are generally not experienced by men. It is hardly surprising, therefore, that academic women are less likely to be married or have children compared to women with comparable training in other professions, or to academic men.[31]

All too often, the choice for academic women is between having a family, having a career or accepting the limitations and stress of trying to combine both. Many of us who were active in the women's movement during the 1970s and early 1980s bought the myth of "superwoman," and believed that if we were organized and efficient we could compete on equal terms with men. We believed that we could be both the "perfect mom" and the highly successful and respected scholar. Perhaps there were some individuals who succeeded. Most of us, however, had to make compromises, often with not very satisfactory results. While some of us have been active in negotiating better maternity and parental leave policies and have argued for the necessity of quality child care, the university as a place of work and study remains a public domain quite separate from the private world of domestic life. The primary assumption is still that issues concerning family responsibilities rest within the family, and that the solutions should be personal and individual.

THE NEED FOR CHILD CARE

As early as the 1970 Report of the Royal Commission on the Status of Women,[32] child care was identified as a major concern for women in the labour force. Fourteen years later, Judge Rosalie Abella stated that child care is a necessity, not a luxury.[33] The Cooke Task Force on Child Care described Canada's child care situation as being in a state of crisis, since the available licensed child care spaces could accommodate less than 9 percent of Canadian children requiring non-parental care on a full-day basis.[34] The crisis in child care persists; in the 1990s, "as many as 3 million children may have been in need of alternate child care arrangements, up from 2.6 million in 1985."[35] Without adequate child care facilities, women will not be able to achieve educational and employment equity.

The establishment of work-related child care is a recognition on the part of employers that society has changed, and that they must deal with the issue of how to integrate work and employees' family responsibilities. However, a report published by the Women's Bureau in 1990 stated that only 3 to 4 percent of licensed child care spaces in Canada were work-related child care programs.[36] How do Canadian universities fare in this regard? According to CAUT's 1992–93 Employee Benefits Survey for Faculty, there were thirty-one universities in Canada (excluding Québec) that reported having child care facilities on campus.[37] These were not evenly distributed in all regions of Canada, and most Maritime universities did not have on-campus child care facilities.

The size of the facilities, the eligibility requirements and the cost per child varied from campus to campus. Only twelve of the facilities provided infant care for children aged seventeen months or under; only one university child care centre indicated that it accepted children at birth. A mere seven centres offered after-school care, and only one mentioned having flexible hours. No university indicated having child care arrangements for sick children.

Given the diversity of child care needs among university women, it is highly unlikely that the majority of child care facilities available on campuses are adequate. For example, not all provide subsidies to students or have sliding fee scales, especially important to staff who may not qualify for subsidies but have difficulty affording the full fee. In most cases, the hours of operation were between 7:30 am or 8:00 am to 5:30 pm or 6:00 pm Monday to Friday. Librarians who work different shifts and graduate students who have evening or weekend labs do not have their child care needs met. Similarly, female administrators and faculty who must attend evening meetings or out-of-town conferences could have considerable difficulty finding adequate child care arrangements.

The shortage of accessible, affordable child care in the general community only exacerbates the child care problem in the university. The Canadian National Child Care Study (CNCCS), based on a survey of 24,155 households and covering a total of 42,131 children, found that in 94.9 percent of the families surveyed, the parent who described him/herself as most responsible for child care arrangements was the mother.[38] The study identified two specific sets of child care needs that were especially problematic: after-school care for children six to twelve years old, for professional development days, days when the children are sick, holidays and the summer break; and child care outside of traditional timeframes, a result of the increasing numbers of parents working non-standard hours.

Not only does the limited nature of child care facilities create a problem for women in university, but often the attitudes and assumptions also cause problems. Without institutional values that support a meshing of family and career, a woman's decision to combine motherhood with an academic career is not legitimized. It is not surprising, therefore, that female faculty, librarians, administrative staff and students experience hostility from their colleagues when they request changes in meeting schedules, work hours or class times in an attempt to juggle their academic and work commitments with family responsibilities. At times this hostility is expressed in terms of questioning women's professional commitment to their career.

A further example of the sorts of androcentric assumptions operating in universities[39] is illustrated by a comment at a meeting of the UNB Senate.[40] In a discussion about a proposed teaching certificate for graduate students, we were told that some of the required teaching workshops for graduate students would be held on Saturdays. When asked why, the faculty member presenting the material responded that "Saturday is a day when everyone is free." For women with children, such a statement is ludicrous and reflects an insensitivity to their situation.

Female graduate students encounter additional problems. Most graduate schools, for example, have a limited timeframe by which students must complete their degree requirements. And, in many instances, it is difficult if not impossible to pursue certain graduate programs on a part-time basis. Given that women are primarily responsible for child care and other domestic activities, both of these policies have a greater adverse effect on women than on men. Not only university policies *per se* create the barriers; the policies of other agencies, such as Employment and Immigration or the Department of Income Assistance, reflect their own notions of what graduate work involves. For example, as the Director of Graduate Studies, I received a call from Employment and Immigration Canada concerning one of our female graduate students. The individual who called was concerned that this student still had not completed her program, and argued that the department would have to cut off her education subsidy. The student, a single mother, had been receiving the subsidy under a re-training grant. Despite my various explanations of why students often do not finish on time, and the particular hardships for single mothers, the official had great difficulty understanding the problem.

At many universities there are no provisions for maternity leave or parental leave for students; therefore, those who bear children while pursuing their studies must return to school quickly after the birth of their children. Students on scholarships or assistantships generally have to give these up if they take time out to have a baby. The fact that very few child care facilities accept small infants further hinders students' ability to pursue their academic studies.

> Without day care, students who are also mothers find it difficult to participate in both the formal (classroom, laboratory, computer and library time) and informal (peer and faculty social activities, informal discussion, attendance at special lectures, workshops, extra-curricular activities) dimensions of their education.[41]

While individual faculty can and do take some of these things into consideration when evaluating their students, the burden still rests with the individual student to request "special consideration" in these circumstances.

A special consideration for post-secondary institutions should be the age distribution of graduate students, which is shifting toward the older end of the range. In 1990–91, for example, 44 percent of female graduate students were older than twenty-nine years of age.[42] With this trend, we can expect that even more students, primarily women, will be faced with the task of combining academic studies with family responsibilities. Hence, adequate child care facilities will be in even greater demand during a period when some universities may be closing their child care facilities because they are not economically viable. If this rumour is true,[43] it suggests that child care is viewed more as an ancillary service, much like a sports arena, than as something essential and a basic prerequisite for achieving educational equity.

On-campus child care can alleviate some, although by no means all, of the problems for women associated with juggling family and career commitments. Access to quality and affordable child care will reduce some of the stress for women with young children. However, more broadly-based societal change is also required. Men must be encouraged to take a larger share of responsibility for parenting and child care; policies such as more extensive and economically viable parental and maternity leave programs must be implemented. Economic incentives should be offered to establish child care centres for children of all ages, including newborn and school-aged children, centres which are available on a twenty-four-hour basis. Institutions should be required to allow flexibility in working hours. The ultimate goal is to change the socialization practices and ideologies in our society that perpetuate the traditional division of labour.

We know that academic women tend to have different career paths than those of men. Women are on average older when they receive their doctoral degrees; they frequently take longer to complete their studies; they often move around more (to follow their male partner); and women's careers are interrupted to have children whereas men's are not. University policies concerning such matters as hiring, promotion and leave arrangements need to be examined to ensure that these are not a form of systemic discrimination. For example, it is often not possible for someone to have a permanent position with a reduced workload for any length of time. However, it is precisely this sort of arrangement that would benefit women who want to spend more time at home while their children are young. While most, if not all, universities have maternity leave provisions for faculty, staff, administrators and librarians, these are often inadequate in terms of the time allowed and the financial compensation received. According to the 1992–93 Employees Benefits Survey, very few institutions have paternity leave provisions, although most provide parental leave in accordance with the relevant Employment Standards legislation.[44] Until men are able and willing to play an equal role in parenting, women will continue to be primarily responsible for juggling their workload.

We have seen that the reward system in the university is such that one's status depends on research and publications. The most critical period in an academic woman's life is at the time she is beginning to establish her career as a scholar in order to obtain tenure. For many women, this occurs when they are in their thirties, and in their childbearing years. A number of women I know consciously chose to postpone having children until tenure was secured; others decided, at that point, that it was too late to have children. Men, however, are not faced with this sort of dilemma. As one female faculty member put it, "for men, family is something to come home to; for women, it's another job on top of whatever we already do."[45]

Clearly, many assumptions, attitudes and policies that govern the university are more likely to benefit men than women. While the "rules of the game" may be applied equally, they are applied to an unequal situation. The consequence of this for women is summed up well in a quotation from a report prepared by the Queen's University Faculty Association Subcommittee on Women and Tenure:

> female faculty members with family commitments are penalized because the number of demands on their time is so great as to almost preclude scholarly interaction with their peers. . . . Women, who traditionally bear the brunt of parenting responsibilities, are thus more likely to be excluded from . . . scholarly functions. As it is well known that interaction with one's peers contributes most to research output, once again it is the woman's research activities which suffer.
>
> It is probably safe to say that "adequate" family life in today's society and "tenure worth" research activities are difficult to balance. Given that women continue to carry major family responsibilities, they pay a price by not being promoted out of the lower ranks, by resigning, or by failing even to consider an academic life as a career choice.[46]

Most female writers who look at the situation of women in university focus on the barriers that confront women in their quest for educational equity. An exception to this approach is found in the Canadian Federation of University Women's report, which defines instead the necessary elements for an ideal "woman-friendly" university.[47] Among the fifty-four features listed were the following: flexible on-campus child care services, including extended and weekend hours; encouragement of male professors to pursue their child-rearing responsibilities; a parental leave policy for students; clauses in hiring and employment equity policies to specifically address different career patterns; criteria to assess qualifications and excellence which recognize women's different career paths; provisions for re-entry fellowships to assist women PhD students or graduates to return to their fields after an absence for child-rearing; and flexible job arrangements for faculty including job-sharing and fractional-load appointments.

CONCLUSION

The roots of the discrimination against women in university are systemic and their origins lie in the social organization of the wider society. To understand the complexity of systemic discrimination and its negative impact on female faculty, librarians, administrators and students, we need to look at all facets of academic life. This includes the existence of perceptual bias, the ways in which women's research and scholarship is devalued and the dual responsibilities women face when combining family and career.

Fundamental changes obviously are needed. For a long time women have attempted to fit into the existing university structure. Some women have "made it" and, while progress is slow, statistics indicate that an increasing number of women are appointed to full-time faculty positions in all disciplines and all ranks. However, we should not assume that simply appointing more women will, in itself, remove the sorts of structural barriers women continue to face. We do need to fundamentally redefine what the university is and who it should serve. Chaviva Hosek summed it up well:

> [Women] can no longer be the grateful guests invited into institutions which continue to belong to men. They [men] have not only the administrative, economic and political power within the university, but most important, they have the power to articulate and enforce their vision of what a university is and what it should be. . . . [T]o divide existing institutional powers more equitably is just one stage of the process we are engaged in. The next step will be to transform the culture of the institution and of learning itself.[48]

If women are to be equal with men in the university, we need a vision of a transformed academy, one that recognizes and makes room for women's and men's family responsibilities on an equal basis. Women's voices need to be heard; women's priorities, responsibilities and concerns need to be validated. Fundamental to achieving this goal are better maternity, paternity and parental leave policies and affordable and accessible child care facilities that meet a diversity of needs. Such facilities would provide regular child care for parents who work evenings and weekends, and sick child care and emergency care for cases where a caregiver becomes ill or quits. Such facilities would have flexibility to ensure that parents could leave their children for the entire day or for just an hour or two as needed during meetings or lectures. Children of all ages, from the newborn to the twelve-year-old, would be accepted in such a child care centre.

If universities implemented these recommendations, we would be one step closer to educational and employment equity for women. Such institutional changes are a necessary, but not a sufficient, condition for equity. Broader societal changes, to undermine the traditional sexual division of labour, also are required to attain complete gender equality. Universities must initiate the sorts of changes required if we hope to find our rightful place in a "woman-friendly" university.

NOTES

1. Canadian Association of University Teachers (CAUT) 1986: 5.
2. Symons and Page 1984.
3. Symons and Page used Statistics Canada data for their comparisons between the status of women and that of men. Their data were for the 1981–82 year.
4. Abella 1984a. The other three designated groups were native people, people with disabilities and visible minorities.
5. Abella 1984a: 1–18.
6. The federal government responded to the recommendations of the Abella Report by passing federal employment equity legislation in 1986. The Federal Contractor's Program, an off-shoot of the legislation, applied to all post-secondary institutions with one hundred employees or more who wanted to bid on government contracts worth more than $200,000. This meant, in effect, that any university in such a position had to sign a statement of commitment to produce and implement employee equity plans at their institution.
7. By feminist pedagogy, I mean the body of writing and research that challenges traditional assumptions about knowledge, learning and what is referred to as the "scientific method."
8. Hollands 1988: 5–7.
9. Statistics Canada 1992b: 19.
10. Statistics Canada 1992b: 12.
11. Symons and Page 1984: 189.
12. Statistics Canada 1993a: 15.
13. Symons and Page 1984: 192.
14. Statistics Canada 1993a: 16, 163.
15. Statistics Canada 1992b: 147.
16. Dubinsky et al. 1990: 9–10.
17. Cited in Canadian Association of University Teachers 1985.
18. Abella 1984: 9.
19. Abella 1984: 4.
20. Ghalem 1993: 3–6.
21. Hosek 1986: 15–16.
22. Smith 1987: 17–18.
23. Sheinin 1988: 9.
24. An excellent study showing the subtle and systemic nature of perceptual bias and its negative impact on women is well-illustrated in a report by Fidell, which is cited in Geis, Carter and Butler 1982.
25. Geramita 1988: 5–6.
26. Cases that come to the CAUT Academic Freedon and Tenure Committee have not been able to be resolved at the local university level. If one compared grievances by gender at the local level, one would also find that a disproportionate number were from female faculty. As an example, at the University of New Brunswick in this past year, four faculty members received tentative negative recommendations concerning their promotion: all four were female.

27. Krahn and Lowe 1993.
28. Simeone 1987: 132.
29. Inch 1985: 6–7.
30. Inch 1985: 6.
31. Simeone 1987: 120.
32. *Report of the Royal Commission on the Status of Women in Canada* 1970
33. Abella 1984.
34. Cooke 1986.
35. Burke 1991: 12–15.
36. Mayfield 1989: 127.
37. The accuracy of the CAUT Employee Benefits Survey depends on how thoroughly association presidents or their designates completed the survey form. Data are not available for Québec universities because they do not participate in these surveys.
38. Goelman et al. 1993.
39. Many of the examples I give are based on my experiences at the University of New Brunswick (UNB). However, I know through talking with colleagues across this country that similar things happen at their institutions.
40. The Senate is the academic decision-making body in the university, and has representatives from faculty, students, administration and the Board of Governors.
41. Canadian Association of University Teachers 1986: 9.
42. Statistics Canada 1992a: 44.
43. This rumour is based on remarks heard at UNB during our discussions about building a child care facility on campus.
44. Canadian Association of University Teachers 1993b.
45. This quotation was obtained from a discussion on the women's studies computer list network. The website address is LISTERV@UMDD.UMD.EDU.
46. Quoted in CAUT 1986: 13–14.
47. Canadian Federation of University Women 1992; see the last article in this book.
48. Hosek 1986: 16.

On the Road to Find Out: Everyday Advice for Working-Class Mothers Returning to School

Eunice Marie Fisher Lavell

Well I hit the rowdy road and many kinds I met there,
and many stories told me of the way to get there.— Cat Stevens

I am a graduate student in education at a prairie university, as well as the mother of three children. When I returned to school eight years ago, I was a single mother from a working-class background. Although I have recently married, I know that being a poor and unmarried mother had everything to do with the difficulties (and probably some of the delights) I have encountered en route to a better life.

I am sharing some stories about my personal experience in the hope that it can be entertaining and instructive. A little later, I also will present more general information about working-class women and post-secondary education, and will make some recommendations to those who advocate for improving the educational situations of women.

STORIES AND THEIR MORALS

I have come to believe that the current organization of university life is spectacularly unresponsive to the needs and lifestyles of working-class mothers. The basic assumption of everyone, from instructors and students to university administration (as evidenced by curriculum development, timetabling and course structure) and funding agencies, is that the primary or only responsibility of "the student" is a commitment to her or his education.

For any student who is a mother, of course, this can hardly be the case. Children have their own impressive array of needs for which mothers are (often solely) responsible. Students who are mothers are responsible for all the practical details of their children's day-to-day lives, for making daycare arrangements and/or interacting with their children's schools and otherwise contributing to their children's education.

But for student mothers who are working-class, such an assumption is clearly ludicrous. The heavier load that we carry along the "road to find out," however, seems often to escape the notice of our fellow travellers—administrators, instructors and other students. At the beginning, it sometimes even eludes us.

"CHEESE AGAIN!"

It took me quite awhile to figure out that myself[1] and most other students at the university just weren't talking the same language when it came to our burden of responsibilities. The first time it really struck me was in second year of the undergraduate program.

Exam season was just around the corner and I was sitting with a group of other women students at the education lounge. We were eating sandwiches and commiserating about our crazy workload. Classes still on, two papers due, teaching experience finishing up and three exams next week. Some fairly cryptic observations about a particular instructor were just beginning to be made when one of the young women, obviously disgusted, tossed her brown bag onto the table muttering, "Great! Just great!"

"What is it?" we all ask solicitously.

"Cheese," she asserts, frowning darkly. "My mother knows I hate cheese, but she's given me cheese sandwiches again. That's twice this week."

"Don't you just hate that," another agrees, and the chatter goes on.

I just sat there, a smile slowly creeping across my face. I was in the throes of a radical shift in perspective.

I was contemplating the larger scenarios in which we were all struggling to survive exam period. For me, going to classes, student teaching, writing two papers and preparing for three exams all resided together in a large but relatively manageable compartment of my life. The rest, my "real" life, was considerably less tidy.

That day, I got to thinking about the relevance of "real" life to being a student. I was thinking about the foundation of work I had to do just to keep my children and myself surviving while I went to university, completely apart from the actual work of going to classes and doing assignments.

This foundational work included weeks, literally weeks, every term during which many hours would be spent filling out application forms, re-application forms and sometimes appeal forms for the several bureaucracies with which I had to deal: Student Aid; government subsidized daycare; government subsidized housing; Child Related Income Support Program (CRISP) and Shelter Allowance for Family Renters (SAFFR), among others.[2] Many more hours would be spent collecting, photocopying and paying for the required documentation for these applications—income tax returns, rent receipts, receipts for tuition, books and supplies, all bank account statements and passbooks, and many others. (I learned the trick of photocopying *everything* after discovering the hard way that when documentation "goes missing," it is always the student's responsibility to replace it.) This foundational work also included planning for and getting my various children to their various daytime arrangements, either daycare or school, and then getting myself to classes. Mostly this would be on foot, pushing a baby stroller since I could rarely afford to purchase the bus pass, which was budgeted by Student Aid.

After this regular morning trek, the actual work of being a university student often seemed like a holiday. During those restful daytime hours, I would go to classes, go to the library, read course material, do research, write papers and do other course-related work. Then would begin the return trek, getting to where my children were and getting us all home. From four o'clock until after ten, I was a mother again. Doing supper, playing with my kids, helping with their homework, doing art, storytime, chats, complaints and fights. Life. Most nights I had my own homework, which sometimes I could attend to for short periods, but mostly I didn't get to it until after the kids' bedtimes. I was often still at my homework early into the morning.

The day of my shift in perspective, when I began to notice the difference in the situations that myself and many of the other students were describing as being "swamped," I began to see the relevance of those contexts for the actual meaning of education to each of us. I began to think about where the other women were coming to university from, and where they were going back to. I thought about the young woman whose "cheese sandwich" angst I had witnessed. I envisioned her after classes driving home in her own car to a house that someone else was paying for, a house that someone else cleaned and someone else maintained for her. Eating a supper that someone else had cooked for her. Having the space to do homework uninterrupted if she so desired or, if not, having the means to do otherwise. Did she sleep, I wondered, in a bed that someone else had made for her?

I was thinking too about the situations of other mothers and poor women I knew who were going to university. I thought about my friend Lorraine, a divorced mother of three teenagers from the northern town of Flin Flon, Manitoba. As a child, her whole conception of herself as a learner had been adversely affected by the racism she was subjected to in school. But many years later, in an upgrading course, she met up with a wonderful instructor who gave her the hope that she could become a teacher and help other children have a better chance. She is supported at university by the Access Program.[3] For a significant part of her first year at university, she was distracted and discouraged by disputes with a foster parenting agency over the care of one of her sons. Just before exams, the agency dumped him in her lap. But she persevered, and she's still here.

I thought about my friend Connie, funded by her Indian band in Northern Ontario. In high school, she had won several awards for academic excellence. Although she now has four little children under the age of seven, and although her husband's grade eight education keeps him from finding any steady employment, she can't take any time off or she will forfeit her funding. She keeps whittling away at her education degree, trying to fit classes and assignments between the cracks of her life.

I thought about my friend Norma, who was an adolescent mother on welfare. She wanted to give her three children a better chance than she had had, so she got herself into the Students on Social Assistance (SOSAR) program,[4] hoping to eventually help others by bringing her hard-won empathy to the field of social work. Right now, it is all uphill but she is determined to do it—and she will.

I thought about my friend Phyllis, a working-class white woman with a grade twelve education, who has worked in construction and on road crews in the North, was once a letter carrier and many times office help. With two children, and divorced from a man who is himself on welfare, she is now getting her bachelor's degree with a major in sociology. She is convinced that she has a valid contribution to make.

I started to think that working-class mothers, while we bring a whole other constellation of personal challenges to university, also often bring a particular kind of perspective to our education. Whereas middle-class people seem to think of university as a part of their entitlement—a foregone conclusion, what "everybody" does or another step to career advancement—working-class people often think of university as a true and valued privilege. The working-class mothers that I know have returned to school to "better themselves," to ensure the survival of their children and often with a sincere desire to improve life for other poor and disadvantaged people. Most of all, I think, working-class mothers at school value learning for its own sake. We want to know, to understand. This is one reason that my title alludes to the old Cat Stevens (1971) song, "On the Road to Find Out." Much of this song, in fact, could be describing my experience—especially the part that goes "many stories told me of the way to get there." You see, in my years at university, it seemed often to happen that when the untidy details of my life found their way into the forum of conversation, other people would hasten to iron out crisp, efficient solutions. I have sometimes been the recipient of astonishing advice from folks who, though they do not have a good grasp of my situation, mistakenly believe they do. Here are just a few stories to illustrate my point.

"Plan Ahead, Take a Course"
On a chilly November day, I am chatting with a fellow student and happen to mention that I haven't yet been able to purchase snowsuits and winter boots for my children.

"You should do what my sister does," she suggests brightly. "Buy your kids' winter clothes the previous spring when they're on sale. That way, you'd save a lot of money."

This is such an amazing, such a foreign concept that I cannot speak—this concept of having any money six months *before* I would need it. I intend to respond to her, but I find that my mind is getting bogged down in numbers. I am thinking that the poverty line for a family of one adult and two children is $25,000[5] and that my income in student loans and bursaries is $10,395, so that, after paying my tuition and books, my children and I are left with $7,900 to live on. We are living this year, I am thinking, on *less than 40 percent* of the bare bones income necessary for survival. I find myself wondering if this person, a sociology major, really understands the concept of "competing resources." I have just succeeded in organizing all these data into some sort of sensible reply but, alas, it is now too late.

"You know what you need?" queries this cheerful person. I blink and open my mouth but, already, more helpful advice is being aimed exuberantly in my direction. "You need to take a money management course."

Now I have encountered this "course" advice many times—although the particulars change. Sometimes, say when I have had to request an extension on an assignment, I am told that I need a time management course or a study skills course. If my appeals to Student Aid for reasonable support have once again been fruitless, folks suggest that I would benefit from a communication skills course. Or from assertiveness training. If my home life is hectic, parenting courses are recommended. "Through courses," these well-meaning people point out to me, "you can really develop a lot of valuable survival skills."

Sometimes I try to paint the "big picture." I try to explain the interaction between the many details of my situation that make things a little more complex than all that, but people like easy solutions. I have found that, if I continue to resist their preferred salvation by referring back to the actual realities of my life, these unsolicited counsellors will soon grow sullen and quiet.

Fortunately, I have a sense of humour and high tolerance for irony. Usually I just shrug and smile, saying, "Maybe you're right."

"GET PRIORITIES STRAIGHT"
I wouldn't want to say that a lot of "parent-bashing" goes on in university courses. But I would say that several prominent theories, in everything from education to psychology and social work, identify the mother's role in every conceivable kind of childhood misadventure. I provide this information only as a point of interest preceding this anecdote.

In early March of my third year at university, my son came down with measles. Although it was a mild case, he was contagious so his daycare couldn't take him. I phoned all my instructors and left messages that I would be missing two classes and why. I got copies of other people's lecture notes and kept up on readings at home.

This arrangement was acceptable to all but one instructor, the teacher of an education course on developing children's reading skills. This particular person had spent considerable time in class pointing out parental contributions to school failure, particularly under the headings "cultural deprivation" and "single mothers." I remember that the word "irresponsible" had often come up in lectures. In the hallway after my return to classes, this instructor stopped me to emphasize that, in her class, attendance was mandatory. Somewhat taken aback, I explained once again my extenuating circumstances—a sick child, no daycare.

"Well, what's more important to you," she asked without a trace of self-consciousness, "your children or your career?"

I looked at her dumbly. "You'd better get your priorities straight," she suggested, striding away from me.

"THINK RESOURCES"

December, April and August are the worst times for people on Student Aid. Not only are these the months when the next round of applications has to be in, they are also the times when the previous period's funding is long gone.

March 31st of my third year is a Friday, and I have been told by a voice on the phone that Student Aid has sent my loan approval document, and that it will be at their office downtown on Monday, April 3rd after 2 p.m. My children and I have been eating sandwiches, soup and rice pudding with powdered milk for a week. My last class on Friday finishes at 3:20, and by 3:40 I am at Safeway. I buy six litres of milk, a dozen eggs, juice, bananas, oranges, two large boxes of generic cereal, and all the fixings for homemade spaghetti. I pay by cheque, gauging that, if all goes smoothly, I'll have it covered before it reaches my bank. This weekend, my family will eat well.

Monday morning, I check with the awards office on campus, and Nancy tells me, "Sorry, the computer went down. Try again Thursday."

After my women's studies class (where we are discussing how the personal is political) I relate this turn of events to a fellow student. "That's one fifteen-dollar service charge I'll owe Safeway and one I'll owe my bank," I say.

"I would never do that," she says briskly. "I never write a cheque until I actually have the money in my account. Otherwise, as far as I'm concerned, it's just like stealing."

I say, "Yeah, but that would have been three more days of going hungry. My kids are funny that way," I joke. "They like to eat every day. Besides, the money was supposed to be there." "Yes, but surely you could have covered it for a few days. Don't you have an overdraft protection on your account?"

"No I don't," I say. "How would I get an overdraft protection?"

"You just apply for one," she explains. "They have the forms at the bank."

I pause. "Well I did and they turned me down. I didn't have any collateral."

"Oh . . . oh so I guess you don't have credit cards either? Well why don't you get a cosigner? I mean, independence is good, I know. It's good to feel independent, but really, wouldn't your parents sign for it?"

"My parents?" I laugh ruefully, "Well they would if they could, I'm sure. But the thing is that they are currently living, the two on them, on dad's part-time income—about five hundred a month. Actually, they've been phoning *me* collect lately. I have more money than they do."

My companion purses her lips. I can tell she's getting irritated with me and my obstinate problems. She's way out of her depth in the waters of simple solutioning here, but for some reason that I just can't fathom, she doesn't want to give it up.

The conversation turns to famous feminists, and I'm glad to let it. She tells a brief, inspirational story about Nellie McClung and the wonderful example she has set for all women. Then I go home.

BUREAUCRATIC ART OF "NOT-SAYING"

As is often the case with bureaucracies, there seems to be a lack of congruence between Student Aid's originally mandated purpose and the one that has eventually evolved. I assume from its name that the former had something to do with offering practical assistance to needy students so that they could get their education. From my experience, I would say that it has strayed somewhat from this function. Being a believer in accuracy when it comes to titles, I have assigned it a more appropriate moniker. I call it Student Aggravation (S.A.). True, S.A. supposedly has provisions for students with children, but as may be apparent to you from the income numbers I provided above, this funding is not even close to sufficient. And when a student is spending more time meeting the requirements of her funding agency than she is doing her course work, she is, in my opinion, not being aided.

Furthermore, an attitude of distrust has often coloured my interactions with the agency. I have often had to go to great lengths to prove to personnel that my children and I are not taking island cruises with the pittance they award me. As my sister Del once pointed out, a person charged with murder is considered innocent until proven guilty, but if S.A. is suspicious of you, it's the other way around.

Of course, none of the tussles I've had with S.A. over the years have been personal. All the times that one swoop of someone's pen threatened to shift me and mine onto the welfare rolls, it was never callousness or a lack of empathy. Only policy.

For instance, the first time I applied for a student loan, I pointed out that I was making payments to Eaton's. "We don't cover that," said the person at the counter.

I said, "But I have to pay them. I owe them."

"Oh we're not saying you can't pay them—we're just saying that we don't cover the payments," she clarified. "Obviously, you'll have to pay them. Just take the payment out of something else."

"But," I point out, "I don't have anything else. I have no husband, no job and poor parents. This is my only source of funding."

"Oh well," she reassures me, turning away, "you'll figure something out."

Similarly, when a health course in second year required that I purchase a sixty dollar pass to the physical education building, S.A. refused to cover it. I took them a copy of the course outline stating that the pass was mandatory and students could not enter the building without it, but the person behind the counter just waved me away. "We don't question that it's required, we know it's required," she said. "We're just saying we won't fund you for it."

In mid-February of my third year, when my daughter's unexpected dental bills wiped out the rest of my term's budget, an S.A. employee asked if I had considered selling my Income Tax return. "Are you saying I have to sell my Income Tax," I asked.

"Oh no. We can't advise you to sell your return—we're not allowed to tell you that. However," she suggested confidentially, "we *can* say that you're not getting any further funding from us this term, and that if you *don't* sell it, you're not going to make it."

Of course, the actual workers at S.A. know that the agency's allowable expenses are not realistic, but individual workers have very little power, and whatever influence they did once have is quickly being eroded. A few years ago, S.A. employed people called student advisors, who would help prospective clients fill out their applications. This was especially important for working-class people and others who might be daunted by the complicated forms, and for people like me who have dependants and therefore might be eligible for extra funding, funding which many people didn't even know existed.

Unfortunately (or fortunately, depending upon whether you are an administrator or a student), the "human element" did sometimes intervene. Even knee-deep in policy, when bureaucratic workers regularly met with applicants face-to-face, they got to thinking of people as human beings—not just a series of numbers on an application form. I think that sometimes the women I dealt with at S.A. actually perceived me as worthy, the sole supporting person for two little children, someone who probably deserved a chance to get a good education. Instead of passing me off to someone else or throwing more paperwork at me, such workers would at times go to considerable trouble to actually help me negotiate my way to reasonable justice.

I suspect that the student advisors, besides truly serving people like me, actually contributed to increased overall efficiency. But S.A. has addressed this glitch in an otherwise perfectly unresponsive system by phasing out the position of student advisor. (Note that it was the positions that were phased out, not the people—nothing personal, just policy.)

CREATIVE COMMUNITY RESPONSES
Oh well, misery loves company. Just look at me and my friends. When working-class mothers meet up at university, we often become fast friends. Those of us who have been around a while have become a regular feature in each other's lives—kind of an amorphous support group.

Big Ones Help the Little Ones

Because many of us live in housing projects, we tend to get to know each other. We have a lot in common—kids, poverty and the excitements and pleasures, worries and disappointments of being students at our age. Besides, we enjoy each other's company.

And we truly help each other. It's not unusual to have neighbourhood sleepovers when the moms' papers are due. Two or three women will spread out their papers in the kitchen, drinking coffee and writing until dawn. Half a dozen kids of various ages range around the house, playing with each other and watching television. If there are problems, the big ones help the little ones. Eventually, they have snacks and crash in their sleeping bags. And the mothers get their work done.

Everybody's Children

If necessity is the mother of invention, then working-class mothers back at school have good cause to be inventive. My friend Connie, for instance, has developed some creative solutions to a common problem. Not only is it the case that she can't afford to pay for child care, but it is also true that she misses and worries about her children when she is away from them. She particularly misses her two littler ones, aged one and two, and she worries about the potential for racism against her Native children in mainstream daycare settings.

Connie addresses these problems by relying on other women. Her mother, herself a survivor of the racist residential schools and with no hope for regular employment, spends many daytime hours with her grandchildren. Connie also applies her energies to organizing and playing in an all-Native women's volleyball team. When she finds that this extra commitment means that she is hardly having a chance to see her children, Connie just brings some of her kids along to games and practices. Everybody pitches in—whoever is on the bench is bound to have a child in her lap from time to time. It's almost like they're everybody's children.

"This Week I'm the Bank"

We are all generally broke, but we are rarely all broke at the same time. So some of us have developed community responses to cashflow problems.

One of the many times my loan document was inexplicably and disastrously delayed, I was over visiting Phyllis. "This week I'm the bank," she announces. "How much do you need?"

"Oh that's okay," I say, "I'll get by."

"Well how about two hundred," she says, heading for the kitchen. I hesitate.

"Look, it's no problem," she says. "Right now, I have it so I give it to you. In a few weeks or months or whatever, when you have it, you pay me back. It's a really nice surprise." She digs down into the cookie jar and hands me a couple of bills. "So in some ways, helping you turns out to be sort of like giving a present to myself."

Going for Coffee
Many of us have coffee "klatches" or meetings on campus. When we go for coffee, we are doing what formal organizations might refer to as "liaising" or networking. We give and get information about courses and tips on assignments. We have discussions about our courses, often complete with scathing critiques of the material and/or instructors. We find out who has which profs, which ones are okay, which few are excellent and which ones to avoid at any cost.

And we talk about who's who in the various agencies we deal with. We are always on the lookout for the real human beings who have so far managed to escape detection inside the bureaucratic machine. When we find one, we remember the name and pass it on; like the people at Awards on campus: Nancy, who throws me a line when I'm going down for the third time in the Sea of Nonsense Policy; and Peter, who dances me outside when I can't get away from the Repeating Dumb Rule Shuffle.

Working-class mothers at university spend a lot of time talking together, and a lot of time listening. The newer ones are listening to learn everything they can about this glorious mess they've gotten themselves into. Those who have been around for awhile spend a lot of time just being a shoulder, listening to frustrations and problems. We often give information but we don't often give advice—either we offer help on the other person's terms or else we just get out of the way.

WORKING-CLASS WOMEN AND POST-SECONDARY EDUCATION
I want to make some suggestions about advocacy for working-class women in post-secondary education, but I should preface these recommendations with some general information about women, social class and education. The belief that education and even higher education are equally available to, and equally benefit, all Canadians is pervasive but not well-founded.[6] Systemic inequality ensures that working-class children, Native children and the children of other racial and ethnic groups are more likely to "fail" at school, to drop out and to achieve marginally than are white, middle-class children.[7] This dynamic affects post-secondary education, to which middle-class white people have greater access and which further privileges them economically.[8]

In 1992, women as a group were more likely than ever before to be present in institutions of higher learning.[9] Like middle-class women, working-class women have tended to discontinue their education during their child-bearing years, but working-class women are much less likely to have completed high school.[10] Consequently, working-class mothers in post-secondary education, who are rarely financially supported by husbands or parents, are unlikely to be able to pay for their own further education. Additionally, working-class women are more likely to have been "streamed" out of university entrance courses, and are also more likely, if they do receive a diploma, to have done so through upgrading courses. So working-class women in post-secondary education are more likely to attend community colleges or vocational training than university.[11]

Furthermore, although much has been made of the fact that women now make up a majority of those attending university, it is important to note that the majority of university women are from the upper-class sector. For instance, according to Guppy, Balson and Vellutini[12] patterns of women's increased enrolments at university "may have resulted not from a growing participation of all women, but of women disproportionately from upper status backgrounds."[13] In my opinion, it is only thanks to a very few innovative programs established in the 1970s and '80s that a hardy handful of non-affluent white, Northern, Native and other working-class people have made their way into universities.[14] Interestingly, women are a firm majority of these.[15] Together with this background picture on working-class women and education, I want to place some general information about women and poverty. Women and their children were a solid majority of those living below the poverty line in 1991 and, with the move toward the so-called global economy, growing unemployment and increased government cuts, the situation is bound to get worse.[16]

Some theorists point out that recent trends in divorce have contributed to women's poverty to the extent that middle-class women face financial hardships after divorce whereas middle-class men do not.[17] Dorothy Smith observes, as well, that we are currently in the midst of a shift in membership of the entire class structure.[18] She says that we may "be seeing shifts in the type of class structure, depressing a whole level of the working class and shifting a section of the middle class into the working class."[19] My own concern here, of course, is not with these newly impoverished women—these *nouvelles pauvres*[20]—but with working-class women, that is, women who come from poorer families and who are well-acquainted with the ongoing struggles of working-class life.

I feel some ambivalence about the increasing attention being given to poverty among the *nouvelles pauvres*. Elizabeth Spelman has pointed out the problematics of collapsing categories such as race, class and sexual orientation to form the supposedly homogeneous group "women."[21] She has asserted that theory thus founded can only lead to perceptions and analyses that are biased in favour of relatively advantaged groups of women.

In discussions of women's poverty, a growing tendency is to focus on the plight of formerly middle-class women now fallen upon hard times, as if they are somehow more worthy of compassion and their poverty somehow a more compelling tragedy. If this tendency continues, already-scarce resources of time and energy will be dedicated to this "special" group at the expense of the equally-deserving majority of working-class women to whom poverty is nothing new.

RECOMMENDATIONS FOR ADVOCATES

What I have hoped to illustrate through the stories I have been telling you is that working-class women face some unique challenges and often also bring unique perspectives and our own kind of lifeskills to our travels on the "road to find out." My basic advice to those who would advocate for such women is to be aware of class and individual differences. Recognize the legitimacy of the strategies for working things out that are often preferred by working-class women—informal arrangements, working in community, inclusion of our children in our work and social lives, and generosity with scarce resources.

Also imperative is an attitude of respect for us and for our abilities. If you see that we are struggling with our load, err on the side of assuming that we are people of considerable ability and that, if we have made it this far, we must be very resourceful indeed. Probably (and I hope not to give offense by saying so) we are not in need of your advice.

There is much that we need, however, and there is certainly work we'd appreciate a hand with, so if you want to help us, help us on our own terms. Don't try to convert us to middle-class ways. There is also much that needs to be done at the institutional level, through channels where most of us have no influence. First, the major obstacle to working-class women's attendance at university is the middle-class bias of the school system.[22] Sweeping changes must be made to the educational system so as to make it more responsive to working-class children. I know this is a tall order and obviously I cannot begin to suggest here how this would be accomplished, but I do know that nothing less will significantly increase the accessibility of university education to working-class women. Perhaps more easily do-able is to stop the *en masse* streaming of working-class children out of university entrance courses.

Second, if working-class women do not have funding, we have *no* access to university. Our access to post-secondary education depends upon funding. Funding programs and other supports to working-class women must be responsive to real life situations, particularly the fact that we usually have children and very, very rarely have familial financial supports to fall back on.

Obviously, government with any true commitment to the education of working-class people would not only stop cutting funding to existing programs, but would expand these programs and create new ones. Any threat to programs such as Access, SOSAR, and the Native pre-medical and pre-law programs available in my province would be unconscionable.[23]

Furthermore, Student Aid funding across Canada must be made available to, and responsive to, the needs of working-class people, particularly sole-support mothers. This would best be accomplished by the creation of a separate department within the existing agency for dealing with this group. Funding rates for working-class mothers who are students should even be made to match those for mothers on welfare ($11,167 annually), which would require raising them by several thousand dollars annually. This would still, however, place them at only 55 percent of the poverty line.[24] For those who qualify, this program should offer non-repayable bursaries instead of, as is currently the case, dispensing bursaries only after the full loan is taken. If loans continued to be made, there would have to be provision for the loans to be "forgiveable," that is, loan repayment would be contingent upon the women's practical ability to make payments. How does it benefit a working-class single mother who has struggled for five years to get a university degree, if her salary (assuming she gets a job) is dedicated to loan repayment for twenty years after graduation?

Finally, I want to emphasize that, although I have made some suggestions about ways of accommodating working-class mothers' educational needs, I am not under the delusion that necessary changes are likely within the existing system. Latter twentieth-century patriarchal capitalism will always relegate large numbers of non-white and working-class people to poverty, and a majority of its victims will always be women and our children. True hope for us can only come with radical change to the system itself.

REPRISE: GRADUATION AND STILL KICKING

The big day arrived at last. I had scrounged a hundred dollars to send to my parents for the Grey Goose bus and they came for my graduation. They were there in the crowd along with my children when my name was called. "Yay mom," I could hear my kids shouting as I was crossing the stage. And I was not the only mom whose kids were cheering for her that day.

I feel sincerely thankful to my kids for bearing with me through all these years of toil, and I feel proud of them too. I am in graduate school now and, after all this time, having a mom who is a student is just normal to them. The other day, I overheard my seven-year-old telling his friend on the phone, "No, don't come over tonight—my mom is studying and it would be too noisy."

My parents don't really understand the ins and outs of acquiring a university education—the volume and complexity of the work I do and the amount of time it consumes. "Why are you always doing your homework at home," my dad wonders. "Why don't you do your work in the classroom like you're supposed to?"

Still, my parents believe in me. They believe that I am doing good for myself, for my kids and for them too. I am doing good for all of us. My parents are proud that I am getting myself educated—my father, who got as far as grade five in school; and my mother, who never finished her second year in grade six.

Last time my mom came for a visit, she was asking again which degree it was that I was working on now. "Is it your doctor's degree," she asks. "I want to know when I can start telling people to call my daughter 'Doctor.'" "Not yet ma," I laugh, giving her a squeeze, "but pretty soon you can tell them to call me Master."

NOTES

1. Since my paper is describing experiences of working-class women from their own perspective, I am using what I would call a working-class voice. When telling stories, for instance, I often refer to "myself" rather than using the more conventional "I." I also reverse the word order at times, as in "myself and my children," rather than "my children and I." At one point, I say that I am "doing good for myself," an expression that carries different connotations from "doing well." These are examples of working-class vernacular as I know it, and I have retained them so as to give both "flavour" and accuracy to my accounts.

   Similarly, since my paper is about the giving and receiving of advice, and since it allows me to pass along my own message, I am using a conversational tone. Early in the paper, I describe what I hope to communicate "a little later on," for instance, as one would in a conversation, instead of saying "below," as is usually done in papers. And I use expressions like "these stories I have been telling you" because I am aware, at the moment that I put each story down, that I am not just casting my words into some vacuum of paper. Rather, as is always the case with storytelling, my stories are being told by someone to someone. Including "you" in the text of my stories from time to time reminds us both of that.

2. CRISP and SAFFR are means-tested income supplements. In 1990, qualified families received up to $30 per child per month from CRISP. SAFFR paid qualified families up to $150 per month to defray the cost of rent.

3. A 1992 University of Manitoba Access Program pamphlet describes Access as "a support program which provides access to a university education for people who otherwise would not have had the chance for such experiences because of social, economic and cultural reasons, lack of formal education, or residence in remote areas."

4. SOSAR is a funding program for qualified individuals who have been on provincial welfare for one year or longer. Other welfare recipients are not allowed to attend schools or universities.

5. Social Planning Council of Winnipeg (SPCW) 1991.

6. Smith 1990.

7. Li 1988.

8. Li 1988.

9. Posen 1990.

10. Posen 1990.

11. Posen 1990.

12. Guppy, Balson and Vellutini 1987.

13. Guppy, Balson and Vellutini, 1987: 179 (emphasis in the original).

14. I am referring here to Access, SOSAR, the Native pre-medical and pre-law programs and, to a lesser extent, Student Aid.

15. Personal communication with D. Sutherland, academic assistant, University of Manitoba Access Program, March 1993.

16. Social Planning Council of Winnipeg 1991.

17. Kitchen 1992.

18. Smith 1990.

19. Smith 1990: 240.

20. *Nouvelles pauvres*—the newly poor (feminine). I mean this term as an allusion to, and play on, the expression "nouveau riche." Webster's defines a nouveau riche as

"a person of newly acquired wealth but limited education or culture." Although my expression "nouvelles pauvres" has other interesting implications, here it will simply imply a female person who has recently come to poverty but whose experience is embedded in middle-class lifestyle, resources and "culture."

21. Spelman 1988.
22. Smith 1990.
23. Since I originally wrote this paper, the SOSAR program has been cancelled, the Native educational program budgets have been seriously threatened and the federal government has announced its "crackdown" on student loans defaulters. Since people on regular social assistance are not allowed to attend any kind of educational program, the end of the SOSAR program effectively curtails the aspirations for higher education of all people on welfare in my province. So much for the current government's social conscience.
24. These calculations are based on figures taken from the SPCW paper.

Let's Start the Revolution*

Jacqueline Stalker

Each individual acts and reacts to life experiences in unique ways. The accumulation of good times and bad times, the sum total of our experiences, shape how we act. My experiences, over many decades in and with our educational systems, have been a rollercoaster ride with dips of disbelief and anger and crests of joy and elation. I have been excluded, frustrated and patronized, but I also have been welcomed, challenged, inspired and rewarded. My post-secondary experiences were not at all unique; they simply indicate how women have been and are treated in academe.

I married at eighteen, a young age. As I had completed all the education that my society deemed appropriate for a young woman in the 1950s, it was not an unusual decision. I had graduated from high school at sixteen, and had been sent to a convent school hundreds of miles from my small Ontario town to obtain a French Grade XIII education. When that was completed with honours, I inquired about university programs. Not surprisingly, I learned that the French university in our capital city accepted only young men. Upon further, and quite aggressive inquiry, university officials reluctantly informed me that they would let me enrol if I agreed to certain stipulations. These included, among other things, living for the duration of the four-year degree program in the local convent with the nuns.

I was Catholic, but I also was in love. The monastic religious life did not appeal to a healthy young woman contemplating marriage. My only choice, therefore, was to go to the university "normal" school to qualify as a teacher. Had the sight of blood and injuries not repelled me, my other choice could have been a nursing school.

This biographical tale of rejection by a university in the early 1950s is supported by Ross who, although he miscalculated by a few years, stated that "before 1950, . . . it was not easy to be admitted to university if one was black, female, a Jew or a Catholic, or from a working- or lower-class family."[1] "Not easy" is an understatement; for me, it was impossible. A university education was not accessible to me or to many others in the 1950s; it was not even accessible for some women in the 1960s, '70s, or '80s.

209

I therefore became a teacher, married the man of my dreams and, shortly thereafter, started a family. Over the years, and as we were transferred from one location to another by my husband's employer, I continued to learn, to teach and to long for a degree. I applied to, and was accepted by, prestigious English universities in Canada. All programs, however, included a residency requirement that would entail my leaving husband and children to meet the degree requirement. I wasn't averse to working hard, but I didn't intend to abandon my family and responsibilities. Thus, for two full decades, I waited.

Finally, we moved to a city that had two universities and where I could enrol and easily fulfill the previously impossible residency requirement. I did just that, acquiring bachelor's and master's degrees on a part-time basis but in record time. I had enroled in a university program primarily intended for men in the Canadian Armed Forces, but which also was available to their "dependants"; in the traditional patriarchal fashion, spouses were deemed to be dependent.

The Armed Forces University Program[2] allowed me to register in an undergraduate degree program and also to take courses from other universities, if and as we moved around the country. Little did the program administrators realize that an ambitious middle-aged woman might use this program to register in courses at five universities at the same time and complete the degree requirements expeditiously and without ever moving. Eighteen months later, I had earned a four-year undergraduate degree, with honours. As it worked so well the first time, I did it again and obtained a graduate degree a couple years later, through the same program and while I was teaching university courses.

I'd like to say that, by the beginning of the 1980s, Canadian universities were sensitive to the needs of women and amended their doctoral program regulations accordingly, but that was not the case. After another thorough two-year investigation of higher education institutional programs and requirements, the only ones combining the desired academic rigour and standards with flexible timetables and schedules amenable to working professionals were found outside of Canada. I therefore enroled in a challenging American program. Four years later, and after a lot of hard work, my dream was realized and I earned a doctorate.

My sense of glee and accomplishment is derived from doing it on my terms. I'm still married; I never abandoned our home to fulfill a residency requirement; and I was able to work within several communities of scholars. It's not impossible, but it did take me thirty years to achieve what I wanted.

My experience may appear to be irrelevant in the 1990s when we have had an increased emphasis on access and equity in Canadian post-secondary education. We hear lots of talk and see many reports, by governments, institutions and the media. Unfortunately, what we don't see is action or significant changes in policies or practices. A glance at historical data reinforces this conclusion. In 1931, before I was even born, female representation among university faculty was 19 percent.[3] More than half a century has elapsed and comparative data indicate that no substantial positive action has taken place to alter the balance of scholars. In 1991, according to federal government data, the percentage of full-time university faculty who were female was 20 percent.[4]

An increase of one percent in female representation among university faculty, over a period of sixty years, is definitely not progress. The cry being heard now is that our institutions need more money for additional academic positions for women.[5] That's a "red herring." When money was flowing freely at times over the past forty years, when the numbers of students increased ninefold,[6] positions certainly were available but no significant gains were made in the percentage of women faculty. Money cannot help when there is simply no will to change.

No crystal ball is needed either; a pencil and paper or calculator will suffice. The result of the calculation is astounding and quite depressing. At the present increase of one percent every sixty years, it will take 1,920 years, or sixty-four generations, before women faculty have representation proportional to their numbers in the general population. Canadians are a tolerant people, but surely everyone's tolerance has a limit.

Does it matter to the general public whether we have women occupying positions as faculty and administrators in our universities and colleges? It should, because it ultimately affects our pocketbooks and taxes. Post-secondary institutions operate on the merit principle. In other words, when new faculty or administrators are hired, a specific process is followed. Faculty members participate in selection committees and recommend the best candidates to the administration. In turn, the administration reviews the process, concurs with, or rejects, the selection and makes a recommendation to the Board of Governors. A board normally agrees with the recommendations put forward by its administrators, and therefore usually hires the recommended individuals to work in the institution. The objective of this process is to ensure that the most meritorious scholars have been hired. In practice, the process has not ensured consistent attainment of the objective.

Indeed, how could any profession undergo the numerical expansion that the Canadian professoriate did in the mid-1960s to mid-1970s, when the number of post-secondary teachers grew from 12,000 to over 62,000, and still maintain quality?[7] To state that only the most meritorious scholars were admitted to academe is sheer sophistry. It does, however, redefine reality and encourage self-congratulation.

Look at the staffing in any post-secondary institution. Does it reflect the Canadian population? Or does it reflect past discriminatory practices that favoured one particular segment of the population in both training and recruitment? If it is still a predominantly male establishment, the merit system at that institution, and at universities and colleges generally, is considering only half of the population meritorious. Essentially, that is discrimination, but discrimination is only a symptom of the real problem.

The fundamental problem is inequality. Inequality exists if all potential scholars do not have equal opportunity for appointments, promotion and tenure. This is serious for all Canadians because inequality means that excellence suffers. To state this in crass terms, if we usually select post-secondary faculty and administrators from the male 48 percent of the population, we are operating at less than half our potential. We are running our universities and colleges at half steam or on half of our cylinders (for industrial age thinkers) or at half the bytes and RAM (for the technological crowd). If we selected and appointed the best and most qualified scholars and administrators from the entire population of qualified men and women, we could operate at full potential and that would reflect excellence!

The consequences of our inequalities in education affect all of us, through our economy, our taxes, our trade and our international status. On a personal level, this inequality ensures a significant number of role models for our sons and grandsons by providing them, during their post-secondary studies, with a supportive history, perspective, curriculum and an environment in which they can be comfortable and succeed.

Our daughters and grandaughters are not as fortunate. They see few role models, rarely have access to an equal number of female advisors, study a male curriculum (his story but not her story), pursue their studies in a relatively unfriendly environment, are sometimes sexually harassed, and therefore question their abilities and competence.

Some scholars, both men and women, are trying to redress the inequities. In some places, small and positive incremental changes are being made. After all, men on the boards, in the administration and on faculty may have wives or significant others, daughters and grandaughters who may be students. They want to be fair, or at least be perceived as being fair. Women scholars, however, are in a dilemma; they frequently are overburdened because of their limited numbers and, just as frequently, they are penalized for it.[8]

When the ratio of female to male faculty is unbalanced, as it is in almost all universities and colleges,[9] women sometimes bear an inequitable burden of responsibilities. Most search, selection, senate and other committees require female representation by women in tenure-stream positions; some even require an impossible male/female balance. As the number of women faculty fluctuates, sometimes reaching but generally always below 20 percent of total faculty (and women in tenure-stream positions are even fewer), a very small number of women spend many hours of the day, and days of the week, on committee work. In addition, as more than half of all post-secondary students are female, women faculty also usually have a larger advising role to fill because many students seek them out. The inequitable allocation of responsibilities exacts a toll. Women have less available time to conduct research and to publish and, for them, that means no promotion and no tenure. What a Catch-22 situation!

In the final years of the twentieth century, access to university for both women and men is no longer the only concern. For some, it will be available; for others, given the escalating tuition fees and the reduced student aid and lack of assistance programs, post-secondary education will remain a dream they can never afford. For those fortunate people who want to and can enrol in university or college programs, a major concern is "what." They have achieved the access denied to many in past, but what does that access provide? If our post-secondary institutions are not leading the way in equity, knowledge, research and excellence, will our students be well-educated and fairly served? Should we question the sincerity and, indeed, the integrity of a system that pays lip service to, but takes no concrete action about, equity and, therefore, excellence?

If we are concerned about these issues, we can do something about them, individually and in groups. As taxpayers, we fund the education system. If we're satisfied with it, no action is required. If we're concerned, however, we can do many things. We can keep education on the political agenda in our country by asking education-related questions of every candidate in every nomination and election. We can use a bit of behaviour modification, and reward through our votes and contributions those members and parties that make education a priority. Within our region or province, we can scrutinize and monitor the conduct and practices at post-secondary institutions. We have a right to know the institutional record, the numbers of women and men on faculty and in administration. If regular reports are not issued, including the numbers in each category of rank and tenure, we can write letters to the institutions requesting such information. Names and salaries may be confidential; impersonal aggregate data are not. We also can get to know who is appointed to the Board of Governors and let them know our concerns so that they can adequately represent us. Again, if we make donations, link them to the desired changes. Otherwise, our funds only help to perpetuate the status quo. These are personal actions that any concerned individual can take.

In addition, groups and organizations can exert more concerted pressure for positive change. Join one or more clubs—male, female or mixed—and ask them to focus their agenda on the state of education in your province or in the country. Better yet, volunteer for their committees and ensure that educational excellence and equity are addressed. Provide organizational and/or monetary support for only those post-secondary initiatives that support excellence through actions, not just words. If you belong to an alumnae association, get them involved. Alumni (men) and alumnae (women) can have a significant impact on institutional policies through the philanthropy of their members, and also through the association's representation on university or college boards, senates and councils. If your organization has the expertise, volunteer members' services to the institution; faculty women will thank you for it. Volunteer to be on selection committees, until such time as the university or college has a number of female staff proportionate to their representation in the general population. The institutions probably won't know what to do with your unusual offer, but it will send a loud and clear message to their administration. Whatever you do, don't let up on your efforts. Change may be a threat to the insecure, but it is a challenge to the adventurous and possibly our only opportunity for achieving excellence.

My personal story is not ended yet, as I plan to live for many more years. For me, life has been and continues to be a challenge and an adventure, which I thoroughly enjoy. It has not always been easy but it has been fun. For more than thirty years, I've taught or been an administrator in schools, community colleges, universities and a Ministry of Education, and in several provinces and countries. As I write this, I am a faculty member in a mid-western university, one of the 20 percent. I realize that, at the present rate of "progress," I won't see equity in our post-secondary institutions during my lifetime, nor will my children or grandchildren during theirs. One thousand, nine hundred and twenty years is a long time to wait. I also know that, when I head into retirement with my husband, I won't have to worry about poverty. Not everyone is as fortunate.

According to a government report, 75 percent of Canadian women will live the last quarter of their lives in poverty. Indeed, many women are living most of their lives in poverty now. Over the past twenty years, the number of women who are working and poor, with earnings below the poverty line, has risen by more than 160 percent, compared to an increase of 24 percent for men in the same situation.[10] This is neither fair nor just.

As education is the major "key" to the labour force, an adequate living and economic security, it's incumbent upon all of us to ensure that this key is available for all people knocking on the education door. We can make a difference.

Women constitute a little more than half of Canada's human resources. We have the potential for providing half of the answers. Alone, we could be a formidable force, but together with supportive men and all people who value excellence, we can start a revolution. And we should.

A century of snail-paced evolution obviously hasn't worked. Although some of the barriers that I encountered, because of gender, language, religion and marital status, have been eliminated, the fundamental problem still has not been addressed. Women do not have equality in post-secondary education, and higher education has never been an enlightened social force leading the way for society.

Therefore, society must lead the way for post-secondary education. As Canadians, we can demand more value for our education tax dollars, more tax dollars for our educational institutions, and institutional action and policies that will shake up the lethargy, comfort and mediocrity of many of our post-secondary institutions. We can support discrimination on the basis of ability, but must insist on both the elimination of other forms of discrimination in academe and the reduction of inequalities in education, so that quality no longer suffers.

Knowledge is power so let's find out what is happening in universities and colleges and use that information to start a revolution. With the public's efforts, excellence can prevail. Of course, equity is a *sine qua non* for excellence.

NOTES

* At Versailles in 1789, upon learning of the fall of the Bastille, Louis XVI asked, "Is it a revolt?" La Rochefoucauld-Liancourt replied, "No, Sir, it is a revolution." The inequalities and injustices of European society had culminated in a revolutionary upheaval in France. Lessons can be derived from history. Perhaps the inequalities and injustices in academe two hundred years later could be eliminated through revolution. If women, who are the majority of our population but the excluded classes in our academic organizations, wish to achieve equality, we can unite in a peaceful variation of revolutionary upheaval. History could beget herstory.

1. Ross 1976.
2. The Armed Forces University Program has been operating for more than twenty years and has attracted over 6,000 members of the armed forces, but fewer than one hundred "dependants" or spouses of the military, to degree programs in arts, sciences, law, medicine, dentistry, human ecology, physical education, commerce, nursing, education, social work, physiotherapy, dental hygiene, music, agriculture and interior design. No similar program is available for the general public.
3. Vickers and Adam 1977.
4. Secretary of State 1992.
5. Canadian Association of University Teachers 1991.
6. Secretary of State 1991.
7. Secretary of State 1991.
8. Park 1996.
9. The unbalanced ratio of female to male faculty is not the case in women's colleges and universities. Canada has one such institution, Mount Saint Vincent University, whereas the United States has more than eighty.
10. Gunderson, Muszynski and Keck 1990.

Creating the "Woman-Friendly" University: A Summary of the CFUW Report*

Mary Saunders, Margaret Therrien and Linda Williams

You have watched your daughter grow into the young woman who stands ready to leave for university. Together you considered the programs and the universities. Perhaps you made suggestions about the classes. Did either of you, in all that preparation, consider the climate into which she would be thrust? Will there be professors who will challenge her to reach her potential? Will her ideas and questions be accepted as readily as those of her brother? Will there be women whose career paths she can emulate? Will she be as free to come and go as her brother? Will the environment nourish her and encourage her to bloom?

Regrettably, the answer to the above questions is usually no. The 1989 murder of fourteen students at the Polytechnique Institute in Montréal *just because they were women* was the most brutal, extreme example of the climate our daughters may face. Spurred on by this tragic incident, then president of the Canadian Federation of University Women (CFUW), Thomasine Irwin, urged CFUW clubs "to contact post-secondary institutions in their communities to determine what actions are being taken concerning sexual discrimination, campus violence, alcohol abuse, and other issues that contribute to the environment on Canadian campuses."[1]

The Canadian Federation of University Women was founded in 1919 by women university graduates as a national, volunteer, non-profit organization. It is committed to the pursuit of knowledge, the promotion of education, the improvement of the status of women and human rights and active participation in public affairs in a spirit of cooperation and friendship. Currently there are 11,000 members in 137 clubs across Canada.

Members of CFUW–Oakville resolved to use the national network of clubs to press politely but firmly for change in the status of women at universities. We knew some universities had instituted excellent programs addressing certain issues, while other universities had not yet acknowledged their existence. Some universities had been "surveyed to death," while others had not yet been offered an opportunity to participate in a study.

A national questionnaire was administered to examine the status of women at Canadian universities and to formulate a qualitative picture of progress in ten areas of academic life.[2] Our objectives were to raise awareness of the struggle of women at universities to achieve equality, to identify creative solutions and to share them with all universities. CFUW hoped that its external concern would complement internal efforts at reform. During the project, we discovered that awareness and delineation of problems were high but the level of action to implement remedies was not, with a handful of exceptions.

METHODOLOGY
The questionnaire was prepared in 1990–1991 by CFUW–Oakville volunteers. Extensive research of relevant literature resulted in a draft questionnaire, which was sent for critical comment to academic women across Canada, several of whom were experts in the area of women's issues on campus. Two versions were prepared, one to be administered to presidents' offices and faculty representatives, the other containing appropriate modifications to be administered to student representatives. Volunteers in francophone CFUW clubs did the French translations. The project was officially launched by CFUW President Peggy Matheson in October 1991.

Questionnaire Subject Areas
Questions were asked on ten areas of university life: what follows is the rationale for the inclusion of each issue.

Support services are among the most important elements in achieving academic success. Without adequate child care, health services, sports facilities and budget, resources, work space and networking opportunities with women's special needs in mind, women have a hard time advancing.

Course content tends to include primarily male-only perspectives and teaching materials. Women's perspectives and contributions are often undervalued and poorly represented on reading lists and in libraries. Curricula, a section that is closely related, refers to whole academic programs rather than single courses. Women's studies courses are sometimes viewed as less equal than other humanities. Women are underrepresented in science, engineering and other technological fields. The use of gender-neutral language was examined because the use of exclusionary or sexist language perpetuates stereotypes based on sex alone and contributes to discriminatory practices.

Harassment on university campuses is well documented. The questionnaire sought information on the existence or lack of policies and procedures as well as the perceived level of awareness. Closely related to harassment is the section on establishing a safe environment, wherein we looked at measures for physical protection.

We had hoped the questions asked about the recognition of work experience would nudge the universities into realizing that women do many useful unpaid or extra-academic activities, which contribute to their careers and should count concretely in hiring or advancement decisions. Women's career paths are often very different from those of men. Job turnover or a gap in relevant career experience is frequently due to family responsibilities or to women following transferred spouses rather than to poor performance. The parallel section on the student questionnaire asked for information about "supervision and guidance."

In the section called incentives, we asked questions about creative and flexible scheduling of courses, part-time students, extending scholarship time limits, expanding the number of awards available to part-time students, the availability of part-time faculty positions and job-sharing.

The area of salary equity addressed the most clearly inequitable and the most galling issue for female academics. Women faculty earn less than their male counterparts at every level. The last section, hiring and tenure, looked at the underrepresentation of women in the professoriate. Women are clustered at the lower ranks and awarding tenure can be a very subjective thing. These sections were omitted from the student's questionnaire.

Questionnaire Administration
Universities surveyed were drawn from the list published by the Association of Universities and Colleges of Canada (AUCC) 1991. CFUW clubs were asked to contact the Status of Women Coordinator (or person responsible for women's issues) at the local university and arrange personal meetings to deliver and then collect the questionnaires. If a similar survey had recently been carried out at the institution, it was requested that the pertinent reports be attached. Completed questionnaires were sent to the CFUW–Oakville committee for analysis and preparation of the national report.

Data Analysis
Eighty-two president's office/faculty and student questionnaires were distributed to CFUW regional directors and clubs. Of these, fifty-one responses were received representing forty-five Canadian universities (55 percent). Forty-two student questionnaires were received, representing thirty-two universities. Data were presented as a description of the situation in 1991–92 at forty-five universities, not as statistically significant numbers. Specific findings are discussed below by section.

DISCUSSION
The response by universities to this CFUW project was positive with a few exceptions. Some respondents were initially reluctant to participate because of internal time constraints or the difficulty of obtaining some of the data. However, after completion, some respondents commented that the exercise nudged them into looking at issues in a different way, gave them new ideas for their status of women committees or brought to the fore previously unrecog-

nized concerns. We have received several expressions of interest in our report from universities and other academic associations.

Support Services
Lack of child care for both faculty and students continues to be a significant problem. More spaces and greater after-hours flexibility are needed for both faculty and students. The area of health services was the most advanced, with almost all institutions providing a reasonable range of services. Athletic facilities were found to be equally accessible to men and women in theory, but some respondents described a low priority of women's programs, unequal sports budgets and lack of sensitivity to women's preferences in athletic activities. Women's centres were reported at half of the responding universities. These centres perform vital functions in promoting networking among women, supplying information and documentation, and/or providing support and life skills training programs. However, only one third of women's centres had secure funding.

Course Content
Much remains to be done to achieve a balance of male/female perspectives and scholarship at Canadian universities. Only one sixth of responding institutions had a general policy encouraging such a balance. Students were acutely aware of variations in the attitudes and course materials used by professors. CFUW recommends that all students be required to take a course in women's perspectives to increase the awareness of women's contributions.

Curricula
Half of the institutions had specific initiatives in place to encourage women to pursue studies in non-traditional fields but it was clear that increased attention to recruitment and publicity is needed. A women's studies program was in place at twenty-eight responding universities but advanced degrees were available at only two. Only one third of women's studies programs had a full-time coordinator.

Gender-Neutral Language
Although 50 percent of universities had a gender-neutral language policy, it was not often seen in action on campus, with the exception of administrative documents. The majority of institutions reported that most of their female faculty used gender-neutral language and encouraged their students to do so, but at fewer than half of the universities did the majority of male faculty comply with the policy. Students lamented the lack of "good examples" in the classroom.

Harassment
The greatest progress has been made in the area of sexual harassment. A sexual

harassment policy was in place at 91 percent of responding universities and 72 percent had a sexual harassment officer responsible for complaints procedures and education programs. Theatre skits, video presentations and workshops were cited as effective means of educating the university community. However, when asked about the level of awareness of what constituted sexual harassment and what to do about it, responses from the faculty and students indicated much less confidence in the awareness of others than responses from the presidents' office. Universities should determine the true effectiveness of their education programs. Mandatory classes for students and workshops for all faculty and staff were suggested. Sanctions for sexual harassment ranged from apology and restitution to the victim to expulsion or dismissal. Several universities mentioned that their sexual harassment officer's emphasis was on educating the harasser rather than punishment. The majority of institutions had measures in place to prevent reprisals against complainants or witnesses. The length of the complaint procedure and the fact that the individual determining the sanction could be the guilty party were identified by some respondents to be problems in the practical application of the policy. Student-produced newspapers, some of the greatest offenders in the past, were covered by the policy in 67 percent of cases but monitored, informally, in only 47 percent.

Safe Environment

Safety measures vary widely among Canadian universities, depending on the nature of the campus, size of the community, etc. Several large urban institutions had major programs in place, stressing zero tolerance of violence against women and supplying information on personal security directly to students. The majority of institutions had fully lit paths around the campus, escort services and well-lit parking lots. Less common were trimmed shrubbery, library security patrols, men's groups concerned with violence against women, emergency phones and TV monitors. Some universities did not have any of these measures (due to underfunding or small campus size) and commented that safety did not appear to be a big issue on their campuses. However, respondents, particularly students, at the same institutions did not share that view. Universities should investigate the perception of personal safety of women on their campuses.

Recognition of Work Experience (Faculty)

Acknowledgement of the differences in career paths between women and men was commencing on some campuses. Thirty-three percent of universities reported that, when hiring, they took into account time taken for child-rearing or other family responsibilities. Only one institution stated that its equity policy contained clauses that specifically mentioned the recognition of different career paths. Recognition of unpaid relevant experience was, at best, informal and highly dependent on the individual and position desired. Unbiased criteria to assess women's qualifications and alternative career paths should be established at all universities.

Supervision and Guidance (Student)

Half of the responding students reported that they had no access to a female faculty member as a mentor. Many respondents lamented the lack of female faculty members available to be mentors and commented that the time permitted with mentors was often too limited to be effective. Only one-sixth of students reported that the ratio of women to men on their committees was the same as the ratio in their department. Such a lack of role models and mentors does a disservice to the young women at our universities, especially those in non-traditional fields.

Incentives

Information on how many students drop out and why was collected by 34 percent of universities but the majority were not able to determine whether more men than women dropped out. Students were very definite that a lack of child care, a lack of flexible timetables and a lack of encouragement by advisors led to a larger number of women than men dropping out. Half of the universities had expanded their scheduling options by offering more evening courses, variable blocks of hours for a course, cooperative work-study programs, correspondence courses and telecollege. Several universities have scholarships and fellowships for part-time undergraduate and graduate students. Job-sharing and "re-entry" fellowships for women PhD students are a rarity at Canadian universities. Even when available (to some degree at 39 percent of institutions), such arrangements were not widespread, tended to be individually negotiated and were not felt to be viewed favourably by others on campus. One university stated that it was incorporating clauses addressing this issue into its employment equity plan.

Salary Equity

Improvement has occurred in salary equity for women faculty but discrepancies are still apparent at every teaching rank. Women's salaries as a percentage of men's ranged from 95 percent at the full and associate professor level to 98 percent at the sessional lecturer level. Women averaged approximately 21 percent of the total faculty hired at responding universities but were still concentrated in the lower teaching ranks (9 percent of full or associate professors, and 12 percent of assistant professors and lecturers). Men were concentrated in the higher teaching ranks (58 percent of full and associate professors, and 21 percent of assistant professors and lecturers). Pay equity plans were in place at 57 percent of universities. A survey to identify salary inequities had been carried out at 58 percent of institutions, and salary inequities were identified at 91 percent of these. Action to implement recommendations from the survey was underway at eighteen universities. Widely applicable recommendations included an equity officer, annual monitoring of salaries and improvements in job classifications.

Hiring and Tenure

Half of responding universities had an affirmative action or employment equity plan. Several universities had established goals and detailed implementation plans for the hiring of women, including penalties for hiring units not complying within a reasonable time. Progress remains slow on the issue of tenure. Of the twenty-nine institutions reporting on hiring in the last five years, only two indicated that they had hired more female than male faculty members in the tenure track; two had hired equal numbers. The number of women achieving tenure in the last five years was 25 percent of the total faculty members. Only seven universities had conducted a study to investigate barriers to women's tenure: male-domination of departments, biased recruitment procedures and difficulties in balancing family, administrative and academic responsibilities were cited as problems. Modified tenure procedures to accommodate faculty with young families were in place at sixteen universities. At 45 percent of responding institutions, efforts were made to include more than one woman on important academic committees. However, 34 percent of universities did not have information on the ratio of female/male faculty on internal review boards allocating funds.

Students' Suggestions

Students felt strongly about several issues raised by the questionnaire. Campus climate was of great concern. Students wanted input into decisions made on safety and harassment. Students perceived that women students were seen as less dedicated to their education and were not encouraged and supported· as much as their male counterparts. Increased access to female mentors was stressed.

RECOMMENDATIONS AND PROFILE

We originally derived from our study over fifty recommendations for action by universities to improve the status of women on campus. A subsequent examination of the documentation forwarded to us by universities led us to conclude that we could recommend very little that was new. Most universities have detailed reports sitting on the shelf, bulging with recommendations that have not been fully implemented. Some institutions even have a later report urging implementation of the reforms in the first report. Therefore, CFUW confines its recommendations to the three listed below.

We felt that a profile of the ideal "woman-friendly" university would be as useful as the recommendations. We present fifty-four features, many of which appear as recommendations in several universities' internal reports. Universities having internal reports can use the profile as a checklist, while those institutions that have not reached the report stage can use it as a blueprint.

Recommendations
1. Implement *now* the recommendations of existing reports or the measures in the following profile.
2. Reorder spending priorities so that measures to improve the situation for women on campus can be managed as far as possible within existing resources.
3. Annually monitor progress in implementing reforms, by striking a committee that is responsible for the monitoring, is accountable and makes the findings public.

Profile of the "Woman-Friendly" University in Canada
What is a "woman-friendly" university? It is a place where every woman feels comfortable living, studying, working and playing; a place where she can reach her full academic and personal potential.

Why be a "woman-friendly" university? If the principle of simple equity is not enough, consider competitive position and self-interest. As the University of Calgary report of March 1991 "Women in the Nineties" stated: "Moving with confidence towards true equality for men and women will help us to attract and retain excellent people even during periods of fiscal restraint, because we will have an edge in creating a supportive working environment, which money does not necessarily provide."

The following profile describes features that would create and *maintain* an environment favourable to women's equality at Canadian universities. To synthesize this list, we have culled good ideas from the relevant literature, from documentation supplied to us in the course of this survey and from our own brainstorming sessions. Many of the same reforms have been cited by other universities and organizations. For convenience, features have been grouped according to the order of issues addressed in the questionnaire.

The ideal "woman-friendly" university would have or ensure:

A. Support Services
1. On-campus child care services with:
   • drop-in capability, extended and weekend hours;
   • enough spaces for faculty, staff and students;
   • subsidies for both graduate and undergraduate students in need;
   • a family housing complex for women with dependants; and
   • a support group for single parents.
2. Encouragement of male professors and lecturers to pursue their child-rearing responsibilities.
3. A parental leave policy for undergraduate and graduate students.
4. A women's centre and/or status of women office on campus that provides a wide range of materials and services of interest to women:
   • speakers, newsletters and workshops;

223

- a library of feminist publications and books, government documents and newspaper articles;
- training in learning skills, time management, assertiveness and leadership;
- career counselling for those in non-traditional fields; and
- a location for support and networking meetings.
5. Secure and adequate funding for the women's centre.
6. A status of women office that:
   - actively works to influence policy in the area of women's issues; and
   - initiates change
   - is independent of faculty association or employment equity office; and
   - has ombuds function.
7. On-campus opportunities for faculty member mentorship and peer support:
   - weekly tutorial/study/discussion groups for encouragement and assistance;
   - specific groups by discipline; and
   - specific groups for female graduate students.
8. Increased accessibility to essential university services for evening students, e.g., registrar's office, deans' offices, libraries and financial aid services.
9. Equality in athletics:
   - equal budgets for men's and women's sports;
   - equal access to, and time in, sports facilities; and
   - women's preferences in sport taken into account.
10. Health services, which include access to birth control methods and psychiatric counselling.
11. Wide publicity of available services.

B. Course Content
12. A university-wide policy emphasizing a balance in course content with regard to male and female scholarship, perspectives and concerns.
13. All instructors to be educated about the negative effects on students of subtle and often inadvertent sexual and racial discrimination.

C. Curriculum
14. A university-wide review of curriculum to increase incorporation of women's scholarship, and remove bias:
    - policies/procedures developed to monitor bias; and
    - heads of departments to be held responsible for review and content of curriculum.
15. Course evaluations with specific questions on gender bias in course materials, class atmosphere and language.
16. A degree requirement that *all* students take at least one course on women's perspectives. This could be adapted for specific disciplines.

17. Increased commitment to the women's studies program:
    • full-time coordinator; and
    • adequate resources and personnel.
18. Initiatives, including wide publicity of available programs, to encourage women to enter and complete degrees in non-traditional fields.

D. Gender-Neutral Language

19. A university-wide policy requiring the use of gender-neutral language in all aspects of campus life and in all documents and media produced at or for the university.
20. Active encouragement of faculty, staff and students to use gender-neutral language on and off campus:
    • education on "how to speak inclusively and gracefully" using work-shops, guest speakers and booklets; and
    • administration, faculty and staff to set "good examples" for students, both in/out of class.
21. Procedures established to hear and deal with complaints.

E. Harassment

22. Creation of an academic, working and living environment based on under-standing and mutual respect:
    • involve more women in decision-making;
    • publicize information on policy and procedures; and
    • conduct standardized triennial survey of all groups of women on campus to assess university climate.
23. A climate of zero tolerance for sexual harassment.
24. A sexual harassment policy that features:
    • a clear definition of sexual harassment, understandable by all, describing types of harassment and penalties;
    • a requirement that the administration or its representatives deal with all complaints expeditiously and fairly;
    • written record of steps taken;
    • involvement of concerned parties in development and review of proce-dures;
    • protection against reprisal;
    • more than one mechanism for complaint resolution; and
    • a perception by all that the policy is effective.
25. A sexual harassment office that consists of one or more full-time positions, preferably filled by females with a background in counselling, social work or mediation.
26. Responsibilities of a sexual harassment officer:
    • provide assistance to complainant and information on procedures to both parties;

- maintain list of support personnel and advocates;
- coordinate formal hearing process;
- educate university community on policy;
- train managers who might have to deal with sexual harassment situations;
- monitor policy effectiveness and recommend changes to administration;
- monitor harassment occurrence and report annually to administration and to university community; and
- maintain statistical and confidential records.

27. Sexual harassment education programs to be delivered:
    - in *mandatory* classes or workshops for all faculty, administration, staff and students;
    - by theatre, video, pamphlet, poster and newspaper;
    - in all languages commonly used on campus;
    - with information from the Criminal Code regarding pornography, libel and slander; and
    - in conjunction with regular surveys to determine whether awareness level is adequate.

28. Sanctions for sexual harassment:
    - to be determined by an independent committee after a formal hearing according to policy;
    - should include a written reprimand, written apology to victim, fine, job transfer, suspension or expulsion; and
    - should include recompense to complainant in form of adjusted grade, salary, restoration of job status or promotion where appropriate.

29. Formal guidelines for acceptable content of publications/skits/computer network material on campus.

30. Published reports of all sexual assaults on campus.

F. Safe Environment

31. A university-wide commitment to the personal safety and security of all on campus, supported by:
    - a committee with representation from across campus, which initiates, monitors, reviews and makes recommendations on all aspects of safety; and
    - a guideline such as the Women's Campus Safety Audit Guide by the Metro [Toronto] Action Committee on Public Violence Against Women and Children and Council of Ontario Universities (METRAC-COU).

32. A survey of female faculty, staff and students to determine their perspective on the safety of the campus.

33. Promotion of the concept that a safe campus is a collective responsibility by clear definitions and visual portrayal of what constitutes violence;
    - *mandatory* education program for all on violence; and
    - orientation package containing pamphlets on personal safety, use of

university safety measures, safety policy and violation penalties.
34. Publication of steps individuals can take, such as:
   - behaving in ways so as to minimize personal risk;
   - looking out for others;
   - reporting all threatening situations and assaults;
   - being prepared to say "no" and hear "no"; and
   - feeling comfortable, not foolish, in seeking help.
35. Encouragement of the growth on campus of men's groups concerned with violence against women.
36. Implementation of safety measures on campus, including:
   - well-lit paths and well-lit parking lots with attendants;
   - trimmed shrubbery in travelled areas of campus;
   - student escort services, both a shuttle van with scheduled route and safe stops, and foot or bicycle escort available on a "call-in" basis;
   - library security patrols, TV monitors and scream-activated alarms/microphones;
   - women's locker rooms with scream-activated alarms; and
   - installation of emergency phones campus-wide and in elevators; phones should be easily identified by colour, and have a direct line to security and call tracing capability.

G. Recognition of Work Experience
37. Clauses in hiring and employment equity policies to specifically address different career patterns and relevant unpaid work experience.
38. Criteria to assess qualifications and excellence, which recognize women's different career paths and appreciate that:
   - women often study non-traditional questions; and that
   - scholarly works published in non-traditional journals can be of equal merit.

H. Incentives
39. A plan to ensure equal representation of women in all courses of study by:
   - assessing admission policies for gender bias;
   - offering greater accessibility for starting, continuing and finishing university degrees;
   - establishing follow-up programs to monitor student progress, especially females in non-traditional fields; and
   - monitoring graduate programs for acceptance, transfer to a higher degree, and graduation rate for women.
40. A determination of whether rates of failure to complete a degree are similar for all students, so as to eliminate any barriers to women.
41. Increased flexibility of scheduling including:
   - courses offered in a variety of times and ways, such as evening, summer,

part-time and correspondence courses, as well as cooperative work-study programs;
- offered in the evenings (or other options) at least once every three years; and
- extended time limits for completion of degrees.

42. Greater variety of scholarships for female students, including:
- specific undergraduate summer research grants;
- scholarships specifically aimed at first-year female students to encourage them to enter graduate studies in non-traditional fields; and
- scholarships extended to high-achieving part-time students, both graduate and undergraduate.

43. Creative and flexible leave provisions, which:
- permit students granted leave to defer or interrupt acceptance of a scholarship; and
- establish "re-entry" fellowships to assist women PhD students or graduates to return to their fields after an absence for child-rearing.

44. Flexible job arrangements for faculty which are viable and respected alternatives, including:
- job-sharing, part-time faculty positions, fractional load appointments with pro-rated salary and benefits; and
- the sharing of research grants and responsibilities.

I. Salary Equity

45. A study to identify salary inequities.

46. A pay equity plan that eliminates gender bias by:
- establishing identical salaries for males and females at each level;
- making sure women's records are not undervalued when evaluating "experience";
- appointing as pay equity officer a high-ranking administrator to monitor salaries; and
- establishing an independent review board to investigate complaints.

47. Lobbying for action by funding agencies by:
- urging government to create incentives for universities actively pursuing equity, e.g., grants specifically for women professors;
- urging agency grant review boards to achieve "research grant equity" for women; and
- urging agencies to open fellowships and grants to part-time academics.

J. Hiring and Tenure

48. Recognition of the importance of having greater numbers of women professors to:
- serve as mentors and role models for students and junior colleagues;
- participate on academic committees; and

- serve in governance and senior administration.
49. An employment equity committee reporting to the president and board with responsibilities to:
    - develop equity programs with timetables and goals;
    - report annually on progress in hiring women; and
    - distribute such reports to all faculty and staff.
50. Collection of information on the numbers of men and women hired, numbers hired into tenure track and numbers achieving tenure, with the goal of achieving proportional or equal representation within five years.
51. Policies and procedures for hiring and recruiting new faculty members to ensure that women are sufficiently represented in all departments, including:
    - *actively* seeking out women and inviting applications;
    - interviewing at least one qualified woman for each position; and
    - hiring a qualified woman over a qualified man and a minority applicant over a white applicant until equity is achieved.
52. Loss of opportunity to fill positions for departments or hiring units that do not hire equitably within a specified time.
53. Inclusion of at least one woman on every important university committee (e.g., faculty appointment, grant review, tenure and promotion committees), with the goal of achieving proportional or equal representation within five years.
54. Encouragement of women to apply for non-traditional positions by:
    - inviting women to apply for senior administration;
    - appointing women as chancellors and presidents;
    - promoting women in non-traditional departments;
    - nominating women for internal and external awards; and
    - accessing a larger pool of women by basing hiring on ability, not rank or classification.

CONCLUSION

The interest in CFUW's survey reflected a concern for the realities of women's lives on Canadian campuses. Several universities have made attempts to redress the historical bias against women. Our data identified ways in which adjustments were being made as well as areas in which little progress has occurred.

WHAT YOU CAN DO

- Take the profile to your alma mater and ask them how they are doing in the various areas.
- Support financially those universities that are implementing the solutions.
- Contact the presidents of the universities, faculty associations and student associations. Ask what is being done to rectify the situation.
- Talk to Boards of Governors about the issues.

• Lobby the federal and provincial governments to require the universities to make changes.

EPILOGUE

We applaud those Canadian institutions that are genuinely making an effort to silence the reactionaries and to offer a more welcoming climate to women on their campuses. We warn those who are not that they are observed by women who increasingly have stronger voices, greater influence and less patience. The universities that will lead the others toward the twenty-first century will be those that acknowledge that 52 percent of the population is too great a resource to be ignored, that women's needs can be different and that their skills complement those of men. We hope that our recommendations and profile of the "woman-friendly" university will be useful to institutions as they work to remove barriers to women on campuses across Canada.

NOTES

*   A summary report of the "Women in Universities: Survey of the Status of Female Faculty and Students at Canadian Universities," conducted in 1992 by the Canadian Federation of University Women.
1.   CFUW President's Address in the CFUW Journal, Vol. 25, No. 7, Spring 1990.
2.   Mary Saunders, Margaret Therrien and Linda Williams. "Women in Universities: Survey of the Status of Female Faculty and Students at Canadian Universities." (The Canadian Federation of University Women: Ottawa, 1992).

Contributors

Without the contributions of authors and reviewers, the Women in Post-Secondary Education (WIPSE) project and this anthology could not have come to fruition. Those authors whose papers were positively evaluated in the double blind peer review process and the reviewers who read and evaluated papers are acknowledged in this section.

Judith Blackwell is an associate professor of sociology at Brock University, St. Catherines, Ontario. She holds a doctorate from the London School of Economics and has published a book and a number of papers on alcohol and illicit drugs, including the drug use of psychiatric patients. She served as a policy advisor on drug and alcohol legislation in England and for the federal government of Canada, and was a research scientist at the Addiction Research Foundation of Ontario. Current research interests include feminist issues in psychiatry and education, the rhetoric surrounding performance-enhancing drugs in sports and drug testing in the workplace.

Mariette Blanchette is the senior legal counsel for the Canadian Association of University Teachers (CAUT). She is a barrister and a solicitor and represents faculty members in arbitration cases. She deals mostly with discrimination, dismissals and denial of tenure cases. She is the CAUT expert on sexual harassment and academic freedom. She is the former secretary of the CAUT Status of Women Committee, as well as the former president of the Canadian Association Against Sexual Harassment in Higher Education. She is presently the secretary of the CAUT Academic Freedom and Tenure Committee. She has worked exclusively with and for faculty members for the past twelve years and was involved in labour relations for another twelve years before that.

Catherine Bray was an associate professor and coordinator of women's studies at Athabasca University from 1989–96. She became a senior lecturer in women's studies at Massey University in New Zealand in 1996.

Helen Breslauer has more than twenty-five years experience working in and on behalf of the university community of Canada. Her PhD, from Rutgers University, is in sociology which she taught for seven years at the University of Toronto. She spent sixteen years as senior research officer for the Ontario Confederation of University Faculty Associations (OCUFA) and is now working as a consultant to university groups on a variety of issues. While at OCUFA, Dr. Breslauer worked with its Status of Women Committee and other equity committees and served as OCUFA observer to the Status of Women Committee of the Canadian Association of University Teachers (CAUT). She has written extensively on equity matters. In 1992 Dr. Breslauer received from CAUT the

231

Sarah Shorten Award "in recognition of an outstanding contribution to the advancement of the status of women in Canadian universities."

Sheila A. Brown is president and vice-chancellor, and professor of business administration, at Mount Saint Vincent University in Halifax, Nova Scotia. Her scholarly interests are in consumer behaviour and marketing, particularly in the not-for-profit sector and in post-secondary education. Dr. Brown is a long time member of the Senior Women Academic Administrators of Canada, chairs the Association of Atlantic Universities' regional Coordinating Committee on Faculty Development and is a member of the executive council of the Canadian Society for the Study of Higher Education.

Teresa Brychcy holds a bachelor of science degree from McGill University and a master of science degree (genetics) from the University of Alberta. After five years at the National Research Council of Canada research laboratories, Ms. Brychcy joined the Natural Sciences and Engineering Research Council of Canada (NSERC) in 1979 where she is currently the director of Scholarships and Fellowships Programs.

Dean Care is an assistant professor in the faculty of nursing at the University of Manitoba. Dr. Care is the program coordinator for the undergraduate nursing program. He teaches leadership and management and his areas of interest are distance education and leadership management. Dr. Care has a doctorate in education from Nova Southeastern University in Florida.

Paula Chegwidden is an associate professor in the department of sociology at Acadia University in Wolfville, Nova Scotia. Her research and teaching interests centre around women in the labour force and women in development. She has been involved in a variety of women's community activities over the years, including the local shelter for abused women, CCLOW, and the Canadian Research Institute for the Advancement of Women (CRIAW). She also has served on the national board of Match International.

Linda Collier teaches humanities and philosophy at John Abbott College in Ste-Anne-de-Bellevue, Québec. Her interest in native peoples originally stemmed from canoe trips in the north. She recently completed a one-year research project culminating in a report entitled, *Teachers' Tales: Teaching Native Students.*

Christine L. Cooper has completed both a master's and a doctoral degree in labour and human resources at the Ohio State University. Dr. Cooper began her academic career at the University of Manitoba, and is currently an associate professor of business at the University of New Brunswick—Saint John. She teaches undergraduate and graduate courses in human resource management, strategic human resource policy, compensation, performance management and organizational behaviour. She conducts research on the procedural and distributive justice of organizational practices (e.g., performance appraisal, compensation schemes and work restructuring) as well as on the comparative industrial relations climates in Canada and the United States. Dr. Cooper's research has been published in *Administrative Science Quarterly, Journal of Applied Psychology* and *Psychological Reports.*

CONTRIBUTORS

Rebecca Priegert Coulter is associate dean of the faculty of education at the University of Western Ontario. She has published articles on the history of youth in Canada, gender and education, and women and educational restructuring. Dr. Coulter is one of the founding editors of *Historical Studies in Education/Revue d'histoire de l'éducation* and, with Linda Briskin, edited a special issue on feminist pedagogy for the *Canadian Journal of Education*. Service on the status of women committees of the Canadian Association of University Teachers and the Ontario Confederation of University Faculty Associations has taught her a great deal about women in post-secondary education.

Susan Hook Czarnocki is the manager of the Faculty of Arts Computing Laboratory of McGill University. She has a master's degree in history from the University of Wisconsin—Madison and a master's degree in sociology from McGill University. She remains involved in various efforts that attempt to ameliorate the "climate" for women across the campus and has served as the chair of the Senate Committee on Women at McGill.

Anne Innis Dagg teaches part-time at the University of Waterloo and is a wildlife biologist who has authored or co-authored: *The Giraffe; The Camel; Running, Walking and Jumping; Canadian Wildlife and Man; Wildlife Management in Europe*; and *Mammals of Ontario*, among other books. Her feminist books include *Harems and Other Horrors* about sexist bias in biology, and *MisEducation: Women and Canadian Universities* with Patricia J. Thompson. Dr. Dagg also has published feminist articles in: *Atlantis; The Canadian Journal of Higher Education; Canadian Woman Studies; The Globe and Mail; Journal of Canadian Studies; Kinesis; Policy Options; The Starting Line*; University of Waterloo *Forum*; and *Women's Education*.

Beth Westfall Davies is an adult educator who has worked in both the university and the community college sectors in British Columbia and Manitoba. She has a particular interest in issues of access to post-secondary education by women, Aboriginal people and residents of remote communities. Dr. Davies has a doctorate in education, specializing in adult education and the support needs of learners-at-a-distance. She is currently acting president of Northwest Community College in British Columbia.

Gail De Chateauvert is a single aboriginal mother. When writing her article, she was in her third year of the bachelor of education progam at the Winnipeg Education Centre, University of Manitoba. She graduated and is now working as a trainer and counsellor in an aboriginal youth program in a western province.

Juanita Ross Epp is associate professor of education at Lakehead University in Thunder Bay, Ontario. She teaches educational administration in both the graduate and undergraduate teacher education programs. She has co-edited two books: *Systemic Violence: How Schools Hurt Children* (Falmer Press, 1996) and *Systemic Violence in Education: Promise Broken* (SUNY Press, 1997).

Dolores Furlong completed her doctorate in education, curriculum development and narrative studies at the Joint Centre for Teacher Development, OISE, University of Toronto. She focuses her research on the personal knowledge of practitioners. Dr. Furlong's career involves twenty years of practice as a nurse, nurse educator and adminis-

233

trator in post-secondary health science programs in hospitals, colleges and universities. She has authored and published articles in educational and nursing journals, presented papers at professional conferences and conducted workshops on curriculum development in nursing. Dr. Furlong is a member of several professional associations including Sigma Theta Tau International Honour Society for Nurses.

Jane Gaskell is a professor and associate dean in the faculty of education at the University of British Columbia. She has published *Gender Matters from School to Work* (1992) and, with John Willinsky, edited *Gender in/Forms Curriculum* (1995). Dr. Gaskell's most recent project was a national study of Canadian secondary schools, published as *Secondary Schools in Canada* (1995). Her current research is on issues of school choice.

Juanita Giesbrecht works as an education development specialist in the Air Traffic Controller Training Division of Nav Canada Central Region located in Winnipeg, Manitoba. In addition to a ten-year teaching career in a community college, she has worked as a staff development consultant and has owned her own professional development consulting business, concentrating primarily on curriculum review and development.

Margaret Gillett, J. William Macdonald Emeritus Professor of Education at McGill University in Montréal, has written extensively on the subject of women in higher education. One of her books, *We Walked Very Warily: A History of Women at McGill* (1981) was the first such work on women at any Canadian university. Dr. Gillett was deeply involved in the establishment of women's studies at McGill and was founding director of the McGill Centre for Research and Teaching on Women. She was also chair of the Canadian Commission for UNESCO's Sub-Commission on the Status of Women and an executive member of the Women's Centre of Montréal. She has been honoured for her work by McGill University (Emeritus Professorship, 1995); the University of Saskatchewan (L.L.D., 1988); Russell Sage College, N.Y. (Sage Medal, 1991); the James McGill Society, the Canadian Society for the Study of Education and the Comparative and International Education Society of Canada (Honorary Life Memberships, 1993–95), the YWCA Women of Distinction Award (1994); and the Governor-General's Persons Award (1996).

Jane Gordon is an associate professor in the department of sociology and anthropology at Mount Saint Vincent University and has also been a member of its women's studies department. Her research interests include issues of gender in higher education and women's voluntary community work. She has been an activist/advocate in a number of areas, including equality in academic life and a term as chair of the Status of Women Committee of the Canadian Association of University Teachers.

Mary Hampton is an assistant professor of psychology at Luther College, University of Regina. Dr. Hampton received her doctorate at Harvard University. The research and teaching areas she is most interested in involve women's studies, adoption issues and cross-cultural counseling.

Jennie Hornosty is a professor of sociology and an employment equity educator for faculty at the University of New Brunswick, Fredericton. She was previously director of graduate studies for the sociology department and coordinator of women's studies.

A mother of two boys, aged twelve and eight, she is actively involved in issues pertaining to the status of women and faculty association affairs. She is a past member of the national executive of the Canadian Association of University Teachers. Her most current research is in the area of violence against women in farm and rural communities, and issues of academic freedon and the inclusive university.

Patricia Hughes is currently the Mary Louise Lynch Chair in Women and Law in the faculty of law at the University of New Brunswick. After teaching political science at the university level, she entered law. On her call to the Ontario bar in 1984, she became counsel in the policy development division of the Ministry of the Attorney General, concentrating on the application of the *Charter of Rights and Freedoms* to Ontario legislation; she subsequently served as a vice-chair of the Ontario Labour Relations Board and alternate chair of the Ontario Pay Equity Hearings Tribunal. Dr. Hughes has been active in the women's movement for over twenty years and is now involved in a number of activities intended to advance diverse women's concerns, both at the university and in the larger community.

Susan Jackel is associate professor of Canadian studies at the University of Alberta. She has been active in women's issues on her own campus, and served a term (1990–92) on the CAUT Status of Women Committee. Dr. Jackel has published on prairie women's history and literature, and is currently working on issues related to Canadian women and citizenship.

Nancy Johnston graduated from York University in 1995 with a doctoral degree in English literature. She currently teaches English for Ryerson Polytechnic University in Toronto.

Sandra Kirby is an associate professor of sociology at the University of Winnipeg. Her areas of interest include research and advocacy about issues of concern to women and sport, and research about feminist methodologies and ethics. Dr. Kirby is a long-time member of the Canadian Research Institute for the Advancement of Women (CRIAW) and of the Canadian Association for the Advancement of Women and Sport (CAAWS); most of her feminist activism is on behalf of those organizations. In her spare time, she coaches rowing at the Winnipeg Rowing Club.

Anne-Marie Weidler Kubanek was born and educated in Sweden. After spending one year as a National Institute of Heath research fellow at Stanford University, she returned to Uppsala University, Sweden, to complete her doctorate in physical organic chemistry. She has worked as an industrial research chemist in the United States and Montréal. Dr. Kubanek has taught at John Abbott College since 1975 and, in addition, pursues an interest in the history of women in science.

Eunice Marie Fisher Lavell, since writing this article, has completed her master's degree in educational psychology. Her thesis is entitled "Doing the Right Thing: Working-Class Feminist Perspectives on the Lives of Adolescent Mothers." Eunice is working as a school counsellor at Hollow Water First Nation and hopes to pay off her student loan by 2013. She listens to country music to remember her home, and Celtic music to remember her history. She writes stories to honour both. She believes in stories.

Ann Manicom is currently an associate professor in the department of education at Mount Saint Vincent University in Halifax. Prior to the restructuring of post-secondary education in Nova Scotia, she served as coordinator of women's studies at Dalhousie University, and helped develop the interuniversity joint master's of arts in women's studies. She writes and teaches in the areas of feminist pedagogy, curriculum critique and feminist research methodologies. With Dr. Marie Campbell, she co-edited the book *Knowledge, Experience and Ruling Relations: Studies in the Socialization of Knowledge*.

Carol McKeen is an associate professor in the school of business at Queen's University. Prior to joining Queen's faculty, she was a member of the audit staff at Deloitte, Haskins and Sells, Minneapolis, and an internal auditor at Honeywell, Inc. Professor McKeen has bachelor's degrees in science and education, and a master's of business administration. She is a certified public accountant and co-author of several articles in the area of women in management, women in the accounting profession and management education for women. She has served as faculty advisor on employment equity to the principal of Queen's University, and is currently working with organizations wishing to improve the career success and satisfaction of their female managers.

Mary Murphy is a registered nurse working in community health care. Her career spans twenty-five years of practice in acute care and community health care settings. She is actively involved in community health programs as a teacher and volunteer. She has four children, two of whom are currently in post-secondary programs. Her particular areas of interest are palliative care and personal agency in health care. Mary is taking courses toward a baccalaureate degree. She is also a member of local advisory committees on hospice and community health care education.

Rachel L. Osborne is a doctoral student in the department of sociology at York University in Toronto. She is the author of "Sexual Harassment in Universities: A Critique of the Institutional Response" in *Canadian Woman Studies*, Volume 12, Number 3, and the co-author of "Women's Fear of Men's Violence" in *Canada Watch*, Volume 1, Number 5. Her ongoing research interests include violence against women and women and post-secondary education.

Karen Pancer is a professor of writing at Humber College of Applied Arts and Technology in Toronto. She holds a bachelor of arts from the University of Toronto, a bachelor of education from the University of Saskatchewan, and a master of arts specializing in language and professional writing from the University of Waterloo. She has been employed in the business and social service fields, has worked as a journalist and teacher, and has taught speech communication courses and writing courses at the college and university level.

Susan Prentice is a member of the department of sociology at the University of Manitoba. From 1993–96, she held the Margaret Laurence Chair in Women's Studies and founded *Backtalk*, the Chair's prairie-region women's studies newsletter. Her research focuses on gender, family and social policy (especially child care), and issues confronting women in post-secondary education. She is the editor of *Sex in Schools: Canadian Education and Sexual Regulation* (Lorimer, 1994). She has been an activist feminist since the early 1980s, and is currently the Manitoba representative on the Child Care Advocacy Association of Canada.

Wendy M. Pullin is a registered clinical psychologist in private practice in Edmonton, Alberta. She has a special interest in women's identity issues—particularly work and family role transitions and intimacy and conflict. She received her master of science degree from the University of Calgary. In her doctoral dissertation research, she examines academic identity formation in Canadian anglophone and francophone women.

Linda Quattrin is a reporter and editor at the *Winnipeg Free Press*. She has a master of journalism degree from Carleton University.

Ruth Rees is an associate professor in the faculty of education, and chair of the University Council on Employment Equity at Queen's University. Her speciality is in the area of educational planning and management, particularly in the area of employment equity in educational systems: elementary, secondary and post-secondary institutions.

Lois Reimer was the University of Toronto's first status of women officer (1984–92). She found the position, with its "rich mix of principles, personalities, and politics," a new learning experience and those eight years the most important over a varied career in university administration. Lois Reimer is enjoying early retirement, currently in her native Winnipeg. Her volunteer interests include the Advisory Panel to the Margaret Laurence Chair in Women's Studies, based jointly at the Universities of Manitoba and Winnipeg, the University of Toronto's National Scholarships program, and the CNIB's university text recording service—all a nice counterpoint to Manitoba blizzards and floods.

Beth Rubin is an assistant professor in the faculty of management at the University of Manitoba. She has a doctorate in industrial/organizational psychology and currently teaches undergraduate and graduate courses in human resource management and organizational power and politics. She conducts research on employment discrimination, gender and differences in values and communication styles, and power in organizations. Having earned a black belt in two different martial arts, Beth spent many years teaching self-defense for women.

Mary Saunders has a background in pure science, including a bachelor of science (honours) degree in genetics from the University of Guelph and a doctorate in biochemical genetics from the University of Toronto. She pursued her interest in things molecular during post-doctoral appointments in interferon research at the Hospital for Sick Children in Toronto and in fungal gene regulation at Allelix Inc., a biotechnology company in Mississauga. Currently she divides her time between her family and two children and serving as scientific editor to Dr.Tak Mak of the Ontario Cancer Institute and the Amgen Institute, editing journal manuscripts and writing books.

Rose Sheinin is an honourary fellow of the Ryerson Polytechnical Institute, a professor in the department of biology, faculty of arts and science, and former vice-rector academic, at Concordia University. She obtained her bachelor of arts in physiology and biochemistry, and master's and doctoral degrees in biochemistry from the University of Toronto. Her scientific career has focused on the study of viruses that cause cancer. Throughout her academic life as undergraduate and graduate student, as post-doctoral fellow, as university professor and as academic administrator, she continually has worked for the advancement of women in the university and in science, engineering and technology and medicine. Dr. Sheinin has been recognized nationally and internationally, and her honours include Doctor of Human Letters, Mount Saint Vincent University, 1985; YWCA Woman of Distinction Award, 1988; Doctor of Science, Acadia University, 1988; Doctor of Science, University of Guelph, 1991; and the Ryerson Honorary Fellowship, 1993.

Bobbi Spark was completing a bachelor of arts (honours) at Queen's University when she wrote this article, and she completed a master of arts degree in 1997. At the 1991 Learneds' Conference, she presented a paper entitled "Uppity Women and the Military." In 1993, she wrote a humorous article about herself called "Cooking at Queen's" for the *Undergraduate Feminist Review*. Bobbi's community work spans twenty-eight years of commitment to working-class women's empowerment in unionism, welfare and tenant rights, legal and community issues, and feminism. She wants to help women to understand their "crazy-making" world of academe.

Jackie Stalker is a wife, mother, grandmother and feminist. During the WIPSE project, she was an associate professor and coordinator of the graduate program in higher education at the University of Manitoba, and also managing editor of *The Canadian Journal of Higher Education*. She is the Manitoba director of the Canadian Congress for Learning Opportunities for Women (1990–97) and, over the years, has had administrative and teaching experience in schools, community colleges, universities, organizations and government in three provinces and several countries. Dr. Stalker's professional and public achievements are listed in *Who's Who in America, in the Midwest, and in American Education, Who's Who of Canadian Women* and *of American Women*, and *The World Who's Who of Women*. She retired, first from government and then from academe, and is now enjoying a stress-free life.

Cannie Stark-Adamec is the director of the Organizational and Social Psychology Unit at the University of Regina and vice-president (women's issues) of the Social Science Federation of Canada. Dr. Stark-Adamec has served as president of the Canadian Psychological Association and as head of the department of psychology at the University of Regina. She was awarded her doctorate from McGill University in the mid-'70s and has published over one hundred articles. Formerly a karate instructor, she now relieves the stress of being a full professor by conducting research on the stress experienced by two misunderstood populations—police officers and women.

Christine Storm is a professor of developmental psychology at Mount Allison University. She has published articles on the language of emotions and on higher education. She has served as coordinator of the Section on Women and Psychology for the Canadian Psychological Association and chair of the President's Advisory Committee on Women's Issues at Mount Allison.

Peta Tancred was the director of the McGill Centre for Research and Teaching on Women from 1990–96, and she is a professor of sociology at McGill University. She is a graduate of McGill, the Université de Montréal and the London School of Economics.

CONTRIBUTORS

Her feminist writings have centred on the *Gendering of Organizational Analysis* (with Albert Mills; Sage, 1992) and *The Sexuality of Organization* (with Hearn et al.; Sage, 1989). She has published extensively on women's work in universities, in state bureaucracies, in banks and with computers. Her current work focusses on women's "exit" from male-dominated workplaces as a means of grasping their comments on masculinist organizations.

Charlene Thacker is an associate professor in the department of sociology at the University of Winnipeg. She has published articles on returning women students and is engaged in research on the multiple roles of returning women students.

Margaret Therrien is a nursing graduate from the Ottawa Civic Hospital. She obtained her bachelor of nursing degree from Dalhousie University in 1985 and has been employed in a variety of nursing positions. Currently she splits her time between her family, a busy part-time career with Canada's Naval reserve and her assorted volunteer positions.

Peggy Tripp-Knowles is a professor cross-appointed to the department of biology and the faculty of forestry at Lakehead University in Thunder Bay, Ontario. She has directed a research program in the evolutionary biology of forest trees using isozyme technology. She chaired the committee that established the women's studies program at Lakehead. A research associateship at the Five Colleges Women's Studies Research Center at Mount Holyoke College in Massachusetts was part of Peggy's recent sabbatical activities in which she examined her scientific subdiscipline for masculine bias. Peggy presently teaches and writes on the topics of science critique, environmental philosophy and the cultural role of science.

Marion Vaisey-Genser is a senior scholar at the University of Manitoba and the past chair of the President's Advisory Council on Women. Her thirty years as a professor have included positions in academic administration as associate vice-president (research), associate dean of the faculty of graduate studies, and head of her home department of foods and nutrition. She currently serves on several health, research and community boards, including the awards committee of the Science Council of British Columbia. Her contributions to research and university development have been recognized by a Queen Elizabeth Silver Jubilee Medal in 1977, a YWCA Woman of the Year Award in 1980, the W.J. Eva Award of the Canadian Institute of Food Science and Technology in 1986, the University of Manitoba Chancellor's Award in 1992, and the Manitoba Home Economics Association Award for Excellence in Teaching in 1993.

Mary Valentich, PhD, is a professor and associate dean (graduate programs) in the faculty of social work at the University of Calgary and former advisor on women's issues to the president of the University of Calgary. Her teaching, practice and scholarly interests are human sexuality, feminist social work practice, organizational development and career management. She has published numerous articles, and co-edited two books and a self-help manual with her partner, James Gripton.

Vande Jane Vezina is a mother of two young children. She has recently relocated from Toronto, Ontario to Edmonton, Alberta where she plans to continue graduate work. Her contribution is based on her master's thesis on the masculinization of higher education and its effects on women graduate students.

Margaret Waller completed both her bachelor and master of arts degrees in Kansas, where she was born, and came to Canada in 1973. She began college-level teaching in 1985 after working as a consultant in social science research. She teaches research methods and sociology of the family at John Abbott College and is active in the women's studies program.

Linda Williams has a doctorate in educational administration from the University of Alberta. She has taught grades one to graduate university classes and has been a workshop designer/leader in personal and professional growth. Throughout her career, she has held various executive positions for professional and volunteer organizations. Linda is presently principal of a private high school.

Peggy Wilson is associate professor of counsellor education at California State University in Sacramento. She was on leave from Sacramento and conducted research at the Saskatchewan Indian Federated College in Regina. Dr. Wilson received her doctorate from the University of California in Santa Barbara. She is a member of the Opaskwayak Cree Nation at The Pas, Manitoba.

S. Catherine Wilson holds a bachelor of arts (English), a bachelor of science (chemistry), and a master of engineering (chemical engineering). Following university, she spent four years in industry, then joined the Scholarships and Fellowships Division of the National Sciences and Engineering Research Council of Canada (NSERC) as a program officer, responsible for the Women's Faculty Awards and Undergraduate Student Research Awards. In 1993, she moved to the Policy, Planning and Evaluation Division as a senior planning analyst.

References

Abell, J. 1991. "Resistance in the Classroom in Feminist Pedagogy: Critique and Commitment." In T. Brettel Dawson (ed.), *Women, Law and Social Change*. North York, ON: Captus.

Abella, R.S. 1984. *Equality in Employment: A Royal Commission Report*. Ottawa: Ministry of Supply and Services.

Aburdene, P., and J. Naisbitt. 1992. *Megatrends for Women*. New York: Random House.

Acker, S. 1992. "New Perspectives on an Old Problem: The Position of Women Academics in British Higher Education." *Higher Education* 24: 60.

Adams, A., and P. Tancred. Forthcoming. *Redesigning the Profession: Canadian Women Architects, 1920–1992*.

Adamson, N., L. Briskin, and M. McPhail. 1988. *Feminist Organizing for Change: The Contemporary Women's Movement in Canada*. Toronto: University of Oxford Press.

Aiken, S.H., K. Anderson, M. Dinnerstein, J.N. Lensink, and P. MacCorquodale. 1988. *Changing Our Minds: Feminist Transformation of Knowledge*. New York: State University of New York Press.

Aisenberg, N., and M. Harrington. 1988. *Women of Academe: Outsiders in the Sacred Grove*. Amherst: University of Massachusetts Press.

Allen, P. 1985. *The Concept of Woman: Classical to Current Concepts, 750 BC–AD 1250*. Montréal: Eden.

American Council on Education. 1985. *Preliminary Report: Senior Women Administrators in Higher Education*. Washington, DC: ACE.

Anderson, D. 1991. *The Unfinished Revolution: The Status of Women in Twelve Countries*. Toronto: Doubleday Canada.

Andrews, A. 1993. "'Chilly Climate' Controversy Sparks Review at UVic." *CAUT Bulletin*, October: 7.

Anonymous. 1990. "The Chilly Climate at a Canadian Business School: Personal Experiences and Reflections." Working Paper. Ontario. June.

Association of Universities and Colleges of Canada. Research, Policy and Planning Division. 1990. *Trends: The Canadian University in Profile*. Ottawa: Association of Universities and Colleges.

Backhouse, C.B. 1988. "Women Faculty at UWO: Reflections on the Employment Equity Award." Unpublished manuscript.

———. 1995. "An Historical Perspective: Reflections on the Western Employment Equity Award." In the Chilly Climate Collective (eds.), *Breaking Anonymity: The Chilly Climate for Women Faculty*. Waterloo: Wilfrid Laurier University Press.

Backhouse, C.B., and D.H. Flaherty, eds. 1992. *Challenging Times: The Women's*

241

Movement in Canada and the USA. Montréal: The McGill-Queen's University Press.

Backhouse, C.B., R. Harris, G. Mitchell, and A. Wylie. 1989. *The Chilly Climate for Faculty Women at the University of Western Ontario*. London: University of Western Ontario.

Baines, B. 1980. *Women, Human Rights and the Constitution*. Ottawa: Canadian Advisory Committee on the Status of Women.

Bannerji, H., L. Carty, K. Delhi, S. Heald, and K. McKenna. 1991. *Unsettling Relations: The University as a Site of Feminist Struggle*. Toronto: Women's Press.

Barman, J., Y. Hébert, and D. McCaskill. 1987. "The Challenge of Indian Education: An Overview." In J. Barman, Y. Hébert and D. McCaskill (eds.), *Indian Education in Canada: Volume 2: The Challenge*. Vancouver: University of British Columbia Press.

Barreca, R. 1991. *They Used to Call Me Snow White... But I Drifted: Women's Strategic Use of Humour*. New York: Penguin.

Basow, S.A., and N.T. Silberg. 1987. "Student Evaluations of College Professors: Are Female and Male Professors Rated Differently?" *Journal of Educational Psychology* 79: 308–14.

Bateson, M.C. 1990. *Composing a Life*. New York: Plume.

Beach, R. 1975. "A Case History of Affirmative Action." In Elga Wasserman et al. (eds.), *Women in Academia*. New York: Praeger.

Beck, E.T., S.C. Greer, D.R. Jackson, and B. Schmitz. 1990. "The Feminist Transformation of a University: A Case Study." *Women's Studies Quarterly* 18(1 & 2): 174–88.

Beecher, C. 1842. *A Treatise on Domestic Economy for the Use of Young Ladies at Home, and at School*. Revised edition. Boston: T.H. Webb.

Beer, A. 1995. "On Being Lucky." In M. Gillett and A. Beer (eds.), *Our Own Agendas: Autobiographical Essays by Women Associated With McGill University*. Montréal: McGill-Queen's University Press.

Belenky, M.F., B.M. Clinchy, N.R. Goldberger, and J.M. Tarule. 1986. *Women's Ways of Knowing*. New York: Basic.

Beresford-Howe, C. 1984. "Stages in an Education." In M. Gillett and K. Sibbald (eds.), *A Fair Shake*. Montréal: Eden.

Berger, T. 1991. *A Long and Terrible Shadow: White Values, Native Rights in the Americas*. Vancouver: Douglas and McIntyre.

Bernard, J. 1964. *Academic Women*. University Park: Pennsylvania State University Press.

Borins, E.M., and G. Feldberg, eds. 1992. "Special Series on Gender and Science." *Women and Therapy* 12(4): 47–125.

Buechler, S.M. 1990. *Women's Movements in the United States: Woman Suffrage, Equal Rights and Beyond*. New Brunswick, NJ: Rutgers University Press.

Burke, M.A. 1991. "Caring for Children." *Canadian Social Trends*. Ottawa: Statistics Canada.

Burtt, E., ed. 1967. *The English Philosophers from Bacon to Mill*. New York: Modern Library.

Byfield, V. 1991. "Fembos in Academe." *Alberta Report*, January 7: 24–30.

Calgary Herald. 1995. "Gender Wars Claim Another Victim." June 4.

Cameron, D.M. 1991. *More Than an Academic Question: Universities, Government, and Public Policy in Canada*. Halifax: The Institute for Research on Public Policy.

Canada, Indian Affairs and Northern Development. 1992. *Basic Departmental Data*. Ottawa: Canada, Indian Affairs and Northern Development.

Canadian Association of University Teachers (CAUT). 1985. *A CAUT Statement on Positive Action to Improve the Status of Women in Canadian Universities*. Ottawa: Canadian Association of University Teachers.

————. 1986. *Brief to the Special Committee on Child Care*. Ottawa: Canadian Association of University Teachers.

————. 1991. "Change or Be Changed." *CAUT Bulletin*, December 10.

————. 1993a. *Profile of the "Woman-Friendly" University in Canada*. Status of Woman Supplement, April. Ottawa: Canadian Association of University Teachers.

————. 1993b. *The CAUT 1992–93 Employee Benefits Survey for Faculty*. Ottawa: Canadian Association of University Teachers.

Canadian Federation of University Women (CFUW). 1992. *Women in Universities: Survey of the Status of Female Faculty and Students at Canadian Universities*. Ottawa: CFUW.

————. 1992. "Profile of the 'Woman-Friendly' University in Canada." *CAUT Bulletin*, Status of Women Supplement.

————. 1990. President's Address in the CFUW Journal, Vol. 25, No. 7, Spring.

Canadian Federation of Students. 1991. *Violence Against Women: A Campus Reality*. Brief presented to the House of Commons Sub-Committee of the Status of Women. Ottawa: CFS.

Canadian Panel on Violence Against Women. 1993. *Changing the Landscape: Ending Violence—Achieving Equality. Final Report*. Ottawa: Ministry of Supply and Services.

Cannon, L.W. 1990. "Fostering Positive Race, Class, and Gender Dynamics in the Classroom." *Women's Studies Quarterly* 18(1 & 2): 126–34.

Caplan, P. 1993. *Lifting a Ton of Feathers: A Woman's Guide to Surviving in the Academic World*. Toronto: University of Toronto Press.

Carasco, E. 1993a. "A Case of Double Jeopardy: Race and Gender." *Canadian Journal of Women and the Law* 6(Dec): 142–52.

————. 1993b. "Anti-Feminism, Racism and Academic Freedom." *OCUFA Forum Supplement: Strategies for the Inclusive University*, December.

Chait, R., and A. Ford. 1982. *Beyond Traditional Tenure*. San Francisco: Jossey-Bass.

Chamberlain, M., ed. 1988. "Task Force on Women in Higher Education." *Women in Academe: Progress and Prospects*. New York: Russell Sage Foundation.

————, ed. 1991. *Women in Academe: Progress and Prospects*. New York: Russell Sage Foundation.

Clarke, E. 1873. *Sex in Education or a Fair Chance for the Girls*. Boston: James R. Osgood.

Clark-Jones, M., and P. Coyne. 1990. "Through the Back Door." *Atlantis* 15(2): 41.

Collective Agreement Between Concordia University and the Concordia University Faculty Association. 1992. Article 16.01.

Collins, P.H. 1992. *Black Feminist Thought: Knowledge, Consciousness and the Politics of Empowerment*. New York: Routledge.

Committee on the Status of Women in Ontario Universities. 1988a. *Attracting and Retaining Women Students for Science and Engineering*. Toronto: Council of Ontario Universities.

————. 1988b. *Employment Equity for Women: A University Handbook*. Toronto: Council of Ontario Universities.

Conway, S. 1991. "Campus Critique Leaves Women on the Margins." *Globe and Mail*, October 24.

Cook, R., and W. Mitchison, eds. 1976. *The Proper Sphere: Women's Place in Canadian Society*. Toronto: Oxford University Press.

Cooke, K. 1986. *Report of the Task Force on Child Care*. Ottawa: Status of Women Canada.

Cornford, F.M. 1922. *Microcosmographia Academica: A Guide for the Young Academic Politician*. Cambridge UK: Bowes and Bowes, reprinted in 1992. Chicago: University of Chicago Press, 1992.

Cott, N. 1984. "The Women's Studies Program: Yale University." In B. Spanier (ed.), *Toward a Balanced Curriculum: A Sourcebook for Initiating Gender Integration Projects*. Cambridge, MA: Schenkman.

Couchmann, J. et al. 1998. "Report to the Faculty of Graduate Studies Council of the Implementation Committee: *Not Satisfied Yet: Report of the Task Force on the Status of Women Graduate Students*." York University, (forthcoming).

Crawley, D., and M. Ecker. 1990. "Integrating Issues of Gender, Race, and Ethnicity into Experimental Psychology and Other Social Science Methodology Courses." *Women's Studies Quarterly* 18(1 & 2): 105–16.

Cross, D. 1992. "A Message from the President. 1990–91 Annual Report." *Chicago State University Magazine*, Fall/Winter.

Cruikshank, M. 1982. "Introduction." In M. Cruikshank (ed.), *Lesbian Studies Present and Future*. Old Westbury, NY: Feminist Press.

Crull, P. 1987. "Searching for the Causes of Sexual Harassment: An Examination of Two Prototypes." In C. Bose et al. (eds.), *Hidden Aspects of Women's Work*. New York: Praeger.

Curzon, Lord of Kedleston. 1909. *Principles and Methods of University Reform*. Oxford: Clarendon.

Dagg, A.I. 1992. "Feminism Reviled: Academic Non-Freedom at Canadian Universities." *Canadian Woman Studies* 12(3): 89–92.

Dagg, A.I., and P.J. Thompson. 1988. *MisEducation: Women and Canadian Universities*. Toronto: Ontario Council on Graduate Studies.

Daly, M. 1973. *Beyond God the Father: Toward a Philosophy of Women's Liberation*. Boston: Beacon.

Daniels, D. 1994. "Climate Audit Will Guide Us Toward Inclusive University." *CAUT Bulletin*, January.

Darsigny, M. 1990. *L'epopée du suffrage feminin au Québec, 1920–1940*. Montréal: UQAM Service aux Collectivités.

Davis, F., and A. Steiger. 1991. "Listening to the Women's Voices." *Women's Education* 9(2): 18–21

Dawson, G.M. 1884. *The Higher Education of Women at McGill*. Ottawa: Public Archives Library.

de Beauvoir, S. 1952. *La Deuxième Sexe*. New York: Knopf.

De Danaan, L. 1990. "From Center to Margin: Dynamics in a Global Classroom." *Women's Studies Quarterly* 18(1 & 2): 135–44.

de la Cour, L., and R. Sheinin. 1986. "The History of the Ontario Medical College for Women: 1883–1906." *Canadian Journal of Women's Studies* 4(3): 73–77.

REFERENCES

Delagrave J. 1990. *Accueil et intégration des étudiants amérindiens au CÉGEP de Sept-Iles, Rapport d'expérimentation, 1989–90.* Sept-Iles, PQ: CÉGEP de Sept-Iles.

Dembski, P.E.P. 1985. "Jenny Kidd Trout and the Foundation of the Women's Medical Colleges at Kingston and Toronto." *Ontario History* 77: 183–206.

de Pizan, C. 1405. *The Treasure of the City of Ladies.* Harmondsworth, Middlesex: Penguin, 1985.

Drakich, J. 1991. "Strategies for a New Equality: Employment Equity for Women in Ontario Universities." In C. Lambert (ed.), *Toward a New Equality.* Ottawa: Social Science Federation of Canada.

Drakich, J., M. Taylor, and J. Bankier. (1993). "Academic Freedom is the Inclusive University." Paper presented at the Canadian Association of University Teachers Status of Women Committee Annual Conference, October 23, Winnipeg.

Dubinsky, K., L. de la Cour, N. Forestell, M. Kelm, C. Morgan, and L. Marks. 1990. "Graduate Student's Comment . . . Here's Where We Separate the Men from the Boys." Preliminary Report on the Status of Women as Graduate Students in History in Canada. Ottawa: *CAUT Bulletin, Status of Women Supplement.*

Dubois, E., G.P. Kelly, E.L. Kennedy, C.W. Koresmeyer, and L.S. Robinson. 1992. *Feminist Scholarship: Kindling in the Groves of Academe.* Champaign, IL: University of Illinois Press.

Echols, A. 1989. *Daring to be Bad: Radical Feminism in America, 1967–1975.* Minneapolis: University of Minnesota Press.

Eichler, M. 1988. *Non-Sexist Research Methods: A Practical Guide.* Boston: Allen and Unwin.

———. 1989. "The Supervision of Theses Adopting Feminist Perspectives or: Jane's Search for a Feminist Supervisor." In C. Filteau (ed.), *Proceedings of a Conference on Women in Graduate Studies in Ontario.* Toronto: Ontario Council of Graduate Studies.

Eichler, M., & Lapointe, J. 1985. *On the Treatment of the Sexes in Research.* Ottawa, ON: Social Sciences and Humanities Research Council of Canada.

Eichler, M., and R. Tite. 1990. "Women's Studies Professors in Canada: A Collective Self-Portrait." *Atlantis* 16: 6–24.

Ellsworth, E. 1992. "Why Doesn't This Feel Empowering? Working Through the Repressive Myths of Critical Pedagogy." In C. Luke and J. Gore (eds.), *Feminisms and Critical Pedagogy.* New York: Routledge.

Emberley, P. 1996. *Zero Tolerance: Hot Button Politics in Canadian Universities.* Toronto: Penguin.

Faragher, J.M., and F. Howe, eds. 1988. *Women and Higher Education in American History: Essays from the Mount Holyoke College Sesquicentennial Symposia.* New York: Norton.

Fausto-Sterling, A. 1985. "The New Research on Women: How Does it Affect the Natural Sciences?" *Women's Studies Quarterly* 13(2): 30–32.

———. 1986. "Women and Minorities in Science: An Interdisciplinary Course." *Radical Teacher* 30: 16–20.

Fee, E. 1982. "A Feminist Critique of Scientific Objectivity." *Science for the People*, July/August: 5–33.

Fekete, J. 1994. *Moral Panics: Biopolitics Rising.* Montréal: Robert Davis.

Feldberg, R., and E. Glenn. 1979. "Male and Female: Job Versus Gender Models in the Sociology of Work." *Social Problems* 26: 524–38.

Feldthusen, B. 1995. "Gender Wars: 'Where the Boys Are.'" In the Chilly Climate Collective (eds.), *Breaking Anonymity: The Chilly Climate for Women Faculty.* Waterloo: Wilfrid Laurier University Press.

Filteau, C, ed. 1989. *Proceedings of a Conference on Women in Graduate Studies in Ontario.* Toronto: Ontario Council on Graduate Studies.

Finkelman, L. 1992. "Report of the Survey of Unwanted Sexual Experiences Among Students of U.N.B.–F. and S.T.U." *Counselling Services Research Report*, October: 1–26.

Fleming, J. 1984. *Blacks in College: A Comparative Study of Students' Success in Black and in White Institutions.* San Francisco: Jossey-Bass.

Flexner, E. 1976. *Century of Struggle: The Women's Rights Movement in the United States.* Cambridge: Harvard University Press.

Ford, A.R. 1984. *A Path Not Strewn With Roses: One Hundred Years of Women at the University of Toronto: 1884–1984.* Toronto: University of Toronto Press.

Fox–Keller, E. 1977. "The Anomaly of a Woman in Physics." In S. Ruddick and P. Daniels (eds.), *Working It Out: 23 Women Writers, Artists, Scientists and Scholars Talk About Their Lives and Work.* New York: Pantheon.

Freeman, M. 1978. *Life among the Qallunaat.* Edmonton, AB: Hurtig.

Friedan, B. 1963. *The Feminine Mystique.* New York: Norton.

Fulton, E.M. 1991. "Alternative University Administrative Structures." In C. Lambert (ed.), *Toward a New Equality: The Status of Women in Canadian Universities.* Ottawa: Social Science Federation of Canada.

Fulton, K.L. 1991. "Journalling Women: The Authentic Voice and Intellectual Cross-Dressing." In Sandra Kirby et al. (eds.), *Women Changing Academe.* Winnipeg: Sororal.

Fulton, K.L., and M. Pujol. 1991. "One Step Forward, Two Steps Back: Twenty Years of Women's Studies at the University of Manitoba." *Resources for Feminist Research* 20(3/4): 31–36.

Gardner, J. 1961. *Excellence: Can We Be Equal and Excellent Too?* New York: Harper and Row.

Gaskell, J., A. McLaren, and M. Novogrodsky. 1989. *Claiming an Education: Feminism and Canadian Schools.* Toronto: Garamond.

Geiger, R.L. 1986. *To Advance Knowledge: The Growth of American Research Universities, 1900–1940.* New York: Oxford University Press.

Geis, F.L., M.R. Carter, and D.J. Butler. 1982. *Seeing and Evaluating People.* Newark de la Cour, DE: Office of Women's Affairs, University of Delaware.

Geramita, Joan. 1988. "Women and Academic Freedom." *CAUT Bulletin Status of Women Supplement*, March: 5–6.

Ghalem, N.Z. 1993. "Women in the Workplace." *Canadian Social Trends.* Ottawa: Statistics Canada.

Gilbert, L.A. 1985. "Dimensions of Same Gender Student–Faculty Role Model Relationships." *Sex Roles* 12(1/2): 111–23.

Gilbert, L.A., J.M. Gallessich, and S.L. Evans. 1983. "Sex of Faculty Role Model and Students' Self Perception of Competency." *Sex Roles* 9: 597–607.

Gill, G., ed. 1992. *1992–1993 Universities Telephone Directory: A Guide to Academic and Administrative Offices at Canadian Universities.* Ottawa: Association of Universities and Colleges of Canada.

Gillett, M. 1981. *We Walked Very Warily: A History of Women at McGill.* Montréal:

REFERENCES

Eden Press.

―――. 1990. "Carrie Derick and the Chair of Botany at McGill." In M.G. Ainley (ed.), *Despite the Odds: Essays on Canadian Women and Science.* Montréal: Vehicule Press.

Gilligan, C. 1982. *In a Different Voice.* Cambridge: Harvard University Press.

Gilmore, M. 1991. *Take Back Toronto: A Guide to Preventing Violence Against Women in Your Community.* Toronto: The City of Toronto Safe City Committee and Healthy City Office.

Gochnauer, M. 1992. "Of Liberty and Social Practices: The Case of Malcolm Ross." *UNB Law Journal* 41: 317–26.

Goelman, H., A.R. Pence, D.S. Lero, L.M. Brockman, N. Glick, and J. Berkowitz. 1993. *Canadian National Child Care Study.* Ottawa: Statistics Canada and Health and Welfare Canada.

Goggin, J. 1992. "Challenging Sexual Discrimination in the Historical Profession: Women Historians and the American Historical Association, 1890–1940." *American Historical Review* 97(3): 769–802.

Goldberg, P. 1969. "Are Women Prejudiced Against Women?" *Transaction*, April: 28–30.

Government of Canada. 1960. *The Canadian Bill of Rights*, S.C., C. 44.

―――. 1977. "Canadian Human Rights Act, 1977 (25–26 Elizabeth II)." *Canada Gazette Part III* (7).

Greenberg, S. 1988. "Education Equity in Early Education Environments." In S.S. Klein (ed.), *Handbook for Achieving Sex Equity Through Education.* Baltimore: Johns Hopkins University Press.

Gruhn, R. 1992. "Radical Feminism Intolerant?" Letter to the editor. *CAUT Bulletin*, September: 2.

Gunderson, M., L. Muszynski, and J. Keck. 1990. *Women and Labour Market Poverty.* Ottawa: Canadian Advisory Council on the Status of Women.

Guppy, N. 1984. "Access to Higher Education in Canada." *The Canadian Journal of Higher Education* 14(3): 79–93.

Guppy, N., D. Balson, and S. Vellutini. 1987. "Women and Higher Education in Canadian Society." In J. Gaskell and A. McLaren (eds.), *Women and Education: A Canadian Perspective.* Calgary: Detselig Enterprises.

Guttentag, M., and H. Bray. 1977. "Teachers as Mediators of Sex-Role Standards." In A.G. Sargent (ed.), *Beyond Sex Roles.* St. Paul, MN: West.

Hahn, C.L., J. Bernard-Powers, L. Hunter, S. Groves, M. MacGregor, and K.P. Scott. 1988. "Sex Equity in Social Science." In S.S. Klein (ed.), *Handbook for Achieving Sex Equity Through Education.* Baltimore: Johns Hopkins University Press.

Hall, R.M., and B.R. Sandler. 1986. *The Campus Climate Revisited.* Washington, DC: Association of American Colleges.

Hamilton, J.A. 1985. "Avoiding Methodological and Policy-Making Biases in Gender Related Research." *Report of the Public Health Service Task Force on Women's Health, Vol. II.* Washington, DC: Government Print Office.

Hanks, P., ed. 1986. *Collins Dictionary of the English Language.* Second edition. London: Collins.

Harding, S. 1984. *The Science Question in Feminism.* New York: Routledge.

Hartman, M.S. 1986. "DOUGLASS Makes a Difference for the Female Student." *Rutgers Alumni Magazine*, December: 17–19.

Haslett, B., F.L. Geis, and M.R. Carter. 1992. *The Organizational Woman: Power and Paradox*. Norwood, NJ: Ablex.

Hebdige, D. 1979. *Subculture: The Meaning of Style*. London: Routledge.

Heilbrun, C.G. 1988. *Writing a Woman's Life*. New York, NY: Ballantine.

Heins, M. 1987. *Cutting the Mustard*. Boston: Faber and Faber.

Higginbotham, E. 1990. "Designing an Inclusive Curriculum: Bringing All Women Into the Core." *Women's Studies Quarterly* 18(1 & 2): 7–23.

Hollands, J. 1988. "Women Teaching at Canadian Universities." *Canadian Social Trends*. Otawa: Statistics Canada.

Hosek, C. 1986. "A New Challenge for Women in Higher Education." *CAUT Bulletin*, November: 15–16.

Hubbard, R. 1989. *The Shape of Red: Insider/Outsider Reflections*. San Francisco: Cleis.

Hudgins, B. 1993. "The Dance Decision." *Faculty Association of the University of Waterloo Forum*, February: 7.

Hughes, H.M. 1977. "Wasp/Woman/Sociologist." *Society* 14: 69–80.

Inch, J. 1985. "Statistics Reflect Dilemma of Women Faculty." *UNB Perspectives*, October: 6–7.

Innis, M.Q., ed. 1970. *Nursing Education in a Changing Society*. Toronto: University of Toronto Press.

Jacobs, J.A. 1989. *Revolving Doors: Sex Segregation and Women's Careers*. Stanford, CA: Stanford University Press.

Johns, W.H. 1981. *A History of the University of Alberta, 1908–1969*. Edmonton: University of Alberta Press.

Johnston, N., and C. Polster. 1992. "Report on the Safety and Security of Graduate Women at York University." *Not Satisfied Yet: Report of the Task Force on the Status of Women Graduate Students*. North York, ON: York University.

Joyce, S. 1991. *The Chilly Climate for Women in Colleges and Universities: Warming the Environment*. Toronto: Ontario Ministry of Colleges and Education and the Ontario Women's Directorate.

Kanter, R.M. 1977. *Men and Women of the Corporation*. New York: Basic.

Keller, E.F. 1985. *Reflections on Gender and Science*. New Haven, CT: Yale University Press.

Keyes, K., Jr. 1982. *The Hundredth Monkey*. Coos Bay, OR: Vision.

Kirby, S. 1992. "The 40 Percent Solution." *Herizons*, Fall: 9.

Kitchen, B. 1992. "Framing the Issues: The Political Economy of Poor Mothers." *Canadian Woman Studies/les cahiers de la femme* 12(4): 10–15.

Kitchener-Waterloo Record. 1993. "Queen's Grievance Board Admits Prof was Victim of Racism, Sexism." January 30.

Klapisch-Zuber, C., ed. 1992. *A History of Women in the West, Vol. II: Silences in the Middle Ages*. Cambridge: Harvard University Press.

Klodawsky, F. 1989. "Parental Leave and Child Care Issues." In C. Filteau (ed.), *Proceedings of a Conference on Women in Graduate Studies in Ontario*. Toronto: Ontario Council on Graduate Studies.

Klotzburger, K. 1973. "Political Action by Academic Women." In A.S. Rossi and A. Calderwood (eds.), *Academic Women on the Move*. New York: Russell Sage Foundation.

Koblitz, A.H. 1984. *A Convergence of Lives: Sofia Kovalevskaia: Scientist, Writer,*

REFERENCES

Revolutionary. Boston: Birkhauser.

Krahn, H., and G. Lowe. 1993. "Women's Employment." *Work, Industry and Canadian Society*. Scarborough, ON: Nelson Canada.

Kranias, G. 1990. "Women and the Changing Faces of Science." In M.G. Ainley (ed.), *Despite the Odds*. Montréal: Véhicule.

Labarge, M.W. 1986. *A Small Sound of the Trumpet: Women in Medieval Life*. Boston: Beacon.

Landes, J.B. 1988. *Women and the Public Sphere in the Age of the French Revolution*. Ithaca, NY: Cornell University Press.

Lauter, P., and F. Howe. 1978. *The Women's Movement: Impact on the Campus and the Curriculum*. Chicago: ERIC ED 193 996.

Leong, F.T.L., C.R. Snodgrass, and W.L. Gardner. 1992. "Management Education: Creating a Gender–Positive Environment." In U. Sekaran and F.T.L. Leong (eds.), *Womanpower: Managing in Times of Demographic Turbulence*. Newbury Park, CA: Sage.

Lewis, M. 1992. "Interrupting Patriarchy: Politics, Resistance and Transformation in the Feminist Classroom." In C. Luke and J. Gore (eds.), *Feminisms and Critical Pedagogy*. New York: Routledge.

Li, P. 1988. *Ethnic Inequality in a Class Society*. Toronto: Wall and Thompson.

Lindberg, D.C., and R.S. Westmen, eds. 1990. *Reappraisals of the Scientific Revolution*. New York: Cambridge University Press.

Little, William, Fowler, H.W.and J. Coulson. Onion, C.T. Reviewer and Editor. 1956. Shorter Oxford Dictionary. Third Edition. Oxford: Clarendon Press.

Logan, H.T. 1958. *Tuum Est: A History of the University of British Columbia*. Vancouver: University of British Columbia.

Looker, E.D. 1990. *The Marginal Majority: A Report to the President on the Status of Women at Acadia*. Wolfville, NS: Acadia University.

———. 1993. "Gender Issues in University: The University as Employer of Academic and Non-Academic Women and Men." *The Canadian Journal of Higher Education* 23(2): 19–43.

Lougheed, T. 1993. "Making Universities More Women-Friendly." *University Affairs*, March.

Luke, C. 1992. "Feminist Politics in Radical Pedagogy." In C. Luke and J. Gore (eds.), *Feminisms and Critical Pedagogy*. New York: Routledge.

Lussier, T. 1995. "Doctoral Students at the University of Manitoba: Factors Affecting Completion Rates and Time to Degree by Gender and by Field of Study." ERIC ED382 148 April.

MacDonald, L., and P. Morris. 1986. "Lack of Child Care: A Barrier to Women Learners." *Women's Education des femmes* 6: 5–9.

MacKinnon, C. 1979. *Sexual Harassment of Working Women*. New Haven, CT: Yale University Press.

MadhavaRau, L. 1995. "Race Relations Policy Brought To Life: A Case Study of One Anti–harassment Protocol." In the Chilly Climate Collective (ed.), *Breaking Anonymity: The Chilly Climate for Women Faculty*. Waterloo: Wilfrid Laurier University Press.

Marchak, P.M. 1996. *Racism, Sexism, and the University: The Political Science Affair at the University of British Columbia*. Montréal and Kingston: McGill-Queen's University Press.

Marshall, S., ed. 1989. *Women in Reformation and Counter-Reformation Europe*. Bloomington: Indiana University Press.

Martin, B.R., and J. Irvine. 1982. "Women in Science: The Astronomical Brain Drain." *Women's Studies International Forum* 5(1): 41–68.

Martyna, W. 1978. "What Does 'He' Mean? Use of the Generic Masculine." *Journal of Communication* 28: 131–38.

Mayfield, M. 1989. *Work-Related Child Care in Canada*. Ottawa: Women's Bureau, Labour Canada.

McCormack, T. 1991. "Politically Correct." *The Canadian Forum* 70(802): 8–10.

McGill Reporter, The. 1995. "1995–96 Preliminary Budget." February 25.

McIntosh, P. 1983. *Interactive Phases of Curricular Revision: A Feminist Perspective*. Wellesley, MA: Wellesley College Center for Research on Women.

McIntyre, S. 1987–88. "Gender Bias Within the Law School: 'The Memo' and its Impact." *Canadian Journal of Women and the Law* 2: 362–407.

McKeen, C.A., and R.J. Burke. 1989. "Mentor Relationships in Organizations: Issues, Strategies and Prospects for Women." *Journal of Management Development* 6(6): 33–42.

———. 1991. "Work Experiences and Career Success of Managerial and Professional Women: Study Design and Preliminary Findings." *Canadian Journal of Administrative Sciences* 8(4): 251–58.

Mikalachki, A., D.R. Mikalachki, and R.J. Burke. 1992. *Gender Issues in Management: Contemporary Cases*. Toronto: McGraw-Hill Ryerson.

Miller, C., ed. 1975. *A History of the McGill Faculty Club*. Montréal: The McGill Faculty Club.

Miller, C., and K. Swift. 1988. *The Handbook of Nonsexist Writing*. Second edition. New York: Harper and Row.

———. 1991. *Words and Women, Updated*. New York: Harper Collins.

Miller, C., and C. Treitel. 1991. *Feminist Research Methods: An Annotated Bibliography*. Westport, CT: Greenwood.

Millet, K. 1974. *Flying*. New York: Knopf.

Mills, C.W. 1959. *The Sociological Imagination*. New York: Oxford University Press.

Milne, P.J. 1995. "Administrative Pimping for Fame and Profit: Part 2." *Women's Education des femmes* 11(3): 35–36.

Minnich, E., J. O'Barr, and R.A. Rosenfeld. 1988. *Reconstructing the Academy: Women's Education and Women's Studies*. Chicago: University of Chicago Press.

Mitchell, F. 1990. "Including Women at Emory and Henry College: Evolution of an Inclusive Language Policy." *Women's Studies Quarterly* 18(1 & 2): 222–30.

Moghissi, H. 1994. "Racism and Sexism in Academic Practice: A Case Study." In H. Afshar and M. Maynard (eds.), *The Dynamics of Race and Gender*. London, ON: Taylor and Francis.

Monson, C.A., ed. 1992. *The Crannied Wall: Women, Religion and the Arts in Early Modern Europe*. Ann Arbor: University of Michigan Press.

Monture, P. 1990. "Now That the Door Is Open: First Nations and the Law School Experience." *Queen's Law Journal* 15: 179–91.

Morgen, S., and M.H. Moran. 1990. "Transforming Introductory Anthropology: The American Anthropological Association Project on Gender and the Curriculum." *Women's Studies Quarterly* 18(1 & 2): 95–104.

Morris, R. 1989. *Report to the Society of Graduate Students on the Problems Faced by*

REFERENCES

Women Graduate Students. London, ON: R. Morris.

————. 1991. *C.U.E.W. Safety and Security Study.* North York, ON: Canadian Union of Educational Workers, CUEW/SCTTE Local 3, September.

Nemiroff, G.H. 1984. "Inventory." In M. Gillett and K. Sibbald (eds.), *A Fair Shake.* Montréal: Eden.

Newman, B. 1988. *Sister of Wisdom: St. Hildegarde's Theology of the Feminine.* Berkeley, CA: University of California Press.

News and Comment. 1991. "Still a 'Chilly Climate' for Women?" *Science* 252 (June): 605.

Newson, J. 1992. "Backlash: A Disempowering Metaphor." *Resources for Feminist Research* 9 (January): 93–97.

Ng, R. 1993. "The Power Dynamics of Racism and Sexism." OCUFA *Forum,* Special Supplement, December.

Noble, D.F. 1992. *A World Without Women: The Christian Clerical Culture of Western Science.* New York: Knopf.

Offerman, L.R., and C. Beil. 1992. "Achievement Styles of Women Leaders and their Peers. Toward an Understanding of Women and Leadership." *Psychological Women Quarterly* 162(1): 37–56.

Orner, M. 1992. "Interrupting the Calls for Student Voice in 'Liberatory' Education: A Feminist Poststructuralist Perspective." In C. Luke and J. Gore (eds.), *Feminisms and Critical Pedagogy.* New York: Routledge.

Pacer. 1973. "Report of the President's Advisory Committee on Equal Rights for Women and Men." Supplement to the *University of Waterloo Gazette,* November 21.

Paige-Pointer, B., and G.S. Auletta. 1990. "Restructuring the Curriculum: Barriers and Bridges." *Women's Studies Quarterly* 18(1 & 2): 86–94.

Palca, J. 1990. "Women Left Out at NIH. A New Study Says the National Institute of Health Does Too Little to Encourage Scientists to Include Women in their Research." *Science* 248 (June 29): 1601–02.

Pantel, P.S., ed. 1992. *A History of Women, Vol. I, From Ancient Goddesses to Christian Saints.* Cambridge: Harvard University Press.

Park, S. 1996. "Research, Teaching and Service: Why Shouldn't Women's Work Count?" *The Journal of Higher Education* 67(1): 46–82.

Parr, J. 1987. *Still Running: Personal Stories by Queen's Women Celebrating the 50th Anniversary of the Marty Scholarship.* Kingston, ON: Queen's Alumnae Association.

————. 1989. "Chilly Climate: the Systemic Dilemma." OCUFA *Forum on Hiring and Retention of Female Faculty,* December.

Pay Equity Act. R.S.O. 1990, Chap. p7.

Pearce, L. 1995. "Gender and the Classroom Climate: Overstepping the Boundaries. Student Demands on Female Staff." Unpublished paper. Montréal: McGill Centre for Research and Teaching on Women.

Perry, K. 1989. *Interim Diagnostic Report on Full-time Faculty at Concordia University at May 31, 1989.* Montréal: Concordia University.

Plasse, M., and C. Simard, eds. 1989. *Gerer au Feminin.* Montréal: Les Editions Agence d'Arc.

Posen, G. 1990. "New Technology and the Education of Female Students." In F. Forman, M. O'Brien, J. Haddad, D. Hallman and P. Masters (eds.), *Feminism and*

Education: A Canadian Perspective. Toronto: Centre for Women's Studies in Education.

Prentice, A., and M. Danylewycz. (1984). "Teachers, Gender and Bureaucratizing School Systems in Nineteenth-Century Montréal and Toronto." *History Education Quarterly,* Spring: 75–100.

Prentice, S. 1994. *Chilly Climates.* Presentation at the June 1994 CWSA Meeting, Calgary.

———. 1995. *Addressing and Redressing Chilly Climates in Higher Education.* Presentation at the June 1995 CWSA Meeting, Montréal.

President's Advisory Committee on the Status of Women. University of Saskatchewan. 1995. "Reinventing our Legacy: The Chills Which Affect Women." In the Chilly Climate Collective (ed.), *Breaking Anonymity: The Chilly Climate for Women Faculty.* Waterloo: Wilfrid Laurier University Press.

Reingold, N. 1987. "Graduate Schools and Doctoral Degrees: European Models and American Realities." In N. Reingold and M. Rothenberg (eds.), *Scientific Colonialism: A Cross-Cultural Comparison.* Washington, DC: Smithsonian Institution.

Rendall, J. 1984. *The Origins of Modern Feminism: Women in Britain, France and the United States, 1780–1860.* New York: Schocken.

Report of the Royal Commission on the Status of Women in Canada. 1970. Ottawa: Information Canada.

Report of the Women in the Faculty of Management Task Force. 1992. Toronto: Faculty of Management, University of Toronto.

Rich, A. 1979. *Lies, Secrets and Silence.* New York: Norton.

Richer, S., and L. Weir, eds. 1995. *Beyond Political Correctness: Toward the Inclusive University.* Toronto: University of Toronto Press.

Ridington, R. 1988. *Trail to Heaven: Knowledge and Narrative in a Northern Native Community.* Vancouver and Toronto: Douglas and McIntyre.

———. 1990. *Little Bit Know Something: Stories in a Language of Anthropology.* Vancouver and Toronto: Douglas and McIntyre.

Riggs, R.O., P.H. Murrell, and J.C. Cutting. 1993. *Sexual Harassment in Higher Education: From Conflict to Community.* Washington, DC: ASHE–ERIC Higher Education Report No. 2.

Robertson, C., C. Dyer, and D. Campbell. 1988. "Campus Harassment: Sexual Harassment Politices and Procedures at Institutions of Higher Learning." *Signs* 13(4): 808–11.

Rosener, J. 1990. "Ways Women Lead." *Harvard Business Review,* November-December: 119–25.

Ross, M.G. 1976. *The University: The Anatomy of Academe.* New York: McGraw-Hill.

Rosser, S.V. 1990. *Female Friendly Science.* New York: Pergamon.

Rossiter, M. 1982. *Women Scientists in America: Struggles and Strategies to 1940.* Baltimore: Johns Hopkins University Press.

Rothblum, E.D. 1988. "Leaving the Ivory Tower: Factors Contributing to Women's Voluntary Resignation from Academia." *Frontiers* 10(2): 14–17.

Rowbotham, S. 1992. *Women in Movement: Feminism and Social Action.* New York: Routledge.

Rowe, M. 1990. "Barriers to Equality: The Power of Subtle Discrimination to Maintain Unequal Opportunity." *Employee Rights and Responsibilities Journal* 3(2): 6.

Royal Commission on the Status of Women. 1970. *Report of the Royal Commission on*

REFERENCES

the Status of Women in Canada. Ottawa: Queen's Printer.

Ruchkall, B. 1997. "The Campus Climate: A Chilly One for Support Staff at the University of Manitoba." Unpublished master's thesis. Winnipeg: The University of Manitoba.

Sadker, M., and D. Sadker. 1985. "Sexism in the Schoolroom of the '80's." *Psychology Today* 19(3): 54–57.

————. 1988. "The Treatment of Sex Equity in Teacher Education." In S.S. Klein (ed.), *Handbook for Achieving Sex Equity Through Education*. Baltimore: Johns Hopkins University Press.

Sandler, B., and R. Hall. 1986. *The Campus Climate Revisited: Chilly for Women Faculty, Administrators and Graduate Students*. Washington, DC: Project of the Status and Education of Women, Association of American Colleges.

Saunders, M., M. Therrien, and L. Williams. 1992. *Women in Universities: Survey of the Status of Female Faculty and Students at Canadian Universities*. Ottawa: Canadian Federation of University Women.

Scassa, Teresa. 1992. "Violence Against Women in Law Schools." *Alberta Law Review* 30: 809–28.

Schele, L., and D. Freidel. 1990. *A Forest of Kings: The Untold Story of the Ancient Maya*. New York: Morrow.

Secretary of State. 1991. *Profile of Higher Education in Canada*. Ottawa: Department of the Secretary of State of Canada.

————. 1992. *Postsecondary Education in Canada: Basic Statistics*. Ottawa: Department of the Secretary of State of Canada.

Sekaran, U., and M. Kassner. 1992. "University Systems for the 21st Century: Proactive Adaptation." In U. Sekaran and F.T.L. Leong (eds.), *Womanpower: Managing in Times of Demographic Turbulence*. Newbury Park, CA: Sage.

Selin, H. 1991. *Science Across Cultures: An Annotated Bibliography*. Hamden, CT: Garland.

Sen, J. 1992. *Women, Unions and the Labour Market: New Perspectives*. New Delhi, India and Acton, MA: Mosaic Books and Copley Publishing.

Serbin, L.A., and K.D. O'Leary. 1979. "How Nursery Schools Teach Girls to Shut Up." In J.H. Williams (ed.), *Psychology of Women: Selected Readings*. New York: Norton.

Sharpe, S. 1994. *The Gilded Ghetto: Woman and Political Power in Canada*. Toronto: Harper Collins.

Shaughnessy, H. 1994. *Annual Report, 1993/94*. Montréal: McGill University Employment Equity Office.

Sheinin, R. 1988. "The Assessment of Excellence." *CAUT Bulletin*, February.

————. 1989. "Women as Scientists: Their Rights and Obligations." *Journal of Business Ethics* 8: 131–55.

————. 1991. "The Theories of Cellular and Molecular Biology and Genetics: Do They Have a Sex?" In A. Decerf (ed.), *Les Théories Scientifiques ont-elles un sexe?* Moncton, NB: Les Editions d'Acadie.

Shortt Smith, E. 1916. *Historical Sketch of Medical Education, Kingston, Canada*. Ottawa: Private Printing.

Signs. 1987. "Editorial." 12(4): 619–20.

Simeone, A. 1987. *Academic Women: Working Towards Equality*. Massachusetts: Bergin and Garvey.

Skilliter, D. 1994. "Studying Science, Playing Politics." *Globe and Mail,* June 13.

Smith, D.E. 1975. "An Analysis of Ideological Structures and How Women are Excluded: Considerations for Academic Women." *Canadian Review of Sociology and Anthropology* 12(4): 353–69.

———. 1987. "A Peculiar Eclipsing: Women's Exclusion from Man's Culture." In D. Smith (ed.), *The Everyday World as Problematic.* Toronto: University of Toronto Press.

———. 1989. "Reflections on Political Economy." *Studies in Political Economy* 30 (Autumn): 37–60.

———. 1990. "Women's Work as Mothers: A New Look at the Relations of Class, Family and School Achievement." In F. Forman, M. O'Brien, J. Haddad, D. Hallman and P. Masters (eds.), *Feminism and Education: A Canadian Perspective.* Toronto: Centre for Women's Studies in Education.

Smith, S.L. 1991. *Report: Commission of Inquiry on Canadian University Education.* Ottawa: Canadian Association of University Teachers.

Social Planning Council of Winnipeg. 1991. "Adequacy of Benefits." Letter to the City of Winnipeg regarding proposed reduction in welfare rates, March. Winnipeg, MB.

Spector, J.D. 1990. "The Minnesota Plan II: A Project to Improve the University Environment for Women Faculty, Administrators, and Academic Professional Staff." *Women's Studies Quarterly* 18(1 & 2): 189–206.

Spelman, E.V. 1988. *Inessential Woman: Problems of Exclusion in Feminist Thought.* Boston: Beacon.

Spender, D. 1980. *Man-made Language.* Boston: Routledge.

———. 1989. *The Writing or the Sex?: Or Why You Don't Have to Read Women's Writing to Know It's No Good.* New York: Pergamon.

Stalker, J. 1993. "Review of *Lifting a Ton of Feathers: An Academic Woman's Guide to Surviving in the Academic World* by P. Caplan." *The Canadian Journal of Higher Education* 23(3): 163–65.

———. 1995. "The Chill Women Feel at Canada's Universities." *Globe and Mail,* July 25.

Stalker, J., and B. Rubin. 1993. "Seeking to Level the Playing Field: Job Equity Rewards Merit." *Winnipeg Free Press,* August 28.

Stanworth, M. 1988. *Gender and Schooling: A Study of Sexual Divisions in the Classroom.* Tiptree, Essex: Anchor Brendon.

Statistics Canada. 1986. *Profile of Ethnic Groups.* Ottawa: Ministry of Industry, Science and Technology.

———. 1990. *Women in Canada: A Statistical Report.* Second edition. Ottawa: Ministry of Industry, Science and Technology.

———. 1991. *Teachers in Universities.* Ottawa: Statistics Canada.

———. 1992a. *Education in Canada: A Statistical Review for 1990–91.* Ottawa: Ministry of Supply and Services, Catalogue No. 81–229.

———. 1992b. *Teachers in Universities. Annual, 1989–90.* Ottawa: Ministry of Industry, Science and Technology, Catalogue No. 81–241.

———. 1992c. *Universities: Enrolment and Degrees. Annual, 1990.* Ottawa: Ministry of Industry, Science and Technology, Catalogue No. 81–204.

———. 1993a. *Education in Canada. Annual, A Statistical Review for 1990–91.* Ottawa: Ministry of Industry, Science and Technology, Catalogue No.81–229.

———. 1993b. *Report on the Survey of Violence Against Women.* Ottawa: Ministry of

REFERENCES

Industry, Science and Technology.

—————. 1993c. *Teachers in Universities, 1990–91.* Ottawa: Ministry of Industry, Science and Technology, Catalogue No. 81–241.

Stevens, C. 1971. "The Road to Find Out." *Tea for the Tillerman.* Hollywood: A & M Records.

Stewart, L. 1990. *It's Up To You: Women at UBC in the Early Years.* Vancouver: University of British Columbia Press.

Stewart, M.L. 1991. "Women Working Together." In C. Lambert (ed)., *Toward a New Equality.* Ottawa: Social Science Federation of Canada.

Stock, P. 1978. *Better Than Rubies: A History of Women's Education.* New York: Capricorn Books, Putnam.

Stowe-Gullen, A. 1898. "Women in the Study and Practice of Medicine." In Rev. B.F. Austin NABD (ed.), *Woman: Maiden, Wife and Mother.* Toronto.

Symons, T., and J. Page. 1984. *Some Questions of Balance: Human Resources, Higher Education and Canadian Studies.* Ottawa: Association of Universities and Colleges of Canada.

—————. 1975. *To Know Ourselves.* Ottawa: Report of the Commission on Canadian Studies, Association of Universities and Colleges Canada.

Tancred, P. 1990. "Harassment and 'Backlash': Common Threads, Any Solution?" *Transactions of the Royal Society of Canada* 1(1): 17–20.

—————. 1992. *Gendering Organizational Analysis.* Newbury Park, NY: Sage.

Tancred, P. et al. 1997. "Les femmes ré-inventent les emplois non-traditionnelles." *L'Agenda des femmes*, novembre–décembre.

Thompson, J.E. 1962. *The Influence of Dr. Emily Howard Stowe on the Woman Suffrage Movement in Canada.* Unpublished master's thesis. Waterloo: Wilfred Laurier University.

Tidball, M.E. 1973. "Perspective on Academic Women and Affirmative Action." *Educational Record* 54: 130–35.

Tierney, W.G., and R.A. Rhoads. 1993. *Enhancing Promotion, Tenure and Beyond: Faculty Socialization as a Cultural Process.* Washington, DC: ASHE–ERIC Higher Education Report No. 6.

Trott, E.A. 1984. *The Faces of Reason: An Essay on Philosophy and Culture in English Canada.* Waterloo: Wilfred Laurier University Press.

Tuana, N. 1993. *The Less Noble Sex: Scientific, Religious and Philosophical Conceptions of Women's Nature.* Bloomington: Indiana University Press.

University Affairs. 1993. "Making Universities More Women–Friendly." March 10.

University of Victoria, Department of Political Science. 1993. *Report of the Climate Committee.* March 23:1.

Urofsky, M.L. 1991. *A Conflict of Rights.* New York: Charles Scribner.

Vickers, J. and J. Adam. 1977. *But Can You Type? Canadian Universities and the Status of Women.* Toronto: Clark, Irwin.

Wayne, L., and R. Ulster. 1991. "High Stakes: The 'Politically Correct' Debate and Feminist Academic Practice." *Resources for Feminist Research: Transforming Knowledge and Politics* 20: 56–61.

Weisstein, N. 1977. "'How Can a Little Girl Like You Teach a Great Big Class of Men?' The Chairman said, and Other Adventures of a Woman in Science." In S. Ruddick and P. Daniels (eds.), *Working It Out: 23 Women Writers, Artists, Scientists and Scholars Talk About Their Lives and Work.* New York: Pantheon.

Weitzman, L.J. 1975. "Legal Requirements, Structure, and Strategies for Eliminating Sex Discrimination in Academe." In E. Wasserman et al. (eds.), *Women in Academia*. New York: Praeger.

Wekerle, G.R., and City of Toronto Planning and Development Department. 1992. *A Working Guide For Planning and Designing Safer Urban Environments*. Toronto: Safe City Committee and Planning and Development Department of the City of Toronto.

Wenneras, C., and A. Wold. 1997. "Nepotism and Sexism in Peer Review." *Nature* 23: 341–43.

Westhues, K. 1989. "Women in Sociology: A Note about the Past." Letter to the editor. *University of Waterloo Gazette*, November 22, 2.

Widnall, S. 1988. "Voices from the Pipeline." *Science*, September: 241.

Williams, K. 1995. "Split Infinitives." In M. Gillett and A. Beer (eds.), *Our Own Agendas: Autobiographical Essays by Women Associated With McGill University*. Montréal: McGill-Queen's University Press.

Williamson, J. 1990. "What is a Nice Feminist Like Me Doing in a Place Like This?" Open Letter. *Seventh Series* 8: 34–59.

Winders, J.A. 1991. *Gender, Theory and Canon*. Madison: University of Wisconsin Press.

Wine, J.D. 1983. "Lesbian Academics in Canada." *Resources for Feminist Research* 12(1): 9–11.

———. 1990. "Outsiders on the Inside: Lesbians in Canadian Academe." In S.D. Stone (ed.), *Lesbians in Canada*. Toronto: Between the Lines.

Winn, C. 1985. "Affirmative Action and Visible Minorities: Eight Premises in Quest of Evidence." *Canadian Public* 11: 684–700.

Women in the Labour Force. 1985–86 edition. Ottawa: Labour Canada.

Woolf, V. 1938. *Three Guineas*. London: Hogarth.

Wylie, A. 1995. "The Context of Activism on 'Climate' Issues." In the Chilly Climate Collective (ed.), *Breaking Anonymity: The Chilly Climate for Women Faculty*. Waterloo: Wilfrid Laurier University Press.

York Federation of Students. 1993. *A Woman's Guide to Safety at York*. North York, ON: York Federation of Students.

York, G., and L. Pindera. 1991. *People of the Pines: The Warriors and the Legacy of Oka*. Boston and Toronto: Little, Brown.

York University Women's Supplement. 1991. *Excalibur*, September.